The Dancer and the Dance

The Dancer and the Dance

A Book of Distinctions

POETRY IN THE NEW CENTRY

Jack Foley

With a Foreword by AL Young

RED HEN PRESS | Los Angeles, California

All the essays in this book have appeared in my column, "Foley's Books", in the online magazine, *The Alsop Review*. Some have also appeared in *Poetry Flash*, *The Contemporary Poetry Review* and in *Italian Americana*. Most of the essays have been considerably rewritten for inclusion here. "Let them print what they want in the magazine," Michael McClure said to me: "Fix it for the book."

Book design: Mark E. Cull

ISBN: 978-1-59709-094-0
Library of Congress Catalog Card Number: 2007935263

The City of Los Angeles Department of Cultural Affairs, Los Angeles County Arts Commission, California Arts Council and the National Endowment for the Arts partially support Red Hen Press.

Published by Red Hen Press
www.redhen.org

First Edition

"These are distinctions in clarity"

—Ezra Pound, "Canto LXXXIV"

Contents

Contemporaries

Foreword

Back before we could Google the worldwide web or access by computer a library's shelves, we leaned on curiosity, happenstance, ingenuity and footwork to zero in on information. Now, at a time when data and knowledge are routinely misconstrued, the picture has changed. The need to make often practically imperceptible distinctions grows. While information technology has hastened the pace at which we bombard ourselves with facts, dates, and endless takes, this same technology threatens not only to slow to a trickle the natural rush of passion, but to dull as well all sense of wonder.

So what?

What do search engines, internet research, iPod, MP3 or DVD have to do with this valuable book you've entered? Many an artist and thinker of my generation might dance around such a question. I can't. Neither can Jack Foley. After all, we both come from a time when practically everything creative — or, in any case, fresh — had to be planted, nurtured and plucked by hand. The telling question to ask is this: What fueled and ignited Jack Foley's interests in the subjects his emotional spark and intellectual flame illuminate in these pages? And in a nation whose intellectuals are oddly anti-intellectual. Whether re-thinking particular poems by William Butler Yeats, John Keats, Stéphane Mallarmé, E.E. Cummings, Louis Zukofsky and Allen Ginsberg, works long regarded as classics, or walking straight down the midway of the contemporary poetry scene (from Garrison Keillor, Adrienne Rich, Francisco X. Alarcón, Diane DiPrima, Dana Gioia, to the late free jazz saxophonist-composer Glenn Spearman on out to slam and spoken word) Foley speaks his whole heart, always cutting his ever-inquiring mind some slack. Plug into Foley a year from now, six months, a few weeks, and chances are he will have shifted position on many opinions he previously championed. He is, after all, his own person: a talented poet, commentator, broadcaster, lecturer, performer, publisher and cultural activist.

⌘

Jack Foley's late-life takes and re-takes on the art and meaning of works by classic and contemporary poets pull you out upon a receding tide, where wonder and passion reside. What's in it for this man, who isn't pumping out commentary and criticism to shore up or defend an academic career? Foley does all this for love. He loves to pull back and take the grand pan-infinity overview of life and art, and he loves just as much to crowd in on technical, esthetic or socially meaningful minutia. It would be easy to trace his allegiance to the performing arts (the song lyrics of Andy Razaf, the music of Glenn Spearman) back to his father, a working vaudevillian. As alert to music, cinema and other dramatic forms as he is to poetry in particular and literature in general, Foley brings his thoughts and feelings for all of the arts into every essay and lecture he delivers. In an age of fractious specialization, Foley slides into place enough little pieces to come up with a big picture.

What makes these pages fun and stimulating is the ever-widening range of Jack Foley's concerns, enthusiasms, passions and loves. The interests of Kenneth Rexroth, the influential 20th century poet and thinker whose work Foley re-assesses, were similarly diffuse. Both men – the one self-educated, the other formally educated – look out at the world with every faculty intact, then translate into fine and lively language what they see, hear, taste, feel and recall. In this collection of warmly crafted essays Foley takes unblinking looks at everything he loves, and this would include plenty of stuff he genuinely doesn't like.

In each of these "classics" Foley either locates a passage he had previously neglected or overlooked, or he brings new personal experience and insight to his re-readings. For example, who but Jack Foley would take the time to point out that poet and essayist Kenneth Rexroth – the flamboyant San Francisco auto-didact whose thought and works influenced what came to called the Beat Generation – had no trouble seeing mysticism as a literary technique rather than as a religious experiences that transcends language. Without literary mysticism, it might be difficult to understand many modernist poets and the confessional vein many of them love to needle and trouble. Foley even caringly questions the presumed greatness of "Howl," Allen Ginsberg's signature flag-raiser for what I used to call Alien Nation.

With equal affection and reverence, Foley looks long and hard at *The Tower*, William Butler Yeats' late-life book in which his timeless "Sailing to Byzantium" debuts. In an autobiographical essay, a chapter from his own intellectual life, Foley doubles back to John Keats' "Ode on a Grecian Urn." While relating personal stories about Matt Phillips, an artist buddy, and critic-professor Paul de Man, one of the youthful author's mentors, Foley plunges fully into the "silence" and "unheard melodies" the famous poem evokes. But before he's through, Foley makes sure we get what he calls "my own feeling," which is that it is the urn itself speaking. It's the urn and not John Keats who delivers the poem's hallmark line: "Beauty is truth, truth beauty."

Reading Foley's pages, the beautiful truths that poetry and storytelling reveal unendingly yanked me back through seasons in heaven and seasons in hell. When, in my own fifties, I revisited some of the reading required of me when I was busy teaching myself to be a writer, but also when I was enrolled in college courses – a Spanish major whose minor was English – I set out delighted. A journey of rediscovery was what I'd anticipated, but discovery was all I got. The teacher of *Don Quixote* to teenagers truly jousts at windmills. Half a century is enough, however, to let any thoughtful observant reader, and rememberer, understand the kind of self-delusion, social shallowness, hypocrisy and folly that Spain's Miguel de Saavedra Cervantes was roasting and sending up centuries ago.

Why does Plato, who loathed democracy, exclude poets from his *Republic,* and yet, in *Ion,* tell us: "Poetry is nearer to vital truth than history"? *Ion* is the dialogue in which Plato's beloved (and, as we later come to find, fascistic) teacher Socrates asks the actor Ion at length why he thinks he's qualified to recite Homer. Contradictions and complexities of this magnitude blind-sided when, in my fifties, I leisurely went back over many of the classics I had dutifully tasted, chewed or swallowed in early youth, reading widely, but largely unsupervised.

✍

It is in the report entitled "Slam," Foley's open-faced account of what happened when he and his wife Adelle attended the "grand slam finals" in San Francisco on April 22, Earth Day, 2000 that the discriminating poet-essayist lays his esthetic criteria on the line. "Though I am a performance poet who has given hundreds of poetry readings," Foley states, "I have a problem with 'slam poetry' and 'spoken word poetry.' Such poetry seems to me little more than the assertion of the 'ego': this is what *I* think, these are *my* feelings. I think the popularity of spoken word is due to that fact.

"Americans like to think of themselves as 'individuals' and feel that 'self-expression' if properly presented is a good thing: after all, everyone is different, we all have individual feelings and they should be expressed. It seems to me that the problem with that formulation is basically that it isn't true – which is why so many 'individuals' end up saying exactly the same things! The 'ego' of 'individuality' is the ego generated by mass culture; it isn't real.

". . . One of the questions my work raises is how can you present spoken poetry, performed poetry, which is *not* an assertion of the ego – which remains true to an understanding of selfhood as multiple."

Although he doesn't agree with so-called language poets (or, rather, L=A=N=G=U=A=G=E poets) who turn their backs on performance to champion "the silence of 'writing,'" Foley, reflecting on his experience with spoken word and slam, fully understands their position.

∞

This brings me to a question Jack Foley put to me some time ago. "Why," he asked, "do you speak so negatively of modernism?"

"I don't speak negatively of it," I explained. "It just seems that poetry was immensely popular with Americans until the 1920's and 30's, when modernism kicked in."

"And so what happened, then?" Foley wanted to know.

"Well," I explained, "people had a hard time understanding what poets like Ezra Pound and T.S. Eliot were driving at, so poetry beat a retreat into college and university classrooms. Modernism gave lit profs something to explain and explicate."

"But I still disagree with you," Foley insisted. "Poetry didn't just go away. You might want to give your views on modernism some further thought."

"Well," I said, "I can tell you that this trend split off in two directions."

"How so?"

"Mandarin and colloquial," I said. "On the one hand you had the enigmatic, writerly modernism of, say, Eliot, Gertrude Stein, Hart Crane, Louis Zukofsky, Marianne Moore. Then, on the other hand, you had poets like Carl Sandburg, Robinson Jeffers, Amy Lowell, Langston Hughes. Poets who thought, "OK, maybe I don't always have to rhyme or count syllables. I can use colloquial speech rhythms and work in free verse.'"

Jack, ever the careful listener, said, "Maybe you'll write about it."

"I will," I said. "It may take some time, but I *will* write about it."

Indeed, while reading Jack Foley's lucid roundup, "Two Modernists & a Beat: Cummings, Zukofsky, and Ginsberg," it struck me why lovers of traditional poetry might have felt a chill when, *circa* 1925 or 1930, it began to look as though modernist practices and affectations were going to take over, be here to stay. That was when page-targeted poems — poetry as voiceless text, that is — began to command intellectual attention and critical respect. Had lovers of recitable poetry dropped out of the picture through some trap-door of fashion? Foley cites "a friend's horrified reaction to E.E. Cummings' "l(a," one of his numerous typographically driven poems. I call it his "loneliness/leaffall" poem. When Foley's unnamed friends gasps and asks, "Is this a poem?" Foley was inspired to pick up his pen.

I happen to be old enough to have been present at a reading Cummings gave at the University of Michigan right after the much studied poem made its first appearance in *95 Poems*, his 1958 collection. During the Q & A interval that followed, more than one student asked him about his typographical esthetics. As a grumpy, distracted undergraduate, I sat in the audience too awed by current events to register for posterity how Cummings had answered those questions.

Modernized and streamlined in the 1500's by Michel de Montaigne, the essay hasn't lost any of its power or persuasion. From *essayer*, a verb meaning to try or attempt, the French derived the noun *essai*, which flowed into English as essay. In vernacular American, it wouldn't be too far off to translate *essai* as "a shot." It was Montaigne's view that his essays not only leave room for response, but that they invite it. Ideally, he thought, the essayist ought to be able to sit down and discuss face to face with readers the essence of a given subject. Erudition eventually had to take a backseat to conversational discourse.

Again and again Jack Foley shoots to illumine and to illuminate. Long opposed to what Ezra Pound calls "the method of infamy" – that is, to lay out two lies, then lay odds on which is the truth – Foley takes delight in looking deeply into a subject. He loves to feel out the fine points, draw meaningful comparisons, then serve up the heartfelt results of his searches to public scrutiny.

Jack Foley's essays reflect the spirit of such a dialectic. In an era when the forms of stand-up, performance, monologue, blog, personal essay, op-ed and commentary have come to overwhelm public discourse, the power of a thoughtfully penned essay persists.

For me what makes these pages fun to read and stimulating to think about is the ever-widening range of Jack Foley's concerns, enthusiasms, passions and loves.

—Al Young,
California Poet Laureate
Summer 2007

Introduction

A book is a mirror in which you see not what you are but what you were. For my sixty-fourth birthday, my son Sean gave me a DVD containing a segment of a 1955 episode of *The Ed Sullivan Show*. (In 1955, Sullivan's show was called *The Toast of the Town*.) Like me, Ed Sullivan was from Port Chester, New York, and he was featuring his home-town high school choir; we sang "You'll Never Walk Alone" and "Beyond the Blue Horizon." I sat watching the segment in my home in California. As the camera projected my fourteen-year-old face, mouth open in song, I felt the sudden shock of the past made vividly present. I think a book is like that: the illusory presence of a past which remains forever out of reach. There were people I recognized on that television segment. But there were others—more fascinating—who are gone forever! Yet I must have known them all. What currents of thought does one recognize after decades of writing? What things stay with you for fifty years? What "re-runs" are possible? Most of the writers I deal with in this book are not New Yorkers like Sullivan but—like me since 1963—Californians.

Among the influences on *The Dancer and the Dance* are the work of Paul de Man, with whom I studied in the early 1960s at Cornell University, and, less obviously, that of Stanley Fish, whose "reader-response" method of textual criticism taught me much when I studied with him at UC Berkeley in 1964. Another influence is the rise of New Formalism—there is an essay on New Formalist poet, Annie Finch—and particularly the work of the Coleridge of New Formalism, Dana Gioia.

Perhaps the deepest influence on the book, however, is the work of the late Father Walter J. Ong. Father Ong's investigation of "the new orality" of the electronic era caused current critics—Dana Gioia among them—to recognize a hidden history of poetry, a history which was not told by those critics for whom the poem was entirely a written object. Though Modernism is permeated by performance—by what we currently call "Spoken Word"—this fact is not generally known because the considerable body of criticism Modernism amassed was completely unaware of it—or regarded orality as unimportant. In a recent review of Ezra Pound's musical productions, Richard Taruskin suggests, "Pound insisted that poetry was not 'literature' but a performance art."[1] One can find such insistence in many other "founding" poets of the twentieth century. Yeats' experiments with the radio are important here—as is Marinetti's equally deep interest in "*La Radia.*" Yeats, Auden, Williams, and Eliot were all interested in the theater; Bertolt Brecht produced plays as well as poetry—not to mention opera libretti. Pound singlehandedly produced an opera. H.D. appeared in a film, *Borderline* (1930). The Dada performances at the Cabaret Voltaire were notorious for their imaginative chaos: "The group," wrote Willard Bohn, "consisted of Romanian expatriates and former German Expressionists. While they were highly accomplished poets and artists, like their colleagues elsewhere, their real specialty was theatrical performance."[2]

These examples suggest that it wasn't Modernism which insisted on the "literary" as *opposed* to "theatrical performance" or "Spoken Word"; rather, it was the influential critics who wrote about Modernism. These critics made Modernism famous (and even gave birth to "Post Modernism"), but they also misunderstood certain aspects of the movement. Father Ong is quite clear about our cultural need to maintain ourselves as a "literate" people while at the same time maintaining our interest in the electronic media. His extraordinarily fertile work, which is firmly in the Modernist tradition, constantly suggests ways in which the electronic and the literary can achieve co-existence, even mutual illumination.

Paul de Man's principal contribution to this book and to my own thought was his discovery of the importance of Porphyry's essay on the cave of the nymphs episode in *The Odyssey* to Yeats' poetic symbolism. Even though Yeats refers to Porphyry's essay in the footnote to "Among School Children" and copiously quotes from it in his essay, "The Philosophy of Shelley's Poetry," few of Yeats' critics noticed that Porphyry's essay also functioned in Yeats' poetry, and no one except de Man noticed *how* it functioned. The crucial moment for Yeats is in "Her Vision in the Wood," particularly the point in the poem at which the old woman says, "They had brought no fabulous symbol there / But my heart's victim and its torturer." The phrase "fabulous symbol" is from Porphyry and implies a kind of gateway to the divine. Yeats may mean that "fabulous symbols" exist despite the fact that, in this particular instance, the old woman is seeing something which isn't one of them. But I think the statement goes further than that. "Fabulous symbols" here turn out to be something other than what Yeats, following Porphyry, initially conceived of them to be. They are not gateways to the divine but merely metaphors for the poet's suffering "heart." But if the symbols are merely metaphors—if in some deep sense they don't work—doesn't that mean that the juice behind them doesn't work either? I think that Yeats' entire career is an extremely reluctant affirmation of the death of God. God is the juice behind the symbols—and if they don't work, God doesn't work either. Similarly, for Mallarmé—with whom Yeats had a considerable affinity—it is not Jesus who comes to save the poet in the terrible "naufrage" of "Brise Marine" but words. Both writers are dealing with a symbolic system which has at its heart the dissolution of the central cultural symbol of the West: God. As the wonderful British children's writer Philip Pullman asks—in a magazine devoted to children's literature—"What happens to the Kingdom of Heaven when the King dies?"[3]

One of the things that happens is that old definitions get reformulated. The notion of selfhood embodied in this book is one of the results of the author's belief in the death (not merely the "absence") of God. The "self" assumed here is not a unified entity—not a "soul"—but something like a "field" in which various elements exist in various relations to one another. Though one can surely find unifying patterns within that field, one cannot find a single pattern which unifies everything. The self of this book is not a unity but a multiplicity—an unstable multiplicity which remains in motion. Many people would of course agree with this idea of selfhood—the self as a "multiplicity of voices"—but clarification is still required as to how this concept of the self as multiplicity affects literary criticism, how the self as multiplicity affects our actual reading of poems. It may be that the self we postulate as we read a poem contradicts the self we experience in the world; it is also possible that familiar poems may be experienced anew by being read in the light of multiplicity. My piece on Keats' great "Ode on a Grecian Urn"—a poem I describe as a "rich incoherence...radically inconsistent in its attitudes"—is meant in part as an exploration of this question.

"These are distinctions in clarity." Anyone who writes a book of criticism hopes to add a candle's worth more light to clarity. In my case, I wish to illuminate something about history—and about my own history. The eyes that looked out at me from that segment of *The Toast of the Town* were lit by a history which intensified and to some degree determined them. My fourteen-year-old self only partially understood that history, though I think he did understand that the history was both personal and cultural. This book is a testimony to whatever progress I have made in these fifty years. It is dedicated to him, that image on the screen whose smile is only tangentially related to my own.

Poetry And The Media

A speech delivered July 19, 2001
at the Sonoma Country Day School Teaching Poetry Conference

The subject of today's panel is "Poetry and the Media." Such a title more or less dictates the subject matter of the response. In one corner, "poetry"— usually encountered in books but sometimes in live performances, in newspapers, or even on television or radio or in films. In the other corner, "the Media"—a term which usually refers to radio, television, and the press, sometimes to films, rarely to books. A panel on "Poetry and the Media" is likely to discuss the presence (or lack of presence) of poetry on the radio—as in Garrison Keillor's recitations—or on television—as in Bob Holman's series, *The USA of Poetry* or Bill Moyers' *The Language of Life*—or in the newspapers—as in Lawrence Ferlinghetti's once intermittent column in *The San Francisco Chronicle*. Such a discussion would also touch on the Internet and on the "Slam" phenomenon. Generally speaking, the *word* "poetry" is avoided in the titles of television programs dealing with the subject; Bob Holman is to be congratulated for actually using the word in his title. The *word* poetry is understood by many to be a turn-off. In the film, *Meet the Parents* (1992), someone announces that the Robert de Niro character is going to read a "poem": we know the horror that is coming!

We could discuss whether poetry is "effectively presented" in these various media, or whether one particular medium presents it better than another. We might suggest that poetry is better suited to one medium than to another: might argue, for example, that it is more effectively presented in the aural world of radio than in the visual world of television—despite the fact that many people talk about a poem's "images" and that world literature boasts an astonishing number of "concrete" or "visual" poems, a resource that has never been exploited by television or film. We could discuss in what manner the kinds of techniques used in presenting radio and television programs have *affected* poetry. Are our attention spans shorter than they used to be? (What *is* an "attention span"?) Do we now need "sound bytes" in our poetry? Is an aphorism a sound byte? How has the complex world of music, of popular song, affected poetry?

1

There is surely much to be said about all these subjects, but I intend to take a somewhat different tack.

It seems to me that in postulating a subject like "Poetry and the Media," we are already thinking of poetry as an aspect of a medium or media, so that the title of the panel should really be "Some Kinds of Media and Other Kinds of Media." A poem *always already exists in a medium*—whether the medium is the page or the mouth of the poet or whatever. A poem of Larry Eigner's was once inscribed on the outside wall of the UC Berkeley Art Museum: that was *its* medium. Indeed, poetry cannot exist *without* a medium: there is no ur-poem or archepoem which exists outside the condition of manifestation; and no poem is anything other than the manifestation of a medium.

My friend Ivan Argüelles handwrote a poem in a spiral notebook while sitting in a UC Berkeley student hang-out called "Kip's." He then phoned me to ask what I thought of the poem. Later, he typed the poem onto a piece of white paper. Using that paper as a "score," he recited the poem at a reading in Berkeley. He also sent "copies" by e-mail to various friends. Later still, he published the poem in a literary magazine. It may have appeared in an online magazine as well. Finally, it became part of a book, in which it would be read and perhaps memorized and recited by other people. Some of these people might like it enough to e-mail it to their friends. Each of these manifestations—spiral notebook, phone call, white paper, recitation, magazine, electronic publication, book—is separate and distinct from all the others. The version of the poem which appears in each of them is separate and distinct from all the others as well.

But, surely, it may be objected, while these various media are all admittedly somewhat different from one another, they are all manifesting *some thing*— and that *thing* exists apart from and prior to any medium. That is a very Platonic idea, and it has considerable appeal in our neo-neo-neo-neo-neo Platonic civilization. But is it true?

We might ask: Doesn't the poem exist first "in the poet's mind"—before it is on paper or spoken? Isn't it there before it shows itself in any medium? These questions can be answered, but the answers require a slight adjustment of our thinking. Rarely is the poem "complete" in the poet's mind: usually it comes into being in a struggle between mind and—a medium: paper, speaking aloud, whatever. That is the period in which the poet is "working on" the poem. But, beyond this, we must understand that *the notion of mind itself is a medium*—or the postulation of a medium—and that it is only by analogy with mind that media exist. Or, more accurately perhaps, it is only by analogy with media that the concept of "mind" exists. We can write a poem only because the poem is already being conceived of as "written." "Mind" is like the paper of a book or like the sound of a speaking voice: it is the primary context within which the verbal or visual event takes place; it is what we *forget* as we listen to the poet describing his wonderful adventures in the world of thought. But without that primary context the poet's description could not exist at all.

In a famous passage from her book, *Everybody's Autobiography*, Gertrude Stein slandered Oakland, California by writing, "There is no there there." The medium is the poem's "there," and it keeps on changing: mind, spiral notebook, phone call, white paper, recitation, magazine, electronic publication, book. These are all media. The poem does not birth itself in the poet's mind and then go on from there to manifest in various media: it simply shifts from one medium to another, as indeed it does when the poet is working on the poem. From this point of view, there is nothing but media—various ways in which the poem shows itself. But there is no poem *apart* from these media. We can of course privilege one medium over another; we can personally prefer one medium to another: each has its strengths and limitations. In our culture, the print medium has enjoyed considerable privilege: fear that this privilege may be ending—or challenged—has brought forth a bevy of cries that our "children don't read enough," that people are becoming "illiterate." But poetry manifests in a number of media—it is not limited to print—and, without the medium, there is no poetry. There is not even silence, which, like everything else, requires a medium.

> Quite unexpectedly, as Vasserot
> The armless ambidextrian was lighting
> A match between his great and second toe,
> And Ralph the lion was engaged in biting
> The neck of Madame Sossman while the drum
> Pointed, and Teeny was about to cough
> In waltz-time swinging Jocko by the thumb—
> Quite unexpectedly the top blew off:
>
> And there, there overhead, there, there hung over
> Those thousands of white faces, those dazed eyes,
> There in the starless dark the poise, the hover,
> There with vast wings across the cancelled skies,
> There in the sudden blackness the black pall
> Of nothing, nothing, nothing—nothing at all.

Archibald MacLeish was writing about "The End of the World." We have had many a *frisson* from literary versions of apocalypse. But 1984 came and went; 2000 came and went; and the world goes on. Perhaps what MacLeish was really writing about was the absence of a medium. I can't tell you where media come from: speculations about that subject go well beyond the boundaries of this panel into the mysterious areas of human thinking and creativity. Even panels must leave themselves open to mystery. But I can tell you this: it is possible, even after all these years, that *Plato was wrong,* and that we must make an effort to think in a different way if we are to encounter reality at all. What I found as I considered the usual view of "poetry and the media" was the concept of mind as something separate and apart from its manifestations—its "media." But what if mind is a kind of medium? What if its manifestations are all we have of mind? In any case, where there are media, there are poems, and where there are no media there are no poems, no thought, no interchange, no ideas, no love, no error, no speech, no intercourse, no—*[gesture towards infinity]*

Classics

William Butler Yeats

The Tower: A Facsimile Edition

> I say to the musicians: 'Lose my words in patterns of sound as the name of God is lost
> in Arabian arabesques. They are a secret between the singers, myself, yourselves. . . .'
> —W.B. YEATS, introduction to *King of the Great Clock Tower*,
>   quoted in F.A.C. Wilson, *W.B. Yeats and Tradition*

In 1928—the year he turned sixty-three—the world-famous poet William Butler Yeats published a slim, beautifully-produced volume called *The Tower*. Yeats had received the Nobel Prize in 1923, and the book was awaited with considerable anticipation. The book's title referred explicitly to "Thoor Ballylee," a derelict Norman stone tower located near Coole Park, the estate owned by Yeats' friend Lady Gregory. Yeats had purchased Thoor Ballylee in 1917. After the tower was restored, it became a summer home for himself and his wife, Georgie Hyde-Lees. T. Sturge Moore's beautiful image on the cover of *The Tower* shows Thoor Ballylee reflected in the still water below it. The image suggests both Yeats' poetic self-reflection—the meditative quality of his verse—and the hermetic tag, "As above, so below."

The Tower contains some of what were to be the poet's most famous, most explicated poems: "Sailing to Byzantium," the title poem, "Meditations in Time of Civil War," "Nineteen Hundred and Nineteen," "Leda and the Swan," and—last but far from least—"Among School Children." Yeats critic M.L. Rosenthal called *The Tower* "Yeats' finest single volume," and the book became, Brenda Maddox tells us in *Yeats's Ghosts: The Secret Life of W.B. Yeats*, the poet's "first best-seller." Yeats himself was very pleased with *The Tower's* reception. He wrote his friend Lady Gregory that "*Tower* is receiving great favour. Perhaps the reviewers know that I am so ill that I can be commended without future inconvenience . . . Even the Catholic Press is enthusiastic." And he told Olivia Shakespear, "*The Tower* is a great success, two thousand copies in the first month, much the largest sale I have ever had. . . ."

Seventy-six years after the first publication of *The Tower*, Scribner's has come out with a facsimile edition with an introduction and two sets of notes by Yeats scholar Richard J. Finneran. (Finneran has supplied us with notes to Yeats' notes as well as notes to the poems themselves.) What can this new volume tell us about Yeats? Are any new insights possible in the case of a poet who has been the subject of so much intense critical scrutiny?

The book opens with the famous opening line of "Sailing to Byzantium"— "That is no country for old men. The young . . ."—and those two terms, "old men," "the young," reverberate throughout the volume. In the very next poem, "The Tower," the poet tells us that, though he is afflicted by "Decrepit age," he is nevertheless in some sense "younger" than he has ever been:

> Never had I more
> Excited, passionate, fantastical
> Imagination, nor an ear and eye
> That more expected the impossible—
> No, not in boyhood when with rod and fly,
> Or the humbler worm, I climbed Ben Bulben's
> back. . . .

Recent biographers have pointed out Yeats' none-too-circumspect, extremely problematical philandering as he aged. Is the combination of "Decrepit age" and violent youth—"Excited, passionate, fantastical / Imagination"—to some degree an indication, even an exploration, of that philandering? "With the easy chauvinism of his time," Brenda Maddox writes,

> [Yeats] used his wife as business manager, nurse, real estate agent, hostess, editor, literary agent, and proofreader while allowing his sexual interests to drift elsewhere. One of his first affairs was with Dolly (Dorothy) Travers-Smith, an artist and scene-painter for the Abbey and the daughter of the automatic-writing medium Hester Travers-Smith. Yeats found Dolly "slim and red-lipped." Friends were amused to watch him one day at a party at Lennox Robinson's cottage try to put her in a trance.

How does this slightly ridiculous philandering—this "faithlessness"—register in his poetry, if indeed it does at all? *The Tower* has one poem, "The Hero, The Girl, and the Fool," which ends with the lines,

> When my days that have
> From cradle run to grave
> From grave to cradle run instead;
> When thoughts that a fool

> Has wound upon a spool
> Are but loose thread, are but loose thread.
>
> When cradle and spool are past
> And I mere shade at last
> Coagulate of stuff
> Transparent like the wind,
> I think that I may find
> A faithful love, a faithful love. . . .

These lines suggest that "a faithful love" is something one can find only after death. Another poem, "The Gift of Harun Al-Rashid," seems to be a transparent tribute to the poet's wife George and her mediumistic abilities:

> was it she that spoke or some great Djinn?
> I say that a Djinn spoke. A live-long hour
> She seemed the learned man and I the child;
> Truths without father came, truths that no book
> Of all the uncounted books that I have read,
> Nor thought out of her mind or mine begot,
> Self-born, high-born, and solitary truths,
> Those terrible implacable straight lines
> Drawn through the wandering vegetative dream. . . .

But "The Gift of Harun Al-Rashid" does not suggest that Yeats has any sexual passion for his wife. "Margot"—a poem written in 1934 but kept unseen until 1970, more than thirty years after the poet's death in 1939—is addressed to Margot Ruddock, one of various "out-of-control" women (Brenda Maddox's phrase) with whom Yeats had extra-marital affairs. It continues *The Tower's* theme of "young" mind and "old" body:

> I
>
> All famine struck sat I, and then
> Those generous eyes on mine were cast,
> Sat like other aged men
> Dumfoundered, gazing on a past
> That appeared constructed of
> Lost opportunities to love.

II

O how can I that interest hold?
What offer to attentive eyes?
Mind grows young and body old;
When half closed her eye-lid lies
A sort of hidden glory shall
About these stooping shoulders fall.

III

The Age of Miracles renew,
Let me be loved as though still young
Or let me fancy that it's true,
When my brief final years are gone
You shall have time to turn away
And cram those open eyes with day.

Though the "tower," the central image of Yeats' book, surely has a number of implications—including the suggestion of the dwelling place of the isolated contemplative—one of its meanings is very obviously the erect phallus. We should note as well that, though Yeats and others have emphasized the historical implications of "Leda and the Swan," not only does this frankly sexual poem depict the revelation of the divine (the "marriage" of mind and matter) as a particularly violent rape: it depicts it as an extra-marital affair. The violent, history-making moment does not arise out of anything Zeus does with his wife; it arises out of his lust (however "indifferent" the god may finally be) for a young woman. Still another poem, "Owen Ahern and His Dancers," deals more or less explicitly with Yeats' "mad" infatuation with Maud Gonne's daughter, Iseult:

I did not find in any cage the woman at my side.
O but her heart would break to learn my thoughts
are far away.

Both the figures of Leda and the swan are important images in *The Tower*. In "Among School Children" Yeats explicitly associates Maud Gonne with Leda's daughter, Helen—an association he made in many poems:

> I dream of a Ledaean body . . .
> For even daughters of the swan can share
> Something of every paddler's heritage. . . .

(Since Helen's mother is mortal, Helen/Maud Gonne is *half* divine—but in her beauty she takes after her mother: she has "a Ledaean body.") The swan appears again in the climactic third section of "The Tower":

> the hour
> When the swan must fix his eye
> Upon a fading gleam,
> Float out upon a long
> Last reach of glittering stream
> And there sing his last song.

And in "Nineteen Hundred and Nineteen" Yeats writes,

> Some moralist or mythological poet
> Compares the solitary soul to a swan;
> I am satisfied with that—

In both these latter passages, the swan is an emblem of the individual (or "solitary") soul. From this point of view (swan as individual soul), the multi-leveled Leda story suggests the immensely problematical attraction of the soul (swan) to matter (Leda)—an attraction Yeats refers to in "Among School Children" as a "drug" whose effects eventually cause the resulting child to "sleep, shriek, struggle to escape." In "Leda and the Swan," the encounter between soul and matter is presented in a primarily mythological/historical context rather than in the context of the individual, but the results are similarly disastrous:

> A shudder in the loins engenders there
> The broken wall, the burning roof and tower
> And Agamemnon dead.

Swans in the context of faithfulness/unfaithfulness suggest an earlier poem which also deals with old age, "The Wild Swans at Coole"—the title poem of a volume Yeats published in 1919. "The Wild Swans at Coole," set at Lady Gregory's estate, is at once autobiographical, descriptive and visionary.

An aging Yeats, remembering his youth, sees the swans "Upon the brimming water among the stones." "All's changed," he writes,

> I have looked upon those brilliant creatures,
> And now my heart is sore.
> All's changed since I, hearing at twilight,
> The first time on this shore,
> The bell-beat of their wings above my head,
> Trod with a lighter tread.

The swans' "hearts," he muses—as opposed to his own—"have not grown old":

> Unwearied still, lover by lover,
> They paddle in the cold
> Companionable streams or climb the air;
> Their hearts have not grown old;
> Passion or conquest, wander where they will,
> Attend upon them still.

The swans present an image of "a faithful love," one which maintains its allegiance to the divine.[1] Yeats himself, on the other hand, has become increasing involved in the beautiful "wood of matter" which surrounds him—"The trees are in their autumn beauty, / The woodland paths are dry"—and, as a consequence, has moved further away from the divine. Here too he is "faithless."

As Paul de Man was the first to notice, shining through Yeats' naturalistic "imagery" is a notion expounded by the Neoplatonist, Porphyry (232/3 - ca. 305) in his *De Antro Nympharum*, a commentary on the Cave of the Nymphs episode in *The Odyssey*. Yeats knew Porphyry's essay through Thomas Taylor's widely-read translation, and he refers explicitly to it in the footnote about "the drug" in "Among School Children." He quotes extensively from the essay in "The Philosophy of Shelley's Poetry"—one of the essays collected in *Ideas of Good and Evil* (1903)—and there are unmistakable references to Porphyry in both Blake and Spenser as well as in Yeats' own work. Though Thomas Taylor "was ridiculed, even persecuted, for bringing to the attention of his age a philosophy so subversive to established values," writes Kathleen Raine in *Blake and Antiquity*,

Coleridge delighted in Taylor's works, Shelley possessed them, Keats too reflected their influence; crossing the Atlantic, they were all-important in the American Transcendentalist movement. To Emerson and Bronson Alcott Taylor was, as George Russell and his friends later called him, "the uncrowned king."

Appearing in *The Witch of Atlas, The Book of Thel,* and in the third Book of *The Faerie Queene,* the cluster of symbols discussed in Porphyry's essay is one of the key items of literary Neoplatonism.

As described by Porphyry, the Cave of the Nymphs is a kind of half-way house for all souls about to be born or about to ascend to heaven; as such it is regarded as the source of all life, which is symbolized by "waters welling everywhere." One of its gates—"the gate of generation"—leads to the earth, and the other—"the gate of ascent through death to the gods"—leads to heaven. The first is "the gate of cold and moisture"—for "cold . . . causes life in the world"—and the second is "the gate of heat and fire." If we keep only these details in mind—and Porphyry goes on to add a great many others—we can see how the Cave of the Nymphs is relevant to "The Wild Swans at Coole." The "brimming water among the stones," for example, is Yeats' equivalent to the water welling among the rocks of the cave, and the two activities of the swans—"They paddle in the cold / Companionable streams or climb the air"— represent respectively the descent of the soul into matter through the gate of cold and moisture and, since air is a purer element than water, the ascent to the divine. Yeats often imagines this ascent as proceeding in "rings" or "gyres" and as accompanied by the sound of a bell—here, "the bell-beat of their wings above my head." (Cf. the bells in "Byzantium" and "All Souls' Night.")[2]

Was the cluster of images in Porphyry's essay a mere "source" for Yeats— something he transformed in the course of writing his poems—or was it something else? That question is another issue raised in *The Tower.* In "Among School Children" the poet makes a careful distinction between two kinds of "images":

> Both nuns and mother worship images,
> But those the candles light are not as those
> That animate a mother's reveries,
> But keep a marble or a bronze repose.

This distinction between different kinds of "images" is no new thing in Yeats' thought. In "Symbolism in Painting," from *Ideas of Good and Evil,* he writes

> All art that is not mere story-telling, or mere portraiture, is symbolic, and has the
> purpose of those symbolic talismans which mediaeval magicians made with complex
> colours and forms, and bade their patients ponder over daily, and guard with holy
> secrecy; for it entangles, in complex colours and forms, a part of the Divine Essence.

"If," he goes on, "you liberate a person or a landscape from the bonds of
motives and their actions, causes and their effects . . . it will change under
your eyes, and become a symbol of an infinite emotion, a perfected emotion,
a part of the Divine Essence. . . ."

The use of mere metaphor, he argues in "Symbolism in Poetry" (also
from *Ideas of Good and Evil*), is not sufficient: "metaphors are not profound
enough to be moving." Symbols "call down among us certain disembodied
powers, whose footsteps over our hearts we call emotions. . . ." Even
Shakespeare is criticized:

> Shakespeare is content with emotional symbols that he may come the nearer to our
> sympathy, but if one is moved by Dante, or by the myth of Demeter, one is mixed
> into the shadow of God.
> ("Symbolism in Poetry")

"Shelley's poetry," Yeats insists in "The Philosophy of Shelley's Poetry,"
"becomes the richer, and loses something of the appearance of idle fantasy,
when I remember that its images are ancient symbols, and still come to
visionaries in their dreams."

The "images" which "animate a mother's reveries" are in the realm of
"mere story-telling, or mere portraiture"; at best, they are in the realm of
metaphor. Images which "keep a marble or a bronze repose"—sacred images
such as the golden bird invoked at the conclusion of "Sailing to Byzantium"—
have another purpose altogether and "call down among us certain
disembodied powers." Yeats' earlier poem, "The Dolls," from *Responsibilities*
(1914), deals with the two kinds of images in a comic way:

> A doll in the doll-maker's house
> Looks at the cradle and bawls:
> 'That is an insult to us.'

The "oldest of all the dolls" describes the baby as "a noisy and filthy thing";
its appearance in the shop brings "disgrace" upon the dolls. Finally, the doll-
maker's wife ends the poem with an apology:

> 'My dear, my dear, O dear,
> It was an accident.'

"The Dolls" demonstrates that Yeats was capable of seeing the comic side of his dilemma, but it is precisely the notion of the sacred but nevertheless *embodied* (*non*abstract) *image* which allows the poet to escape from the situation he describes at the beginning of "The Tower":

> It seems that I must bid the Muse go pack,
> Choose Plato and Plotinus for a friend
> Until imagination, ear and eye,
> Can be content with argument and deal
> In abstract things; or be derided by
> A sort of battered kettle at the heel.

At the conclusion of the poem, the "learned school" in which the soul studies is not the "school" of Plato and Plotinus, with their "abstract things," but something closer to the "school" of Porphyry, with its insistence that Homer "has obscurely indicated the images of things of a more divine nature in the fiction of a fable"—its insistence that Homer was, in effect, in Yeats' terms, a Symbolist poet. Porphyry's term for Homer's sacred imagery is in fact, in Taylor's translation, "fabulous symbols"—a phrase which shows up in a horrific context when Yeats comes to write "Her Vision in the Wood." (Yeats' interest in finding a "school" is also something to be kept in mind when we arrive at "Among School Children": the title refers not only to the "children" the poet meets in Reverend Mother Philomena's Montessori school but to the poet himself, who is still looking for a proper "school." Cf. the line in "The Gift of Harun Al-Rashid," the penultimate poem of *The Tower*: "She seemed the learned man and I the child. . . .")

At the conclusion of "The Tower," Yeats pours forth a number of what are for him "fabulous symbols":

> Pride, like that of the morn,
> When the headlong light is loose,
> Or that of the fabulous horn,
> Or that of the sudden shower
> When all streams are dry,
> Or that of the hour
> When the swan must fix his eye

> Upon a fading gleam,
> Float out upon a long
> Last reach of glittering stream
> And there sing his last song.

Nor is Porphyry absent from Yeats' list. The lines,

> I choose upstanding men,
> That climb the streams until
> The fountain leap, and at dawn
> Drop their cast at the side
> Of dripping stone. . . .

in part refer back to an earlier, nostalgic passage in the poem,

> in boyhood when with rod and fly,
> Or the humbler worm, I climbed Ben Bulben's back
> And had the livelong summer day to spend,

but both the "fountain" and the "dripping stone" (not mentioned in the earlier passage) are details from Porphyry, "fabulous symbols" which show up often in Yeats. (The "dripping stone" is equivalent to "the brimming water among the stones" in "The Wild Swans at Coole.") Here and elsewhere, Yeats is attempting, through the use of "symbols," "to liberate a person or a landscape from the bonds of motives and their actions, causes and their effects" and to allow the person or landscape to "change under your eyes."

"Among School Children" is the poem in *The Tower* which has been most explicated and, to my mind, most misunderstood. I wrote about the poem at some length in my essay, "Yeats' Poetic Art" (available from the archives of my online column, "Foley's Books," in my book, *Foley's Books*, and in *The Yeats Eliot Review*, vol. 18, no. 4, April 2002). The problem of the poem is not so much old age as it is the difficulty of distinguishing between kinds of "images." Yeats' intense infatuation with Maud Gonne's beauty (her "Ledaean body") led him to believe that she was an embodiment of the divine—a "fabulous symbol." As she ages, however, she seems anything but such an "image":

> Her present image floats into the mind—
> Did Quattrocento finger fashion it
> Hollow of cheek as though it drank the wind
> And took a mess of shadows for its meat?

Indeed, the once beautiful, "Ledaean" woman now seems, like Yeats himself, a scarecrow: "Old clothes upon old sticks to scare a bird." Not something to attract a bird like the swan but something to scare it away.

In this context, the concluding lines of the poem take on a meaning which is very different from the one which is usually ascribed to them:

> O chestnut-tree, great-rooted blossomer,
> Are you the leaf, the blossom or the bole?
> O body swayed to music, O brightening glance,
> How can we know the dancer from the dance?

Are these lines the expression of "organic unity" that critics usually take them to be? Isn't a chestnut-tree (like any tree) an expression of the ultimate unity of leaf, blossom and bole? Aren't leaf, blossom and bole parts of the whole? Are the two aspects of Maud Gonne—her divinity and her humanity—in a state of harmony or are they in conflict with one another? Aren't the dancer and the dance identical, since we can experience the dance only *through* the dancer?

A bole is "the stem or trunk of a tree." A leaf is "one of the expanded, usually green organs borne by the stem of a plant." A blossom is "the flower of a plant, esp. of one producing an edible fruit . . . *The apple tree is in blossom.*" (Definitions from *The Random House Dictionary*). As time passes, as the tree "grows," we experience bole, leaf and blossom. But that is the point: *as time passes*. I think that the answer to Yeats' first question is *No*: his "great-rooted blossomer" is precisely *not* "the leaf, the blossom or the bole"— not the tree that exists in time. Rather, it is a "fabulous symbol"—something existing outside of time, or in a different temporal order from the human and the natural. The elevated tone of "great-rooted blossomer" (as opposed to the mere "blossom" of the next line) suggests the difference. The "great-rooted blossomer" is, in effect, *nothing but* a "blossomer." Unlike Maud Gonne, it never ceases to manifest the divine; it never grows old, and it constantly points to what Yeats calls in "The Gift of Harun Al-Rashid" "Self-born, high-born, and solitary truths, / Those terrible implacable straight lines / Drawn through the wandering vegetative dream."

The meaning of the chestnut image is suggested by a passage in Basho's *The Narrow Road to the Deep North*: "The chestnut is a holy tree, for the Chinese ideograph for chestnut is Tree placed directly below West, the direction of the holy land." The "great-rooted blossomer" is like those images which "keep a marble or a bronze repose." The organic tree, on the other hand, is an image like those worshiped by mothers—an image whose reflection of the divine is essentially mutable.

A similar distinction can be made between the dancer and the dance. "The dance," writes Paul de Man in "Image and Emblem in Yeats,"

> is a recurrent emblem for contact with the divine; the following early quotation describes it well: "Men who lived in a world where anything might flow and change . . . had always, as it seems, for a supreme ritual that tumultuous dance among the hills or in the depths of the woods, where unearthly ecstasy fell upon the dancers, until they seemed the gods or the godlike beasts, and felt their souls overtopping the moon; and, as some think, imaged for the first time in the world the blessed country of the gods and of the happy dead" . . . The "dancer" on the other hand . . . is associated with the symbol of the "body" and appears as a real woman in the generated world of matter, capable of giving the "pleasure of generation."

Maud Gonne may well have functioned as Yeats' Muse—and may well be to some degree responsible for some of his finest poetry. His "worship" of her physical beauty may have led him to a kind of "perfection." At the same time, however, that very quest meant that he had to abandon something—and it is that "something" which is the great issue of his later poetry. Was Yeats' interest in Maud Gonne spiritual or libidinous? What kind of "image"—what kind of "body"—has been the constant subject of his work? "Her Vision in the Wood" (from *The Winding Stair and Other Poems*, 1933) contains the heart-rending admission that the poet's attempt to become an archetype—"to liberate a person or a landscape from the bonds of motives and their actions, causes and their effects"—ends in woeful failure; the poem even contains Porphyry's significant phrase, "fabulous symbol," now not spoken in triumph but in despair:

> That thing all blood and mire, that beast-torn wreck,
> Half turned and fixed a glazing eye on mine,
> And, though love's bitter-sweet had all come back,
> Those bodies from a picture or a coin
> Nor saw my body fall nor heard it shriek,
> Nor knew, drunken with singing as with wine,
> That they had brought no fabulous symbol there
> But my heart's victim and its torturer.

"How can we know the dancer from the dance?" The line is not a mere piece of rhetoric but a genuine, anguished question: the burden of the poem is that Yeats has *failed to know* the answer to that question, and it has cost him dearly.

Despite his sixty years, Yeats remains at the end of "Among School Children" not a figure of wisdom but a learner—"among school children," asking questions to which he has no real answer. His stance at the end of the poem is no different than it was at the beginning: "I walk through the long schoolroom *questioning*," though it is true that our experience of the poem has deepened our sense of the importance of that questioning.

Yeats himself remarked upon the "bitterness" he found in *The Tower;* bitterness is definitely one of the volume's themes:

> Death and life were not
> Till man made up the whole,
> Made lock, stock and barrel
> Out of his bitter soul,
> Aye, sun and moon and star, all . . .
> ("The Tower")

❧

> Some violent bitter man, some powerful man
> Called architect and artist in, that they,
> Bitter and violent men, might rear in stone
> The sweetness that all longed for night and day . . .
>
> What if those things the greatest of mankind,
> Consider most to magnify, or to bless,
> But take our greatness with our bitterness!
> ("Meditations in Time of Civil War")

❧

> All, all those gyres and cubes and midnight things
> Are but a new expression of her body
> Drunk with the bitter sweetness of her youth.
> ("The Gift of Harun Al-Rashid")

But "bitterness" and "sweetness" are merely two examples of Yeats' constantly oppositional thinking—what he calls his "continual oscillations" (quoted in

F.A.C. Wilson, *W.B. Yeats and Tradition*); they correspond roughly to "this world" and "the next world." Cf. The remarkable concluding lines to "Demon and Beast" from *Michael Robartes and the Dancer* (1921):

> O what a sweetness strayed
> Through barren Thebaid,
> Or by the Mareotic sea
> When that exultant Anthony
> And twice a thousand more
> Starved upon the shore
> And withered to a bag of bones!
> What had the Caesars but their thrones?

There is perhaps an even deeper "bitterness" at work in *The Tower*. Yeats' language as he attempts to define the functioning of the symbol—the symbol "*entangles*, in complex colours and forms, a part of the Divine Essence"; symbols "*call down among us* certain disembodied powers, whose footsteps over our hearts we call emotions" (my italics)—suggests one of his primary themes: the descent of spirit into matter, often referred to in esoteric writing as "the fall of man" or "the tragedy." The many oppositions which inhabit Yeats' poetry are all versions of this primary opposition, this "tragedy," which, Yeats argues in *The Tower*, is ultimately not worth it: [3]

> Never to have lived is best, ancient writers say;
> Never to have drawn the breath of life, never to have looked into
>   the eye of day;
> The second best's a gay goodnight and quickly turn away.
> ("From 'Oedipus at Colonus'")

∽

> What youthful mother, a shape upon her lap
> Honey of generation had betrayed,
> And that must sleep, shriek, struggle to escape
> As recollection or the drug decide,
> Would think her son, did she but see that shape
> With sixty or more winters on its head,
> A compensation for the pang of his birth,
> Or the uncertainty of his setting forth?
> ("Among School Children")

Yeats' conception of "the symbol" was in effect Porphyry's cave all over again. If the symbol could "attract" spirit to it—emulate in little the "fall of man"—it could also lead man back to the divine. But what if the symbol couldn't accomplish this? What if all that happens is merely the fall? Worse, what if the poem achieves not cosmic revelation but only self-awareness? In this context, the lines, "the tragedy began / With Homer that was a blind man" ("The Tower"), take on an added dimension. Was Homer "blind" to the consequences of his actions? If even the much-lauded "symbol" involves "the tragedy," what hope is there for literature? The first stanza of "Two Songs From a Play" concludes,

> And then did all the Muses sing
> Of Magnus Annus at the spring,
> As though God's death were but a play.

Is "God's death" not, as Yeats once hoped, a "symbolic talisman," a genuinely magical event, but merely an esthetic matter—"but a play"? Was that in fact the primary revelation of his poetry?

With *The Tower* Yeats begins a passionate exploration of his entire career which brings him finally to the perception of an intense, monumental *lack* of unity, to the realization of a fundamental confusion among his impulses—a confusion which is at best masked by his doctrine of oppositions. "Why should not old men be mad?" he asks in *Last Poems* (1936-1939),

> No single story would they find
> Of an unbroken happy mind,
> A finish worthy of the start.
> Young men know nothing of this sort,
> Observant old men know it well;
> And when they know what old books tell,
> And that no better can be had,
> Know why an old man should be mad.

In the introduction to *King of the Great Clock Tower* (1935), Yeats wrote, "I say to the musicians: 'Lose my words in patterns of sound as the name of God is lost in Arabian arabesques.'" The paradox of Yeats' poetry, of which he was fully aware, was that it was conceived not as self-expression but as divine song—a celebration of those "powers" which he sensed operating "behind" nature; *yet it was everywhere fueled by a transgressive impulse which he could not escape if he were to write the poetry at all.* This paradox is constantly present in Yeats' work, which remains tremendously exciting but which nowhere arrives at that "unity of being" for which some critics wish to praise him.

If in Yeats' early work the poet is imagined as a "priest"—"The arts are . . . about to take upon their shoulders the burdens that have fallen from the shoulders of priests" ("The Autumn of the Body," 1898); "We who care deeply about the arts find ourselves the priesthood of an almost forgotten faith, and we must . . . take upon ourselves the method and the fervour of a priesthood" ("Ireland and the Arts," 1901)—in his later work the poet is a "wild old wicked man." Yeats' late "affairs" (not to mention his delight in "dirty stories") were, at least in part, an exploration on "the biographical level" of this lifelong spiritual paradox—a paradox which resulted both in great poetry and in a fearful spiritual enterprise which was anything but "unified":

> The intellect of man is forced to choose
> Perfection of the life, or of the work,
> Yet if it chose the second must refuse
> A heavenly mansion, raging in the dark.
> ("The Choice," from
> *The Winding Stair and Other Poems*, 1933)

∽

> But Love has pitched his mansion in
> The place of excrement. . . .
> ("Crazy Jane Talks with the Bishop," from
> *The Winding Stair and Other Poems*, 1933)

Yeats

evasive,
he answered questions
deceitfully
like a politician . . .
love
fades

looking
he found her brown
hair
inescapable . . .
try as he may . . .
love
fades

God
addressed him
when he was a child
assuring him
of a lifetime of visions
and endless
love
he said, "God, I will love You always"
God
fades

Two Classics Revisited

1. *Keats' Great Ode*

for Matt Phillips

ODE ON A GRECIAN URN

1

Thou still unravished bride of quietness,
      Thou foster child of silence and slow time,
Sylvan historian, who canst thus express
      A flowery tale more sweetly than our rhyme:
What leaf-fringed legend haunts about thy shape
      Of deities or mortals, or of both,
            In Tempe or the dales of Arcady?
What men or gods are these? What maidens loth?
      What mad pursuit? What struggle to escape?
         What pipes and timbrels? What wild ecstasy?

2

Heard melodies are sweet, but those unheard
      Are sweeter; therefore, ye soft pipes, play on;
Not to the sensual ear, but, more endeared,
      Pipe to the spirit ditties of no tone:
Fair youth, beneath the trees, thou canst not leave
      Thy song, nor ever can those trees be bare;
         Bold Lover, never, never canst thou kiss,
Though winning near the goal—yet, do not grieve;
      She cannot fade, though thou hast not thy bliss,
        Forever wilt thou love, and she be fair!

3

Ah, happy, happy boughs! that cannot shed
      Your leaves, nor ever bid the spring adieu;
And, happy melodist, unwearied,
      Forever piping songs forever new;
More happy love! more happy, happy love!
      Forever warm and still to be enjoyed,
          Forever panting, and forever young;
All breathing human passion far above,
      That leaves a heart high-sorrowful and cloyed,
          A burning forehead, and a parching tongue.

4

Who are these coming to the sacrifice?
      To what green altar, O mysterious priest,
Lead'st thou that heifer lowing at the skies,
      And all her silken flanks with garlands dressed?
What little town by river or sea shore,
      Or mountain-built with peaceful citadel,
          Is emptied of this folk, this pious morn?
And, little town, thy streets for evermore
      Will silent be; and not a soul to tell
          Why thou art desolate, can e'er return.

5

O Attic shape! Fair attitude! with brede
      Of marble men and maidens overwrought,
With forest branches and the trodden weed;
      Thou, silent form, dost tease us out of thought
As doth eternity: Cold Pastoral!
      When old age shall this generation waste,
          Thou shalt remain, in midst of other woe
Than ours, a friend to man, to whom thou say'st,
      Beauty is truth, truth beauty—that is all
          Ye know on earth, and all ye need to know.

My friend the artist Matt Phillips told me recently of his great admiration for John Keats. Phillips had written a short essay about Keats to accompany his illustrations to "Ode on a Grecian Urn." Phillips' comments sent me back to Keats' great poem and then to a particular edition of Keats' work published by Signet in 1966 and edited by an old mentor of mine, Paul de Man (1919-1983). I knew de Man when he was at Cornell University, where he taught from 1960 to 1966. I had heard about him earlier, when I spent a summer at Harvard. I was speaking to a friend about William Butler Yeats. The friend said, "You sound a bit like Paul de Man." When I asked who Paul de Man was, my friend explained that he was a brilliant teacher who had a particularly brilliant version of Yeats. When I returned to Cornell, I was surprised to find de Man teaching there.

I remembered two things about de Man's introduction to his edition of Keats. The first was de Man's insistence that "Time and again, literary and critical movements set out with the avowed aim of moving beyond romantic attitudes and ideas":

> But time and again, it turns out that the new conceptions that thus assert themselves were in fact already present in the full context of European romanticism; instead of moving beyond these problems, we are merely becoming aware of certain aspects of romanticism that had remained hidden from our perception . . . What sets out as a claim to overcome romanticism often turns out to be merely an expansion of our understanding of the movement, leading inevitably to changes in our images of individual poets.

The second thing I remembered was de Man's assertion that the "striking fact about Keats's last poems is that they contain an attack on much that had been held sacred in the earlier work; one is reminded, at moments, of Yeats's savagely derisive treatment of his own myths in some of the *Last Poems*":

> There is something indecorous in the spectacle of a poet thus turning against himself and one can understand the desire of commentators to play down this episode in Keats's history. . . .

Paul de Man's own last book, *The Rhetoric of Romanticism* (1984), contains an equally "indecorous" attack upon his life's work—or at least upon the work collected in *The Rhetoric of Romanticism*:

> Such massive evidence of the failure to make the various individual readings coalesce is a somewhat melancholy spectacle. The fragmentary aspect of the whole is made more obvious still by the hypotactic manner that prevails in each of the essays taken in isolation, by the continued attempt, however ironized, to present a closed and

linear argument. This apparent coherence *within* each essay is not matched by a corresponding coherence *between* them . . . Rather, it seems that they always start again from scratch and that their conclusions fail to add up to anything.

I thought of such passages when I came upon Hegel's remark in the *Phenomenology* that man "sunders himself to self-realization"—the notion that self-realization involves a violent turning away from all those things one earlier held dear.

"The mixture of emotions" in Keats' great odes, de Man argues, "is subtle and self-deceiving":

[T]he poet's sympathy for the suffering of mankind gives him the kind of moral authority that allows him to call authoritatively for a lucid acceptance of human limitations. It is this morally responsible voice that warns his fellow men against the danger of giving in to the deceptive quality of poetic symbols: they "tease" and "deceive" in foreshadowing an eternity that is not within our reach; the urn and the nightingale finally act as powers of death and, in this sense, these poems are also written against the objects they set out to praise.

I'm not in complete agreement with de Man's remarks, but I find them still of considerable interest.

∽

Keats begins with desire, sexuality—even rape: "Thou still unravished bride. . . ." The violence implied by the word "ravished" is immediately "quieted," however, with an abstraction: "of quietness." In the second line, the phrase "foster child"—a phenomenon of *our* world, Keats' world—is balanced against the abstractions "silence and slow time." Each stanza—an Italian sonnet minus a quatrain—has a feeling of great formality: one *expects* abstractions and elegance from such forms, and Keats supplies them in abundance. Though Keats includes glancing references to the world we experience daily, nothing is terribly "real" in this deliberately artificial context.

Paul de Man points out that "Tempe and Arcady are the domains of Pan and Apollo, where Ovid describes them pursuing the mortal nymphs Syrinx and Daphne." The poet's evocation of an Ovidian "leaf-fringed legend" is very well suited to the antiquity and elegance of the form, and the evocation is followed by a slightly playful series of paradoxes. The assertion that the urn can "express . . . A flowery tale more sweetly than our rhyme" is a graceful compliment—the sort of "flowery" compliment one might pay to a woman one wishes to interest, not something anyone takes to be quite true. Indeed, "flowery tales" are often expressed in rhyme, and, if de Man is correct, Ovid is as much in Keats' mind as the urn itself. Something of the same thing can be said of Keats' "deities or mortals": we understand that these are literary or "artistic" figures—figures, not people—though the sexuality of "still unravished" is now given greater emphasis: "What maidens loth? / What mad pursuit? . . . What wild ecstasy?"

The second and third stanzas gave us light paradoxes which are not meant to be thought of too deeply or challenged in any way. *Are* "unheard" melodies sweeter than "heard melodies"? What is an unheard melody anyway? Keats assures us with a cliché: an unheard melody is something addressed "not to the sensual ear" but "to the spirit." Again, we are not to question too much. We are in some sort of vague version of idealism—some sort of conception in which the "ideal" is to be preferred to the "real." And the urn seems to express that idealism. Nothing is ever consummated—we are still in the realm of the "unravished bride"—but, on the other hand, desire is never quenched. Such a state, Keats argues lightly, is *better* than a situation in which consummation occurs. Had the scene on the urn presented an image of what Blake called "gratified desire," Keats' poem would have been profoundly altered: instead of perpetual desire we would have had perpetual orgasm—a state which is not so easily identified with "idealism." One can hear the voice of D.H. Lawrence or E.E. Cummings screaming at Keats' easy acceptance of sexual frustration—and his identification of it with the ideal. "Talk about your Sal- / Sal- /- Sal-," writes Cummings,

> talk
> about your Salo
> -mes but gimmie Jimmie's gal.
> ("Jimmie's got a goil")

Against this, Keats' assertions sound almost idiotic:

> Fair youth, beneath the trees, thou canst not leave
> Thy song, nor ever can those trees be bare;
> Bold lover, never, never canst thou kiss,
> Though winning near the goal—yet, do not grieve;
> She cannot fade, though thou hast not thy bliss,
> Forever wilt thou love, and she be fair!

Doesn't Keats have a body?

He does, and it will surface a few lines later. He attempts to put the best face possible on his assertion about the desirability of a state of perpetual sexual frustration by linking it to a state of eternal springtime—a state of paradise, though not quite the paradise of *Genesis*. He remains in a Classical, Ovidian context:

> Ah, happy, happy boughs! That cannot shed
>> Your leaves, nor ever bid the spring adieu;
> And, happy melodist, unwearied,
>> Forever piping songs forever new . . .

The "melodist" reminds us of the "shepherd" of pastoral poetry—the kind of thing both Spenser and Milton wrote. Yet the moment "human passion" is mentioned, the poem suddenly takes on a quality it has not had before. These lines are not Classical, fanciful, artificial or playfully paradoxical; they are utterly real:

> That leaves a heart high-sorrowful and cloyed,
>> A burning forehead, and a parching tongue.

That "burning forehead" and "parching tongue" might well be characteristics of a frustrated lover, but they also suggest the human diseases with which Keats was certainly familiar. It is as if the poet's own sexual frustration, which he has been attempting to disguise as idealism, suddenly bursts forth in the form of bodily illness. (In fact Keats once contracted a venereal disease.)

But like the earlier phrase, "foster child," the lines' touch of reality is only momentary; the poem is not yet ready to take on such questions. In relief perhaps, Keats turns to another side of the urn and attempts to regain the balance and control of the opening lines:

> Who are these coming to the sacrifice?
>> To what green altar, O mysterious priest,
> Lead'st thou that heifer lowing at the skies,
>> And all her silken flanks with garlands dressed?
> What little town by river or sea shore,
>> Or mountain-built with peaceful citadel,
>>> Is emptied of this folk, this pious morn?

Yet coming after assertions of intense bodily distress, the word "sacrifice" and the heifer's noisy "lowing at the skies" have overtones they would not have had under other circumstances. Doesn't disease cause the "sacrifice" of people? Wasn't Keats, who had been trained as a doctor, aware of such sacrifice? The feelings of desolation, of pain and sacrifice which have entered the poem almost against the poet's wishes suddenly have a new place to express themselves. The town the people leave—*which isn't even represented on the urn*—is suddenly seen not merely as empty but as *desolate*:

> And, little town, thy streets for evermore
> Will silent be; and not a soul to tell
> Why thou art desolate, can e'er return.

"Death," says Hamlet, "is the undiscovered country from whose bourn / No traveler returns" (III, i, 56). Death has suddenly entered Keats' poem: "not a soul to tell / Why thou art desolate, can e'er return." The artificiality of the paradise Keats was trying to describe protects us against death: "Ah, happy, happy boughs! That cannot shed / Your leaves, nor ever bid the spring adieu." Yet that paradise utterly shatters against the actual presence of death in the poem—a presence which both we and Keats know to the bone and which is linked to sexual frustration, itself a kind of death. Keats, born in 1795, was a young man when he wrote this poem in 1819, so it is not surprising that themes of sexual desire and frustration should be in his mind. He was also, as people often are in their early life, acutely aware of death. (Keats' father died in an accident when the poet was eight years old; his mother died of consumption in 1810; his brother Tom died of the disease in 1818).

To paraphrase Keats' "Ode to a Nightingale," the word "desolate" "is like a bell / To toll [the poet] back from thee to my sole self"—to the very mortality Keats has been trying to escape by writing the poem. "The fancy," he complains in the Nightingale Ode, "cannot cheat so well / As she is famed to do." What began as simple description—this is what is on the urn, it's only a description—has suddenly turned upon him and revealed the very sources which the poem existed to evade. *Keats didn't know why he was writing the poem, and the poem's language is now telling him something about his own consciousness.* He has nowhere to go but back to a confrontation with the urn as a whole—with this enigmatic *thing* which, like Poe's raven, has brought him mysterious news of his own death:

> O Attic shape! Fair attitude! with brede
>   Of marble men and maidens overwrought,
> With forest branches and the trodden weed;
>   Thou, silent form, dost tease us out of thought
> As doth eternity: Cold Pastoral!
>   When old age shall this generation waste,
>   Thou shalt remain, in midst of other woe
> Than ours, a friend to man, to whom thou say'st,
>   Beauty is truth, truth beauty—that is all
>   Ye know on earth, and all ye need to know.

The idea of "silence" is important to the poem. The urn is the "foster child of silence"; Keats writes of "unheard melodies"—silent ones; the streets of the town "for evermore / Will silent be"; there is "not a soul to tell / Why thou art desolate." In the last stanza the urn itself is called a "silent form," though in the concluding lines it "speaks": "thou say'st." Perhaps the most telling phrase of the stanza, however, is "Cold Pastoral!" At this point the urn is almost a tombstone, something which—like a published poem—extends beyond the life of the humans who constructed it and extends as well into the midst of "other woe / Than ours." If it is "a friend to man," it is also cold, like stone, lacking human warmth. Paul de Man glosses the celebrated concluding lines of the poem as follows:

> Stimulated by the gnomic character of the line and by the textual uncertainty, hundreds of pages have been written on the passage. If one ignores the quotation marks, then the entire statement would be made by the urn, including the following line "that is all ye know on earth and all ye need to know." If one keeps the quotation marks, then the remaining part of the sentence may not be said by the urn; it can either be addressed by Keats to the urn (or the figures on the urn) or, more likely, addressed by Keats to the reader. One can also question, in that case, what the antecedent of "that" would be. . . .

If we have to choose who exactly is saying the line, my own feeling—or part of my feeling—is that the statement "Beauty is truth, truth beauty" is said entirely by the urn, and that Keats is addressing the urn when he says, "That is all *ye* know on earth, and all *ye* need to know." Humans, who suffer and die like the lowing "heifer," have very different modes of knowledge from that of the urn. For the urn, "beauty" and "truth" can be identical because the "truth" expressed there is of a limited, artificial sort—something which evades the "truth" of mortality:

> Ah, happy, happy boughs! that cannot shed
> Your leaves, nor ever bid the spring adieu. . . .

Such a "truth" is by no means comforting since a good deal of the poem is devoted to demonstrating its limitations—even its inadequacy. Yet the lines,

> Beauty is truth, truth beauty—that is all
> Ye know on earth, and all ye need to know,

sound as though they ought to be comforting: they sound like a simplistic moral, something along the lines of Kipling's

> Yours is the Earth and everything that's in it,
> And—which is more—you'll be a Man, my son!
> ("If")

or like a sermon which asserts that the limitations of knowledge are a good thing: *Seek not to know too much*—that sort of thing. Keats' designation of the urn as "a friend to man"—as opposed to a "Cold Pastoral!"—now becomes important. Surely a "friend" would not attack us: it would offer us comfort in our misery. The concluding lines of the poem are not only, as de Man says, "gnomic" but deliberately evasive. There is no comfort against mortality; it is a stark fact which cannot be avoided—and there is nothing in the poem which suggests the possibility of a blissful afterlife. The poem is without comfort of any kind. And yet: the concluding lines don't "know" that. We are given a "moral" which is in fact not the moral of the poem at all—and it allows us, in its deception, to exit without tears or anger. Beauty, truth—how nice to think that they are identical, and how nice not to have to think anything more about it.

❧

A friend wrote me about my paper on Keats. I answered as follows:

I think perhaps that both your suggestions are rooted in a determination to keep the poem somehow in Keats' control (or in someone's control). You write of "a sense of superiority as one unmasks the self-deceptions of the material" and of "an appreciation for the way the poem dramatizes its own unmasking for the reader's delight and appreciation"—Keats as audience for his own poem.

In the latter case, as audience, his identity is not placed in question—in fact, his "appreciation" affirms him as an ego. In the former case, he feels "a sense of superiority"—again an affirmation of his ego. And ego means control.

I am suggesting that Keats is to some extent *abnegating* control: he is writing his poem as a kind of field in which various things may happen—opening a space in which various possibilities arise. He is not "unmasking" anything but radically shifting contexts. What results is a kind of rich incoherence in which various incompatible positions are all expressed—but none so emphatically that we are forced to choose one as opposed to the others. As Keats writes his poem, the words he selects lead him into contexts which are different from the one in which he began—and, instead of trying to control this tendency and force the words back into the original context, he simply allows the process to happen. What appears as a kind of "summary" of the poem—the "beauty is truth" passage—is in fact no summary at all, but it does allow us to exit from the poem without tears or anger at the fact of human mortality— to *pretend* that the lines are summarizing the poem and that they are a comfort.

Because the poem is radically inconsistent in its attitudes, it does not allow for an assertion of Keats as any kind of "unified ego"—no clear "self," no final "position" appears.

What I'm describing here seems to me quite compatible with Keats' description of "the Poetical Character" (Letter to Richard Woodhouse, October, 1818):

> It [the poetical character] has no self—it is everything and nothing—It has no character—it enjoys light and shade; it lives in gusto, be it foul or fair, high or low, rich or poor, mean or elevated—It has as much delight in conceiving an Iago as an Imogen. What shocks the virtuous philosopher, delights the chameleon Poet. It does no harm from its relish of the dark side of things any more than from its taste for the bright one; because they both end in speculation. A Poet is the most unpoetical of any thing in existence; because he has no Identity—he is continually in for—and filling some other Body. . . .

It also goes well, I think, with Keats' idea of "Negative Capability" (Letter to George and Tom Keats, December, 1817):

> when a man is capable of being in uncertainties, Mysteries, doubts, without any irritable reaching after fact & reason—Coleridge, for instance, would let go by a fine isolated verisimilitude caught from the Penetralium of mystery, for being incapable of remaining content with half knowledge.

That this very same letter suggest that Keats believes that, for a poet at least, beauty and truth *are* identical—"with a great poet the sense of Beauty overcomes every other consideration, or rather obliterates all consideration"— makes it all the more remarkable that "Ode on a Grecian Urn" does *not* believe that, or at least does not fully believe it. Even this position—this "belief" in Beauty—is an instance of "half knowledge."

2. Mallarmé's "Brise Marine" ("Sea Breeze")

L'oeuvre pure implique la disparition élocutoire du poète, qui cède l'initiative aux mots. . . .
("The pure work implies the disappearance of the poet as speaker, yielding his initiative to words. . . .")
—MALLARMÉ, "Crise de vers" (1886-1896)

The great French Symbolist poet Stéphanes Mallarmé (1842-1898) is one of the most fascinating, complex figures in French literature. Influenced by Charles Baudelaire, he went on to influence such diverse figures as Paul Valéry and André Gide. In an 1891 interview, Mallarmé told journalist Jules Huret, "I believe there must only be allusion. The contemplation of objects, the images that soar from the reveries they have induced, constitute the song . . . To *name* an object is to suppress three quarters of the enjoyment of the poem, which derives from the pleasure of step-by-step discovery; to *suggest*, that is the dream. It is the perfect use of . . . mystery that constitutes the symbol . . . There must always be enigma in poetry."

After reading Mallarmé's extraordinary and extremely experimental late poem, "Un Coup de Dés" (published in 1897), Paul Valéry remarked, "'He has undertaken,' I thought, '*finally to raise a printed page to the power of the midnight sky.*'"

The work of a poet like Mallarmé necessarily resists translation, but his productions are so fascinating that many writers, including myself, have made the attempt. Recently, a friend asked me to comment on Richard Wilbur's translation of an early, relatively straightforward poem by Mallarmé, "Brise Marine" ("Sea Breeze"), written in 1865. Here is the original poem:

Brise Marine

La chair est triste, hélas! et j'ai lu tous les livres.
Fuir! là-bas fuir! Je sens que des oiseaux sont ivres
D'être parmi l'écume inconnue et les cieux!
Rien, ni les vieux jardins reflétés par les yeux
Ne retiendra ce coeur qui dans la mer se trempe
Ô nuits! ni la clarté déserte de ma lampe
Sur le vide papier que la blancheur défend,
Et ni la jeune femme allaitant son enfant.
Je partirai! Steamer balancant ta mâture,
Lève l'ancre pour une exotique nature!
Un Ennui, désolé par les cruels espoirs,
Croit encore à l'adieu suprême des mouchoirs!
Et, peut-être, les mâts, invitant les orages
Sont-ils de ceux qu'un vent penche sur les naufrages
Perdus, sans mâts, sans mâts, ni fertiles îlots . . .
Mais, ô mon coeur, entends le chant des matelots!

Here is Richard Wilbur's translation, originally published in *The New Yorker* in 1999:

The flesh grows weary. And books, I've read them all.
Off, then, to where I glimpse through spray and squall
Strange birds delighting in their unknown skies!
No antique gardens mirrored in my eyes
Can stay my sea-changed spirit, nor the light
Of my abstracted lamp which shines (O Night!)
On the guardian whiteness of the empty sheet,
Nor the young wife who gives the babe her teat.
Come, ship whose masts now gently rock and sway,
Raise anchor for a stranger world! Away!

How strange that Boredom, all its hopes run dry,
Still dreams of handkerchiefs that wave good-bye!
Those gale-inviting masts might creak and bend
In seas where many a craft has met its end,
Dismasted, lost, with no green island near it . . .
But hear the sailors singing, O my spirit!

This is a blank verse version of the poem by Peter and Mary Ann Caws. It was published in *Stéphane Mallarmé: Selected Poetry and Prose* (1982), edited by Mary Ann Caws.

> How sad the flesh! and there's no more to read.
> Escape, far off! I feel that somewhere birds
> Are drunk to be amid strange spray and skies!
> Nothing, not those old gardens eyes reflect
> Can now restrain this heart steeped in the sea
> Oh nights! Nor the lone brightness of my lamp
> On the blank paper which its whiteness shields
> Nor the young wife, her baby at her breast.
> I shall depart! Steamer with swaying masts,
> Raise anchor for exotic wilderness!
>
> Tedium, desolated by cruel hope,
> Has faith still in great fluttering farewells!
> And, it may be, the masts, inviting storms
> Are of the sort that wind inclines to wrecks
> Lost, with no mast, no mast, or verdant isle . . .
> But listen, oh my heart, the sailors sing!

Richard Wilbur is a fine poet and does a good job with the form; his poem is genuinely graceful. I think it's generally better than the Caws' version—though Wilbur has to resort to "teats" rather than "breasts" (for rhyme) and though his concluding line, "But hear the sailors singing, O my spirit!," contains an ambiguity which is not in the original: in his version it is possible that the *sailors* are singing "O my spirit!" In addition, he changes "heart" ("coeur") to "spirit"—again for the rhyme.

The translation of the opening line in both the Wilbur and Caws versions seems to me a far cry from the compelling—even astonishing—statement with which Mallarmé opens his poem: "La chair est triste, hélas! et j'ai lu tous les livres." Better a straight literal translation, "The flesh is sad, alas! and I've read all the books." In the version of the poem I produced, I italicized "all"—as I italicized "down there," a resonant phrase in French literature. Oddly, the word "strange" keeps coming back in Wilbur's version though it does not in Mallarmé: "Strange birds," "a stranger world," and "How strange that Boredom." Mallarmé states that he thinks *all* birds—birds in general, not just "strange birds"—are drunk, intoxicated ("ivres"); they all want to be in unknown foam and skies. The word "drunk" is somewhat different from Wilbur's "delighting in"; the original suggests that Mallarmé is deliberately recalling some of Baudelaire's reflections on the charms of drunkenness, as in "Enivrez-Vous" ("Get Drunk"): "Il faut être toujours ivre," "One must always be drunk." Wilbur's "a stranger world" is also somewhat different from the original: "une exotique nature" ("exotic wilderness" in Caws). And "How strange that Boredom" is in Mallarmé simply "Un Ennui"—Boredom, "Tedium" in Caws. There's no equivalent in Mallarmé to "How strange." ("Ennui" is of course an important word in Baudelaire's work.)

I think that the main problem with both versions of Mallarmé's poem is that they fail to catch the genuine poignancy of the penultimate line, "Perdus, sans mâts, sans mâts, ni fertiles îlots. . . ." (Note that the line is only eleven syllables: it breaks off. The ". . ." is the twelfth syllable.) Wilbur's "Dismasted, lost" is certainly no match for Mallarmé's plaintive "Perdus, sans mâts, sans mâts. . . ." (Mallarmé deliberately repeats the phrase "sans mâts"; and nothing in his poem is as harsh, even ugly as Wilbur's word "dismasted.") The Caws version is better than Wilbur's because it's more literal: "Lost, with no mast, no mast, or verdant isle . . ." But the English here is rather clumsy: in the French, Mallarmé's line is a genuine *cri de coeur: everything* is *perdu,* lost. In effect, the poem ends at that moment: the poet has absolutely nothing left.

Then, out of nowhere, there occurs a new movement: "Mais, ô mon coeur, entends le chant des matelots!"

As far as I know, none of Mallarmé's many commentators has noticed the extraordinary pun in the concluding line. In the penultimate line, everything is lost ("perdus"): there are no masts ("mâts") and no isles ("îlots"). Yet in a sense the concluding word gives the poet back the very things he has lost: the *sound* of "matelot" contains "mâts" + "îlots." The "lost" masts and isles are not restored to the poet as entities, only as names, echoing words. *But that is all they were to begin with.* In a way, the proper translation of the concluding line is, "But, oh my heart, listen to the song of 'mâts' + 'îlots.'" One can sense in this early poem—written when the author was in his twenties—an extraordinary shift from a focus on "things" to a focus on "words." If, from one point of view, the poet's fear of action propels him towards language— forces him to take refuge in the qualities of words—from another point of view the poem enunciates a new mode of beauty. Mallarmé's "mâts-îlots" / "matelot," is obvious once you point it out, but, amazingly, as far as I know, it has never been pointed out. Why? Perhaps because to notice it, one must move away, as Mallarmé does, from the referential quality of "matelot" and must "cède l'initiative aux mots," "yield the initiative to words."

Nothing in the Wilbur or Caws translations suggests that the authors have noticed the pun; they make no attempt to reproduce it. In addition, Wilbur's version is oddly *jaunty*—far too much so: it's as if Mallarmé were saying, "Oh well, it may be that 'those gale-inviting masts might creak and bend,' but, really, that happens to lots of ships ('where many a craft has met its end'), and, as I was saying at the beginning, 'But hear the sailors singing, O my spirit.'" But the last line isn't a return to the beginning of the poem: it's a genuinely new movement; it exists to find a way of dealing with that plaintive word, "*perdus*." It is not religion which saves the "lost" Mallarmé—not a sudden revelation of Jesus—but a sudden revelation of the power of words.

This is my translation of the complete poem. I couldn't keep the form as Wilbur did—though I did try for end rhymes—and I had to change "masts" to "sails" for my reproduction of the pun. (I italicize "sailors" at the end to draw the reader's attention to the word: sail/oars; sailors.) The loss of Mallarmé's fine word, "Steamer" is unfortunate.

The flesh is sad, alas! and I've read *all* the books.
Run away—run away *down there*. I think that birds are drunk
They want to be in unknown foam and skies!
Nothing—not even the gardens reflected in your eyes—
Will hold this heart that drenches in the sea—
(Ah, nights!)—not even the desolate brilliance of the lamp by which I see
The blank paper whose white-
Ness defends it, nor the young wife
With her child suckling: I'm leaving—
Weigh anchor!—going to a place where there is no grieving.
An immense Boredom—thrust from Hopes to Griefs—
Believes still in the supreme goodbye of waving handkerchiefs!

. . . And yet the masts may summon storms
That blast the sails and wreck the oars:
Lost, without sail, without sail, or beating oars . . .
But oh, my heart, listen to the song of *sailors*.

Two Modernists & A Beat

Cummings, Zukofsky, and Ginsberg

1. *A Poem By E.E. Cummings*

A friend's horrified reaction to this poem—"Is this a poem?"—made me want to write about it. The poem appeared in E.E. Cummings' book, *95 Poems* (1958).

l(a

le
af
fa

ll

s)
one
l

iness

Cummings insists, rightly, that what we encounter in a text is not "words"— the products of our breaths and bodies—but "letters." ("Language" is something you do with your "langue," your tongue; reading is something you do with your eyes.) The primary verbal components of this poem are the words "loneliness" and "a leaf falls," but Cummings has rearranged the letters of these words so that new patterns emerge. What he has produced is a formal poem, but its formality is an arrangement of letters rather than words. The poem has nine lines: a single line is followed by a space and then by three lines throughout: one line, three lines, one line, three lines, one line.

It takes a moment to see the two statements. "A leaf falls" is within the parenthesis; "loneliness" is outside the parenthesis. Because Cummings has rearranged the spacing of these words, he can find other words within them. "One" appears in "loneliness," for example. The French words "la" and "le" appear in the opening lines. "Af" from "leaf" and "fa" from "falls" are inverted mirrors of one another. It is as if Cummings finds the beginning of the word "falls"—fa—within the word "leaf"—af. "One" is also important. On the typewriter—the instrument Cummings used to produce his poems—an l (first letter of the word "loneliness") and a 1 (the numeral) are the same symbol. The "one" who is lonely is both "one" and "1." The poem is a sort of haiku—it's as if the ideogram for the word "loneliness" were a falling leaf. Indeed, the poem's very shape suggests the downward falling of a leaf. Further: the French words "la" and "le"—words meaning, respectively, "the" (feminine) and "the" (masculine)—point to the poem's central problem: male and female are separated from one another, a fact which gives rise to "loneliness." Line five, the very center of the nine-line poem, has "ll": a "one" (1) and a "one" next to one another—which is what the poem longs for. The two l's are letters in the word "falls" but they are also both letters in the word "loneliness"; in "loneliness," however, the letters are widely separated from each other.

Cummings' little poem—the opening of the volume in which it originally appeared—seems to me a brilliant and dazzling display of new possibilities of text even as it names one of the oldest of human problems: loneliness. (The "title" of the poem is the numeral "1": it is the *first* of the "95 Poems.")

Loneliness: You can feel it in the fall of a leaf, in the disconnection of an isolated part from the whole in which it once functioned—which, incidentally, is also a description of Cummings' technique: isolated letters are separated off from the words of which they were part—and so they make new words. Finally, Cummings allows us to return them to what they originally were: a leaf falls; loneliness. Further: Isn't a page—the thing on which the poem manifests—also a "leaf"? In a very short space, Cummings forces us to attend to what we are doing *right now*: reading. And he insists that reading is an isolating experience: it doesn't involve another person, only letters, text. Isn't reading itself therefore a mode of loneliness? To do it we have to be "by ourselves"—alone. Reading allows us to contact another—in this case E.E. Cummings—but it is not the same kind of contact we would have if Cummings were standing before us in living presence speaking his poem. Reading gives us letters, not words. As author, Cummings is absent, not there—and he knows it: his little poem is an acknowledgement of the distance between writer and reader, while at the same time, of course, it brings writer and reader together. A leaf falls. *We turn the page*. Loneliness.

2. *Louis Zukofsky: A Poet Worth Fighting For*
A Review Of *Louis Zukofsky: Selected Poems*, Edited By Charles Bernstein
(The Library Of America American Poets Project)

In *Ulysses*, to depict the babbling of a woman going to sleep, I had sought to end with the least forceful word I could possibly find. I had found the word 'yes,' which is barely pronounced, which denotes acquiescence, self-abandon, relaxation, the end of all resistance. In *Work in Progress*, I've tried to do better if I could. This time, I have found the word which is the most slippery, the least accented, the weakest word in English, a word which is not even a word, which is scarcely sounded between the teeth, a breath, a nothing, the article *the*.
—JAMES JOYCE, quoted in Richard Ellmann, *James Joyce*

People referred to Gertrude Stein as "ahead of her time." In fact, Stein—like Joyce or Pound—was entirely of her time: she was living within twentieth-century assumptions whereas most of the people around her were living within nineteenth-century assumptions. "Modernism" was in part an attempt to find forms which expressed the assumptions of the twentieth century. "The child born in 1900," wrote Henry Adams at the very dawn of the century, "would. . . be born into a new world which would not be a unity but a multiple. Adams. . . could not deny that the law of the new multiverse explained much that had been most obscure. . . ."
—JACK FOLEY, from a journal

In December 1978, a few months after Louis Zukofsky's death, a soon to be notorious event occurred, shaking the foundations of the anything-but-homogeneous group of poets living in and near San Francisco. Outtakes of Louis Zukofsky's appearance in a 1966 NET television documentary, *USA Poetry*, produced by Richard Moore, were being shown at the San Francisco Art Institute under the auspices of the Poetry Center. Tom Mandel, director of the Poetry Center and a poet associated with the L=A=N=G=U=A=G=E group, introduced Barrett Watten (himself a prominent L=A=N=G=U=A=G=E poet) to speak about Zukofsky's work. As Watten spoke, the distinguished (and older) San Francisco poet Robert Duncan—who had championed Zukofsky's poetry but who was no friend to L=A=N=G=U=A=G=E poets—grew more and more impatient. Finally, in an astonishing move, Duncan seized the stage from Watten and began himself to speak about Zukofsky. "I in no way believe that there is such a thing as 'just language,'" Duncan insisted, "any more than there is 'just footprints.'"

Duncan's action was both passionately defended—Watten, Duncan felt, was desecrating Zukofsky's work—and passionately rejected. "Duncan's interference and reseizure of the stage," writes Eleana Kim in "Language Poetry: Dissident Practices and the Makings of a Movement" (1994), "was seen by some to be indicative of the fear and reactionary censorship characterizing the general attitude of the New Americans [poets associated with the 1960 anthology, *The New American Poetry*] to the Language project. But also at stake were questions of tradition, the implications of poetic assumptions and alliances."

Now, Louis Zukofsky's work has been edited and selected for the Library of America's American Poetry Project by another prominent L=A=N=G=U=A=G=E poet, Charles Bernstein, and he has done a superb job. It is no easy task to deal with a writer as enigmatic, even chameleonic as Louis Zukofsky. Zukofsky's poetry alone ranges from something like light verse to an immensely complex, dense medium. It operates in both formal modes and free verse. This amazing passage (eight lines, approximately five words in each line) is the opening poem of *80 Flowers*— a book originally meant to have been published in the year of the poet's eightieth birthday, 1984. The passage is reminiscent of Gertrude Stein's *Tender Buttons*:

> Heart us invisibly thyme time
> round rose bud fire downland
> bird tread quagmire dry gill-over-the-ground
> stem-square leaves-cordate earth race horsethyme
> breath neighbors a mace nays
> sorrow of harness pulses pent
> *thus* fruit pod split four
> one-fourth *ripens* unwithering gaping

In addition to poetry, Zukofsky published a short story, a play, critical writing (including the formidable *Bottom on Shakespeare*), translations, even a novel. His extraordinary early work, "Poem Beginning 'The,'" was first printed in 1927 in Ezra Pound's magazine, *The Exile*. Zukofsky wrote the poem in 1926; when it appeared, he was twenty-three years old. The poem's title is generally believed to refer somewhat ironically to *The Waste Land*—the phrase, "the waste land" occurs in the work—but it perhaps also has a relationship to the concluding word of *Finnegans Wake*. (Joyce's novel had begun to appear as *Work in Progress* in 1924). James Joyce is perhaps the one modernist whose work is as various and complex as Zukofsky's, and it's as if Zukofsky simply picks up where Joyce leaves off. (It's a short step from *the* to *a*). A more certain influence on Zukofsky is Henry Adams, whose great book, *The Education of Henry Adams* was completed in 1907 and published in 1918, after the author's death. Zukofsky wrote a Master's thesis on Adams and maintained a lifelong interest in him. One way of seeing the body of Zukofsky's work is as a series of attempts to give form to what Adams called "the multiverse." Zukofsky's work may well be—in Adams' phrase—"not . . . a unity but a multiple."

In any case, "Language" in one form or another is definitely at the center of Zukofsky's work, and translation is a major element of his use of language. If James Joyce had an uneasy relationship to the oppressor language, English, so did Louis Zukofsky, whose parents spoke only Yiddish. Charles Bernstein writes, "For *Catullus*, the Zukofskys developed a technique that has come to be called homophonic translation—translation with special emphasis on the sound rather the lexical meaning." The purpose of such translation, writes Mark Scroggins in "A Biographical Essay on Zukofsky" is "'to breathe the 'literal' meaning' of the Latin original, adhering as closely as possible to the sounds and rhythms of Catullus, and letting the meaning take a distant back seat." Scroggins' comments are accurate and helpful, but there are many moments in *Catullus* when Zukofsky deliberately chooses "lexical meaning" over sound. The opening line of *Catullus* 3, "Lugete, o Veneres Cupidinesque," is not sonically very close to the opening line of Zukofsky's version: "Lament, o graves of Venus, and Cupids." Zukofsky's version of the poem is in fact a more or less literal translation, though with some interesting added attractions. This is the supposedly "literal" Loeb Classical Library version of the poem; it was written by F.W. Cornish:

> Mourn, ye Graces and Loves, and all you whom the Graces love. My lady's sparrow is dead, the sparrow my lady's pet, whom she loved more than her very eyes; for honey-sweet he was, and knew his mistress as well as a girl knows her own mother. Nor would he stir from her lap, but hopping now here, now there, would still chirp to his mistress alone. Now he goes along the dark road, thither whence they say no one returns. But curse upon you, cursed shades of Orcus, which devour all pretty things! My pretty sparrow, you have taken him away. Ah, cruel! Ah, poor little bird! All because of you my lady's darling eyes are heavy and red with weeping.

This is Zukofsky's version (not included in the *Selected Poems*):

Lament, o graces of Venus, and Cupids,
and cry out loud, men beloved by Her graces.
Pass here, it's dead, meant so much to my girl, the
sparrow, the jewel that delighted my girl,
that lovable in her eyes she loved them less:
like honey so sweet he was sure to know her,
with her ever as a girl's with her mother;
not seizing a moment to stray from her lap,
silly crazy to hop up here and down there,
one endless solo to his only goddess.
Who now? it's hard to walk thru tenebrous flume
down there, where it is granted not one comes back.
On you be the curse of the blind and dead shade
Orcus, hell that destroys all beautiful things:
so you stole my beautiful sparrow from me.
Why pick evil? why my little fool sparrow
It's your doing—my girl's own, darling's sweet
excellent eyes a little swollen and red.

"Pass here" is Zukofsky's version of the Latin "passer," sparrow, a word which may have reversed some of its letters as it found its way into English. (Another example would be the Greek "morph"—m sound at the beginning, f sound at the end—which became the English "form"—f sound at the beginning, m sound at the end.)[1] Zukofsky's "one endless solo to his only goddess" is a marvelous transmutation of Catullus's "ad solam dominam usque pipiabat" and far better than the Loeb version of the line. In addition, Zukofsky's word "goddess" may be a kind of historical joke. The Latin word for "lord" is *dominus*. The corresponding female word is *domina*, the word Catullus uses. The two words would be accurately translated into English as "lord" and "lady," as in "the lady of the house" or, as the Loeb translation has it, "mistress." With Christianity, the word *dominus* took on the meaning of "God," as in the Latin Mass: "Dominus vobiscum," "The Lord be with you." Zukofsky's translation is perhaps the only example in English of a corresponding change of meaning for *domina*. If *dominus* means god, shouldn't *domina* mean goddess? Another marvelous Zukofsky translation occurs in *Catullus* 115. Catullus calls his acquaintance Mamurra "Mentula." "Mentula" is used here as a proper noun, but the joke is that the word means "penis." The Loeb translation, acutely aware of propriety, translates the word only as a proper noun and leaves it at that. Peter Whigham's translation is more accurate: "Mentula" becomes "O'Toole." But Zukofsky clearly gets the prize: in his version "Mentula" becomes "Meantool." ("Non homo sed vero mentula magna minax" becomes "known *homo* said hero Meantool a man gnawn mean ax.")

Zukofsky's playfulness and his interest in sound—in evidence throughout his Catullus translation—is matched by a deeply historical consciousness which constantly interrogates the words he uses. In the television documentary the poet remarks, "[Erik] Sati said it very nicely: he was born very young in a world that was already very old." What is a poet's relationship to history—to the entire burden of poetry he inherits?

Zukofsky's historical consciousness also takes the form of what Harold Bloom called "the anxiety of influence." Catullus is one of many "precursor poets" for Zukofsky. (Another is William Shakespeare. Still another is the Yiddish-American poet, cited and translated in *A*, Solomon Bloomgarden or "Yehoash.") Zukofsky's *Catullus* insists on *both* the similarity of his American English to the Latin and its utter, appalling distance. The American poet "breathes with" Catullus as he makes similar sounds to the Latin, but he also frequently creates a "meaning" which has nothing to do with anything Catullus meant to say—a "meaning" which is in some ways liberating but in others approaches nonsense.

In the television documentary, Zukofsky quotes a poem by the English poet Robert Herrick (1591-1674):

To Daffodils

When a daffodil I see
Hanging down his head t'wards me,
Guess I may what I must be:
First, I shall decline my head;
Secondly, I shall be dead;
Lastly, safely buried.

Zukofsky comments, "I wanted to do something as good as that, if possible." He then reads his own "Little Wrists" (later titled "So That Even a Lover"):

Little wrists,
Is your content
My sight or hold,

Or your small air
That lights and trysts?

Red alder berry
Will singly break;
But you—how slight—do:
So that even
A lover exists.

(The two poems are also juxtaposed in Zukofsky's book, *A Test of Poetry*.) Grousing about "this *horror* of explaining a text—especially one's own," Zukofsky comments ruefully, "You think I made it. I just wonder." Zukofsky's poem, which is about his son Paul, is quite beautiful and complex, playing on various meanings of the word "do," a word emphasized by the sudden shift in the poem's rhythm. (Paul may "break" in various senses—as he "does" in various senses.) The poem is *different* from Herrick's. It's not a question of whether Zukofsky succeeded in equaling Herrick, whether he "made it." The more interesting point is that Zukofsky initially felt himself to be in competition with Herrick, and, even upon completion of the poem, he wasn't sure that he had won the competition. The poet's sense of competitiveness is very likely part of what led him to the "bitterness" he experienced in his later years—years in which he was nonetheless enthusiastically "discovered" by younger poets such as Robert Duncan and Robert Creeley. Zukofsky "seemed to many to have become irremediably bitter," writes Mark Scroggins, "convinced that he had somehow been unreasonably passed over by the powers that conveyed poetic recognition." The poet's sense of exile from those powers—not to mention his equally intense sense of exile from the dominant power structures of America—was, among other things, *linguistic*. He was not only born young into a world that was already very old; he was born as a necessarily English-speaking American into a household of Yiddish-speaking immigrants. The "past" was palpably present in every sound his parents made. He experienced Shakespeare's works in Yiddish before he experienced them in English. In "Poem Beginning 'The'"—sometimes directly addressed to his mother, who would not have been able to read it—Zukofsky momentarily (and ironically) takes on the persona of Shakespeare's Shylock:

251   Assimilation is not hard,
252   And once the Faith's askew
253   I might as well look Shagetz just as much as Jew

254	I'll read their Donne as mine,
255	And leopard in their spots
256	I'll do what says their Coleridge,
257	Twist red hot pokers into knots.
258	The villainy they teach me I will execute
259	And it shall go hard with them,
260	For I'll better the instruction,
261	Having learned, so to speak, in their colleges . . .
266	I, Senora, am the Son of the Respected Rabbi,
267	Israel of Saragossa,
268	Not that the Rabbis give a damn,
269	Keine Kadish wird man sagen.

The concluding line is a quotation from Heine and is simultaneously defiant and submissive: after all, wasn't Heine also a Jew?

In his later years Zukofsky moved away from the radical political consciousness of his youth—a consciousness which sometimes shows up in the extremely complex context of his poetry—into the comforts of his immediate family life, as his musician wife Celia and his son Paul (later to become a well-known violinist) became (in all senses of the word) figures in his poetry:

for Celia and Paul

River that must turn full after I stop dying
Song, my song, raise grief to music
Light as my loves' thought, the few sick
So sick of wrangling: thus weeping,
Sounds of light, stay in her keeping
And my son's face—this much for honor. . .

Honor

His voice in me, the river's turn that finds the
Grace in you, four notes first too full for talk, leaf
Lighting stem, stems bound to the branch that binds the
Tree, and then as from the same root we talk, leaf
After leaf of your mind's music, page, walk leaf
Over leaf of his thought, sounding
The grace that comes from knowing

Things, her love our own showing
Her love in all her honor.

As both these lines and "Little Wrists" suggest, the poetry about family is not sentimental but frequently daunting, difficult, if ultimately positive. Charles Bernstein remarks, "Often Zukofsky's poems have no speaker"—the poems in *80 Flowers* would be a good example—but it is also true that the figure of "Zukofsky the poet" haunts the poet's work. The opening poem of *A* depends on our understanding exactly who the speaker is and his relationship not only to "A / Round of fiddles playing Bach" but to the "Black full dress of the audience." And there are many other poems in which persona is important: "A Song for the Year's End," Section nine of "Light," "The Old Poet Moves to a New Apartment 14 Times," the title poem of *Barely and Widely*. There is even a poem (happily included in *Selected Poems*) which imitates the sound of a person sneezing:

> *To Friends, For Good Health*
>
> (*Sneezing on it:*)
>
> And the
>   best
>
> To
> you
>   too

In his introduction to the *Selected Poems* Charles Bernstein remarks on "the intricate patterning of sound that everywhere pervades [Zukofsky's] work," on "the microtonal shifting of vowels," and goes on to write of "the syntactic rotation of the same words shifting to different parts of speech." One of the great examples of this latter technique is Zukofsky's famous, kaleidoscopic "A Song of Degrees":

> Hear her
> (Clear mirror)
> Care.
> His error.
> In her care—
> Is clear.

Hear, her
Clear
Mirror,
Care
His error.
In her,
Care
Is clear.

Hear her
Clear mirror
Care his error
In her care
Is clear

Hear
Her
Clear
Mirror
Care
His
Error in
Her
Care
Is clear

Hear
Her
Clear,
Mirror,
Care
His
Error in
Her—
Care
Is
Clear.

In the TV documentary Zukofsky recites the poem and adds, "The effect—I don't know if you pray these days—is something like a prayer." It is not the *content* which gives the poem a religious quality—the content perhaps has something to do with a family argument or Celia's relationship to Louis—but the *sound* and the *repetition* of the words. Zukofsky's title emphasizes the religious aspect of the poem. In the Old Testament, Psalms 120 to 134 are each called "A Song of Degrees." *The New Scofield Reference Bible* comments that the word "degrees" is better rendered by "ascents": "these Psalms were either sung by pilgrims on the ascending march from the Babylonian captivity to Jerusalem, or. . . were sung by worshipers from all parts of Palestine as they went up to Jerusalem for the great festivals. An alternate view is that the headings, 'A Song of Ascents,' refer to the fifteen steps leading to Court of Israel in the Temple, and that these Psalms were sung on these steps." In Zukofsky's case, the poem suggests some sort of purification process—a movement from "error" to "clarity"—and the "degrees" are perhaps the different modes of understanding we have as the poem's syntax constantly causes the words to change contexts. The twelve individual words of the poem are each understood, as Henry Adams puts it, as a "multiple."

Louis Zukofsky: Selected Poems is an absolutely necessary book for anyone seeking to understand twentieth-century American poetry. Zukofsky is a master, but he is definitely a formidable master. Charles Bernstein's selection guides us through both accessible and "difficult" aspects of Zukofsky and does it in a way that constantly sheds light on the work as a whole. Bernstein's introduction is also excellent: well written and, in general, compelling. I do have some problems with some of his specific readings, however. Often the difficulty of dealing with Zukofsky is the difficulty of *why* Zukofsky chooses to use the words he does. Bernstein quotes this short poem (which, he notes, arose from the poet's thinking of a tugboat),

THE

The
desire
of
towing

and offers this commentary:

I love the simple fact of the title, *The*, by the author of "*A*". . . Is the title pronounced *thuh* or *thee?* Beats me. Both. Syllable count: 1/2/1/2. [I hear "desire" as three syllables, not two—JF] Tow the line?; but, they say it's supposed to be *toe the line*. So much depends upon . . . whether you want to be towed, since this is *the* desire, not *a* desire. Now, go back to the image: *Tiny tug drags large barge.* Perhaps this poem's a counter-poetics: Do you want a poem to tow you or to do some towing yourself? A Zukofsky poem does not tow you along for a ride; that's what [Peter] Quartermain means by emphasizing "thinking *with* the poem." In contrast to *the* desire of towing, we might speak of *a* desire not to be towed. Or anyway, told.

This seems to me more to trivialize the poem than it does to illuminate it. Everyone knows that Zukofsky plays on various meanings of words, so often critics do a kind of free-associating around a particular word in a poem. But what if the critic chooses the wrong word? The problem, I think, is that Bernstein thinks the operative word of "THE" is "towing," and so he expends all his critical energy on that word. (Zukofsky does pun on "tow" in section nine of "Light," but it's "two" and "tow-headed" that he chooses, not "toe.") What if the operative word of "THE" is "desire"—a word which shows up on the very first page of *Bottom on Shakespeare* and, as the index indicates, is repeated frequently throughout the book. Zukofsky quotes Spinoza, "Desire which arises from reason can have no excess" and insists that "the art of the poet must be to inform and delight with Love's strength"; he cites Aristotle on "those things, which we desire with such affection that nothing can obliterate them from the mind." Why does a tugboat tow? Is it because the boat or its captain is being paid to do it? Or is there a "desire of towing"? Does a tugboat operate the way a poem does—through desire, love, and not through money? The tugboat, Zukofsky suggests, tows not through economic necessity but for another reason—and the poet writes for that very same reason. Desire is central to any genuine activity. The title of the poem suggests that it can go in any direction: *the* . . . whatever. *This* happens to be the subject matter the poet chooses, but other subject matter is possible. There are myriad modes of desire. Of course the poem may also "tug at your heartstrings," and if this sounds like an overly sentimental formulation for such a radically experimental poet, we should remember that Zukofsky specialized in writing "valentines"— poems of love, poems which "inform and delight with Love's strength."

Louis Zukofsky's deep interest in text, in the complexities of scholarship, is, like his sense of language, in part a reflection of his Jewishness. There is a definite Kabbalistic side to this poet. (*A* is partly a playful title: the poem is *A* by Z . . .) But the poet's interest in breath, in sound, points in a somewhat different direction from his interest in the "literal." In the TV documentary Zukofsky refers to his Catullus translation as "noise." An insistence on the poet's "breath"—on "voices"—on "noise"—suggests an emphasis on what the voice proceeds out of: the body. It suggests as well an emphasis on immediacy and on the aliveness of the present moment— the moment in which we are breathing and speaking. Such an emphasis necessarily moves towards "performance," a condition in which the speaker's "breath" is immediately present and no longer dependent upon the text-interpreting actions of "eyes." (Homer, one remembers, was blind.) The performative element which haunts modernism—and which was ignored by most of modernism's explainers—haunts this poet as well. Zukofsky's son Paul became not a poet but a performer, and the grand concluding movement of Louis's life-poem, *A*, is a complex performance piece utilizing texts by the poet but entirely "composed" by Celia and meant to be presented *aloud.* The following poem from *Bottom on Shakespeare* is Louis's take on a line from *Two Gentlemen of Verona*—significantly, a line from a play. Like much (but not all) of his work, it cries out to be spoken, to be heard. Just before reciting it Zukofsky remarked, "I've taken liberties."

> Come shadow, come, and take this shadow up,
> Come shadow shadow, come and take this up,
> Come, shadow, come, and take this shadow up,
> Come, come shadow, and take this shadow up,
> Come, come and shadow, take this shadow up,
> Come, up, come shadow and take this shadow,
> And up, come, take shadow, come this shadow,
> And up, come, come shadow, take this shadow,
> And come shadow, come up, take this shadow,
> Come up, come shadow this, and take shadow,
> Up, shadow this, come and take shadow, come
> Shadow this, take and come up shadow, come
> Take and come, shadow, come up, shadow this,
> Up, come and take shadow, come this shadow,
> Come up, take shadow, and come this shadow,
> Come and take shadow, come up this shadow,
> Shadow, shadow come, come and take this up,
> Come, shadow, take, and come this shadow, up,
> Come shadow, come, and take this shadow up,
> Come, shadow, come, and take this shadow up.

3. *"Howl" And The Howlers*
Ginsberg's Poem Fifty Plus Years Later

> If it's true that the road to originality lies in imitation, then it wasn't an utter waste of time for a Catholic high school boy from the suburbs to try to sound in his poems like a downtown homosexual Jewish beatnik intimate in the ways of pot and Benzedrine.
> —BILLY COLLINS, "My 'Howl'" (2006)

> Don't hide the madness.
> —ALLEN GINSBERG, "On Burroughs' Work" (1954)

"The Beat Generation" was one of the most publicized, misunderstood, attacked, understood, deeply considered, cannibalized, ripped-off art movements of the twentieth-century. Its influence extends from the adolescent troubled about sexuality and identity to the dry-as-dust scholar looking for history and significance in old books and papers. Whereas the "hippies" seem somewhat passé, sentimental, and—worst of all—old, the even-older Beats (some of whom were also hippies) have passed into history as American artists of considerable importance. Like Elvis, Jack Kerouac is now forever young, intense and handsome—a symbol of American success—and only occasionally remembered as the middle-aged, fat, lonely man he became. He has in fact become exactly what he wished to be: a great American writer. But he has also become more than that: an icon. If America has secular saints, he is surely one. But, like many prophets perhaps, he has become a saint of a religion he would have despised: his image is used to sell things; he is the American bourgeoisie raised to cosmic proportions.

From its inception, the Beat Generation was a testimony to the power of the fuzzy definition. Intensely meaningful—and with certain aspects continually but not always manifesting—"Beat" has never been adequately defined. Had it been adequately defined, it might have been long dead as a movement. Though everyone would agree that *something* took place in the middle of the twentieth century, after the war, it would be difficult to find agreement about exactly what that something was. Was it a rebellion, as people often claimed? Kerouac announced, with some justice, that he was never a "rebel." In his late bitterness but with some irony still, he told Bruce Cook in *The Beat Generation*, "The Beat Generation?—That was just a bunch of guys trying to get laid." He also wrote,

The Beat Generation, that was a vision that we had, John Clellon Holmes and I, and Allen Ginsberg in an even wilder way, in the late Forties, of a generation of crazy, illuminated hipsters suddenly rising and roaming America, serious, curious, bumming and hitchhiking everywhere, ragged, beatific, beautiful in an ugly graceful new way.

"About the Beat Generation" (1957)

ॐ

On October 7 or October 13, 1955, a poetry reading was held at The Six Gallery, a cooperative art gallery in San Francisco. Different sources list different dates. Allen Ginsberg's postcard announcing the event says October 7th–and that is almost certainly the correct date–but his biographer, Barry Miles, says October 13th. (I've been told that Ginsberg claimed that the reading had to be postponed for six days—so the postcard was inaccurate. No one else seems to mention the postponement.) The featured readers were Allen Ginsberg (the organizer), Michael McClure (whose first reading it was), Gary Snyder, Philip Whalen, and Philip Lamantia. Jack Kerouac was visiting Ginsberg at the time and attended, though he did not read. Kenneth Rexroth was Master of Ceremonies.

Ann Charters writes in *The Beat Reader*, "The 'Six Poets at the Six Gallery' reading was the catalyst that dramatically revealed what Ginsberg later called the 'natural affinity of modes of thought or literary style or planetary perspective' between the East Coast writers and the West Coast poets."

Both Jack Kerouac and Michael McClure wrote about the Six Gallery event, Kerouac in *The Dharma Bums* (1958)—in which he calls the Six Gallery the Gallery Six—and McClure in *Scratching the Beat Surface* (1982). The event soon became famous as the first public reading of "Howl" (though Ginsberg read only the first section of the poem that night). Ginsberg's poem created a sensation. Kerouac collected money for wine and passed around gallon jugs of California Burgundy. When Ginsberg's turn came, writes Barry Miles, "he read with a small, intense voice, but the alcohol and the emotional intensity of the poem quickly took over, and he was soon swaying to its powerful rhythm, chanting like a Jewish cantor, sustaining his long breath length, savoring the outrageous language. Kerouac began cheering him on, yelling 'Go!' at the end of each line, and soon the audience joined in. Allen was completely transported. At each line he took a deep breath, glanced at the manuscript, then delivered it, arms outstretched, eyes gleaming, swaying from one foot to the other with the rhythm of the words."

All descriptions of the Six Gallery event emphasize the transformative character of Ginsberg's reading. Michael McClure writes that "'Howl' . . . was Allen's metamorphosis from quiet, brilliant, burning bohemian scholar trapped by his flames and repressions to epic vocal bard." Kerouac's communal wine-drinking gave the event a Bacchanalian, Dionysian quality. (Wine is of course associated with various religions, including Kerouac's own, Catholicism; in a 1958 letter to John Hollander, Ginsberg himself refers to "Howl" as "rather like a jazz mass.") Barry Miles too attests to both transformation and religious associations. These various elements coalesce into a single image: *what the audience at the Six Gallery was witnessing was the metamorphosis of Allen Ginsberg, "hornrimmed intellectual hepcat with wild black hair" (in Kerouac's phrase), into Allen Ginsberg, "epic vocal bard."*

Ann Charters remarks that Ginsberg "found the audience so fervently sympathetic to his words that he discovered his unrecognized talents as a performance artist"; his "predecessor as an incandescent performer of poetry was the Welsh poet Dylan Thomas, whose widely acclaimed reading tours of American cities in the early 1950s . . . and his best-selling recordings had revolutionized the way his audiences thought of poetry."

True enough, but Kerouac's and the audience's shouts of "Go!" indicate that Ginsberg had taken on the persona not only of the rhapsodic poet but of the jazz musician. Though Ginsberg wasn't reading his poem to jazz accompaniment (as Ruth Weiss, Kenneth Rexroth and others were soon to do at The Cellar), his unaccompanied reading was alive with a sense of music—even with a sense of bebop: "who poverty and tatters and hollow-eyed and high sat up smoking in the supernatural darkness of cold-water flats floating across the tops of cities contemplating jazz."

In his notes to the LP album, *Allen Ginsberg Reads Howl and Other Poems* (1959), Ginsberg describes his poem as full of "long saxophone-like chorus lines" and suggests that writing it was equivalent to the experience of a jazz musician improvising. Like the hipster, who, Norman Mailer wrote in "The White Negro" (1957), "absorbed the existentialist synapses of the Negro," Ginsberg's performance at the Six Gallery took on the aura of the hippest of public performers: in Mailer's formulation, "for practical purposes [he] could be considered a white Negro." Instead of being the observer of what Kerouac called in *On the Road* "the happy, true-hearted Negroes of America," Ginsberg became the authentic conveyer of their power.[1] Like

Neal Cassady—the "secret hero of these poems"—the sensitive, gay, bespectacled, hustling, funny, lonely, fiercely intellectual, convivial, drug-taking ex-student of Lionel Trilling's stood before his audience as something equivalent to Charlie Parker. For one of the very few times in the twentieth century, poetry seemed *cool*.

And—most importantly—if Ginsberg could do it, so could we.

Kerouac's *San Francisco Blues* and *Mexico City Blues* had already presented the jazz musician as analogous to the poet, but Kerouac was not yet widely known. (*On the Road* did not appear until 1957; *Mexico City Blues* was not published until 1959). "Howl" was written at a time when influential critics such as Arthur Mizener were saying, "The age of Yeats is over; we are in the age of Auden"—by which Mizener meant that Romanticism had been replaced by irony and *sotto voce*. Ginsberg sent "Howl" to a critic even more distinguished than Mizener, his old Columbia mentor Lionel Trilling. Trilling was—as the poet knew he would be—horrified:

> I'm afraid I have to tell you that I don't like the poems at all. I hesitate before saying that they seem to me quite dull, for to say of a work which undertakes to be violent and shocking that it is dull is, I am aware, a well known and all too easy device. But perhaps you will believe that I am being sincere when I say they are dull. They are not like Whitman. . . .

Poet John Hollander, writing in the *Partisan Review*, was even harsher:

> It is only fair to Allen Ginsberg . . . to remark on the utter lack of decorum of any kind in his dreadful little volume.

In "The White Negro," Norman Mailer asserted that after the Second World War and the revelation of what went on in concentration camps "one could hardly maintain the courage to be individual, to speak with one's own voice": these years, he complained, are "the years of conformity and depression. A stench of fear has come out of every pore of American life, and we suffer from a collective failure of nerve. . . The only courage, with rare exceptions . . . has been the isolated courage of isolated people":

> If the fate of twentieth century man is to live with death from adolescence to premature senescence, why then the only life-giving answer is to accept the terms of death, to live with death as immediate danger, to divorce oneself from society,

to exist without roots, to set out on that uncharted journey into the rebellious imperatives of the self.

In such a climate, Ginsberg could appear not only as an immensely talented poet but as a harbinger of cultural change. "Howl" too "lives with death as immediate danger" and insists on "the rebellious imperatives of the self." The poet's LP liner notes indicate that writing "Howl" was a kind of conversion experience, a personal transformation: "I suddenly turned aside in San Francisco . . . to follow my romantic inspiration—Hebraic-Melvillian bardic breath." The extraordinary thing about the event at the Six Gallery was that the audience could *witness* Ginsberg's transformation: they could actually *see* the poet become jazz musician. Ginsberg's powerful reading, "arms outstretched, eyes gleaming," was not only the presentation of a poem but a living emblem of the possibility of change. Through rhythm (the "beat") it turned being "beaten down" ("I saw the best minds of my generation destroyed by madness") into, in Kerouac's French pun, "*béat*"—blessedness. The poet's longing for the visionary transforms him, *through* the jazz musician, into active, epic, Whitmanic, visionary bard. This transformation experience is at the absolute center of "Howl" and is in fact its primary subject. The "Footnote to Howl," completed after the Six Gallery reading, makes the transformation explicit:

> Holy! Holy! Holy! Holy! Holy! Holy! Holy! Holy! Holy! Holy!
> > Holy! Holy! Holy! Holy! Holy!
> The world is holy! The soul is holy! The skin is holy! The nose
> > is holy! The tongue and cock and hand and asshole holy!
> Everything is holy! everybody's holy! everywhere is holy! everyday is in eternity! Everyman's
> > an angel!
> The bum's as holy as the seraphim!

"A human voice and body," commented McClure, "had been hurled against the harsh wall of America."

∽

And what of "Howl" these days—more than fifty years after the poem was written?

On October 7, 2005—the opening night of "Litquake," San Francisco's city-wide celebration of literature—"Howl Redux" was presented at the city's elegant Herbst Theatre. "Redux" means brought back, coming alive again, and "Howl Redux" took place exactly fifty years after the Six Gallery event. The event was meant not only as a celebration but a mirroring of the Six Gallery event. Unfortunately, one was constantly reminded of the differences between the two events. The Six Gallery was an auto repair garage that had been converted into an art gallery. The building still stands. It was not a small space, but it boasted a kind of cavernous intimacy. You could see the people who were listening to you and the crowd was active—encouraging readers, making remarks. This was not the case with Herbst Theater, in which the audience—some of whom had paid two hundred dollars for the privilege of attending—was largely passive, as if it were attending a concert of Classical music. There were "refreshments" in the lobby, but certainly no one was passing around a jug of homemade "Dago Red," as Jack Kerouac had done at the original reading. Michael McClure remarked, "There are a lot more people here tonight" than there were at the Six Gallery. There were indeed about a thousand people in Herbst Hall's ample, packed space, though no one had to stand, as they had at the Six Gallery reading. Earlier in 1955, McClure writes in *Scratching the Beat Surface,* the Anarchist poet Robert Duncan had performed at the Six Gallery and "had stripped off his clothes at the end of [his play, *Foust Foutu* (*Faust Fucked*)]." One could have the sense of doing something *illicit,* even "subversive" at the Six Gallery. Not at Herbst Theater.

"Howl Redux" was subtitled "Allen Ginsberg's 'Howl' and Other San Francisco Revolutionary Writings." Scarcely a month goes by in San Francisco without a newspaper article announcing that "The Beat Goes On": literature, and particularly Beat literature, has become part of the city's tourist industry. San Francisco *wants* "Howl" to be "Redux," and so it isn't surprising that a genteel, officially-sponsored, city-wide event like Litquake should celebrate the fiftieth anniversary of Ginsberg's great, anarchic, thumb-nosing poem— a blast of language directed *against* gentility, "overturning," Ginsberg wrote to Richard Eberhart in March 1956, "any notion of propriety, moral 'value,' superficial 'maturity,' Trilling-esque sense of 'civilization.'" The poem celebrates those

> who passed through universities with radiant cool eyes hallucinating Ar-
>   kansas and Blake-light tragedy among the scholars of war,
> who were expelled from the academies for crazy & publishing obscene
>   odes on the windows of the skull,
> who cowered in unshaven rooms in underwear, burning their money in
>   wastebaskets and listening to the Terror through the wall,

> who got busted in their pubic beards returning through Laredo with a belt
>   of marijuana for New York,
> who ate fire in paint hotels or drank turpentine in Paradise Alley, death, or
>   purgatoried their torsos night after night
> with dreams, with drugs, with waking nightmares, alcohol and cock and
>   endless balls. . . .

The event at Herbst Theater was unfortunately more like the embalming of "Howl" than like its revivification. There was certainly no mention of "drugs"—even though drugs (heroin and peyote in addition to marijuana) were an important aspect of the early work of both Lamantia and McClure, who were celebrated along with Ginsberg. Beat historian Ann Charters attended the first complete reading of "Howl" in March, 1956 in Berkeley—the first attempt to "repeat" the Six Gallery reading—and remarked to me in an interview that, while she was impressed with the poetry of Ginsberg, Whalen, Snyder, and McClure, she was "unnerved by the drunken wildness of their friends in the audience and Robert LaVigne's drawings of Orlovsky [her date for the evening] making love with Ginsberg." Robert LaVigne corrected Charters' remark—Ginsberg's partner in the drawings was not Peter Orlovsky but someone else—but wildness, nakedness, drunkenness, and eroticism were all aspects of what the Six Poets at the Six Gallery were doing. Like Ginsberg's poem, the event was meant to shock. It was certainly not meant to assure a city's bourgeoisie that Great Literature continued to be produced within city limits. The audience at Herbst Theater tittered when mention was made of U.S. Customs Officer Chester McPhee's opinion that "Howl" was "obscene," but none of the poem's genuine and deliberate obscenities—imagination's grenades hurled at propriety—were present in Herbst Hall. The people in Ginsberg's poem

> howled on their knees in the subway and were dragged off the roof
>   waving genitals and manuscripts. . .
> let themselves be fucked in the ass by saintly motorcyclists, and
>   screamed with joy. . .
> blew and were blown by those human seraphim, the sailors, caresses of
>   Atlantic and Caribbean love. . . .

No one was doing anything like that at Herbst Theater. Though we were shown film of Ginsberg reading from the first section of "Howl"—which was all that was read at the Six Gallery—such passages were edited out of the footage. The "secret hero" of the evening was definitely not "N.C. . . . cocksman and Adonis of Denver" who "sweetened the snatches of a million girls trembling in the sunset" and "went out whoring through Colorado in myriad stolen night-cars." At Litquake, all of the rough edges—where subversion happens—were carefully smoothed over. The organizers of Litquake undoubtedly meant well, but Jack Kerouac's Allen Ginsberg—"Allen Ginsberg in an even wilder way"—was definitely not present. "Howl" is a wonderfully subversive poem—and part of what it is subverting is "literature," what Ginsberg called "civilization." *Tout le reste est littérature* (Verlaine)— but not "Howl." It maintains its power not through genteel public presentation but through the secret, quasi-illicit longings of generations of readers who believe that the poem speaks precisely, and uniquely, to them. For all its fame, "Howl" is not a public poem—though it became a public poem in every possible way. As Ginsberg himself understood, "Howl" is fundamentally a "guilty pleasure":

> I thought I wouldn't write a *poem* but just write what I wanted to without fear, let my imagination go, open secrecy, and scribble magic lines from my real mind— sum up my life—something I wouldn't be able to show anybody, writ for my own soul's ear and a few other golden ears. So the first line of *Howl*, "I saw the best minds etc.," the whole first section typed out madly in one afternoon, a huge sad comedy of wild phrasing, meaningless images for the beauty of abstract poetry of mind running along making awkward combinations like Charlie Chaplin's walk, long saxophone-like chorus lines I knew Kerouac would hear *sound* of—taking off from his own inspired prose line really a new poetry . . . Have I really been attacked for this sort of joy?
> (Notes to the LP, *Allen Ginsberg reads HOWL and Other Poems*)

∾

But even a guilty pleasure can be a testimony to human freedom. "Howl" is closer to the writings of the Marquis de Sade than it is to *The Waste Land*. It is not surprising that such a poem, like the writings of de Sade, should run afoul of the law, but it is certainly ironic that "Howl" had to be defended not as a great blast of anarchic (even pornographic) freedom—which is what it is—but as an outstanding piece of "literature," a monument to the "civilization" that good liberals like Lionel Trilling were strenuously upholding. (The difference between Trilling and Kerouac is immediately apparent if you compare the titles of their novels: both titles invoke the metaphor of travel, but Trilling wrote "The Middle of the Journey," with its quietly genteel reference to Dante; Kerouac wrote the more demotic—and memorable—"On the Road.")

It's not that "Howl" isn't "literature"—of course it is—but it is not genteel literature; it is in some deep sense *illegal*, but it had to be defended as if it were *A Tale of Two Cities*. The people who attacked it were in a certain sense correct. Ginsberg (who did not attend the trial) is saying, "*Yes, I am* being obscene—*and I don't care if you think so.*" Of course the book should not have been banned, but the terms in which it had to be defended were necessarily to some degree a betrayal of the very energy which gave the poem life. David Gates is surely correct when, in "Welcoming 'Howl' Into the Canon" (in *The Poem That Changed America: 'Howl" Fifty Years Later*, ed. Jason Shinder), he writes, "Ginsberg *meant* the poem to be obscene":

> not merely offensive in its forbidden words describing forbidden acts but offensive to intellect, to common sense, to all our consensual realities, to all the boundaries we believe necessary to civilized life. This is not, at bottom, a poem holding up liberal, or libertarian, pieties against conservative pieties, although that's how it had to be sold to the judge and the public, and it's what Ginsberg himself sometimes seemed to argue when he put on his crusader-for-free-speech hat. It's a *radically* offensive poem, or used to be—offensive even to received notions of what poetry is, and it needs offended readers whose fear and outrage bring it most fully to life.

Ginsberg always insisted on the structure of "Howl" and tirelessly pointed it out: "The Poem," he told Richard Eberhart, "is really built like a brick shithouse." But in fact the thrill of "Howl" does not reside in its structure but in its astonishing and exhilarating approach to sheer chaos, to madness—its "*radical* offensiveness."

∽

City Lights' new *Howl on Trial: The Battle for Free Expression*, edited by Bill Morgan and Nancy J. Peters, definitely wears the crusader-for-free-speech hat. But this too is an aspect of Ginsberg's poem—if not exactly of what he originally wrote, at least of the poem's tangled, intricate history.

The book begins with a brief introduction by Lawrence Ferlinghetti. The celebrated poet/publisher reminisces about his involvement with the publication of "Howl"—"the repressive, conformist, racist, homophobic world of the 1950's cried out for it"—and denounces "this time of rampant materialism, militarism, nationalism, and omnivorous corporate monoculture eating up the world." It's interesting to note that Ferlinghetti didn't really "get" "Howl" until he heard Ginsberg read it: "Ginsberg handed me 'Howl' with some hesitation, as if wondering whether I would know what to do with it. I didn't. But later that week when I heard him read it at the Six Gallery, I suddenly knew what had to be done." (In a 1956 letter to Lucien Carr, Ginsberg himself notes that "Howl" is "very good read aloud cause it's got swing." And Gregory Corso's review of the poem—included in *Howl on Trial*—asserts, "'Howl' is essentially a poem to be read aloud, but only by the Howler . . . any other Howler would screw it up . . .").

Ferlinghetti's remarks are followed by a useful chronology of "Howl" and then by Nancy J. Peters' searing essay, "Milestones of Literary Censorship." "And so it went," she writes, "American law continuing to be shaped by a small group of evangelistic zealots that claimed to represent everyone in the country." The essay gives us a fascinating chronology, "The Struggle for Free Expression," which begins in 1821 with John Cleland's *Fanny Hill: Memoirs of a Woman of Pleasure* and ends with the chilling assertion, "Under present law, Allen Ginsberg's 'Howl' could be subject to censorship once again if offered on City Lights' web site."

One of the dates mentioned in "The Struggle for Free Expression" is 1978:

> *F.C.C. v. Pacifica Foundation.* The Court held that the F.C.C. could create time, place, and matter restrictions on literary and other material to be broadcast. For example, Ginsberg's "Howl" was among the works restricted to the early morning hours when children would presumably be asleep.

This twenty-eight-year-old ruling continues to create problems for people attempting to broadcast literature on stations such as KPFA.

The longest sections of *Howl on Trial* are "The *Howl* Letters," edited by Bill Morgan, and "Excerpts from the Trial Testimony." The letters extend from August 16, 1955, when Ginsberg was living at 1010 Montgomery in San Francisco—where he wrote the opening section of "Howl"—to September 7, 1958, when he was living in New York and wrote a long letter in defense of his poem to his friend John Hollander, who had reviewed *Howl and Other Poems* unfavorably. The letters are for the most part written by Ginsberg but there are also letters from friends such as Gregory Corso and from Ginsberg's publisher, Lawrence Ferlinghetti. The letters cover the period when "Howl" is read at the Six Gallery (October 7, 1955); when it finally makes its way into print (November 1, 1956); when 520 copies of the book are confiscated by San Francisco Collector of Customs Chester MacPhee (March 25, 1957); when City Lights employee Shigeyoshi Murao is arrested for selling a copy of the book (June 3, 1957); when it comes to trial (August 8, 1957); and when Judge Clayton W. Horn issues his enlightened decision finding Lawrence Ferlinghetti not guilty of publishing and selling obscene writings (October 3, 1957). *Howl on Trial* includes passages from Judge Horn's decision. In part the decision reads,

> The theme of "Howl" presents "unorthodox and controversial ideas." Coarse and vulgar language is used in treatment and sex acts are mentioned, but unless the book is entirely lacking in "social importance," it cannot be held obscene. . . The book or material must be judged as a whole by its effect on the *average adult* in the community. If the material is objectionable only because of coarse and vulgar language which is not erotic or aphrodisiac in character it is not obscene. . . The People state that it is not necessary to use such words and that others would be more palatable to good taste. The answer is that life is not encased in one formula whereby everyone acts the same or conforms to a particular pattern. No two persons think alike; we were all made from the same mold but in different patterns. Would there be any freedom of press or speech if one must reduce his vocabulary to vapid innocuous euphemism?

Ginsberg's letters are enjoyable and interesting. Many of them are about money, which was a factor for both Ferlinghetti and Ginsberg. Ginsberg defends his work but occasionally has doubts about it too: "The poems are actually sloppy enough written," he admits, "without sloppiness made worse by typographical arrangement." He generously credits Jack Kerouac for the technique in "Howl": "I realize how right you are, that was the first time I sat down to blow, it came out in your method, sounding like you, an imitation practically." There are amusing moments, tech talk about poetry ("The technical problem raised and partially solved is the break-through begun by Whitman but never carried forward, from both iambic stultification and literary automatism, and unrhythmical shortline verse, which does not yet offer any kind of *base* cyclical flow for the build up of a powerful rhythm"), and the long, impassioned defense of his work to John Hollander. In fact, one could wish for even more letters. Louis Ginsberg's 1956 letter to his son, for example, in which the father commends the son's "wild, rhapsodic, explosive outpouring" but deplores his foul language: "I still insist . . . there is no need for dirty, ugly, words, as they will entangle you unnecessarily in trouble. Try to cut them out. . . ." Or

Allen's 1955 letter to his previous mentor William Carlos Williams—a poet noted for his "shortline verse":

> The key is in Jazz choruses to some extent; also to reliance on spontaneity & expressiveness which long line encourages; also to attention to interior unchecked logical mental stream. With a long line comes a return [to], (caused by) expressive human feeling, it's generally lacking in poetry now, which is inhuman. The release of emotion is one with rhythmical buildup of long line.

Or for a more generous selection from Ginsberg's important letter to Richard Eberhart. (The line about "Howl" being "built like a brick shithouse" is not included here.) These letters are available in the original draft facsimile edition of "Howl," but it would have been nice had they been included in *Howl on Trial* as well.

The excerpts from the trial testimony are fascinating and well edited, so that one has a sense of the progress of the trial. Judge Horn's statements are always balanced and interesting, and he emerges as a literate, intelligent man. "It is obvious," he states, "that you are never going to get unanimous consent on anything that is involved in this case. That's the reason it is such a difficult question. That's the reason why the freedom of the press should be so stringently protected, so that no one segment of the country can censor to the injury of the rest, what they can read, see and hear and so forth. That is why this case is such an important one, why I am giving it such a lot of time and consideration." Notable writers—some of them now more or less forgotten—come forth to praise Ginsberg's poem. Mark Schorer—who had written a book on Blake—speaks of "The language of the street, which is absolutely essential to the esthetic purpose of the work"; Kenneth Rexroth describes "Howl" as "prophetic literature": "the theme is the denunciation of evil and a pointing out of the consequences and a call to repent and a pointing out of the way out . . . 'Woe! Woe! Woe! The City of Jerusalem! The Syrian is about to come down or has already, and you are to do such and such a thing and you must repent and do thus and so.'" He describes "Howl" as a poem of "extraordinarily high" merit and calls it "probably the most remarkable single poem, published by a young man since the second war." At one point, reading a passage from the poem, the attorney for the prosecution finds himself unable to pronounce the word "solipsism." He is instructed by the attorney for the defense while Judge Horn points out that the word is misspelled in City Lights' text. Defense attorney Jake Ehrlich is able to make mincemeat out of the witnesses for the prosecution. One, Gail

Potter, announces that she has rewritten both *Faust* and *Everyman* ("Now, that isn't as funny as you might think") and assures the Court that "you feel like you are going through the gutter when you have to read that stuff ['Howl']. I didn't linger on it too long, I assure you." Ehrlich declines to cross-examine her. In the case of another such witness, David Kirk, the lawyer seems better acquainted with literary history than the "expert":

> *Mr. Ehrlich*: Now, you have heard of Erasmus, haven't you?
>
> *Mr. Kirk*: I have.
>
> Q. And Erasmus was quite a writer, wasn't he?
>
> A. I have little acquaintance with Erasmus. My study begins with 1660.
>
> Q. 1660. You wouldn't dare go back a day before 1660, would you?
>
> *Mr. McIntosh* [attorney for the prosecution]: Object to that, your Honor.

Given such witnesses, there is little doubt that Ginsberg's poem will emerge triumphant, though one of the glories of *Howl on Trial* is the presentation of Jake Ehrlich's eloquent closing statement; surprisingly, the lawyer quotes from Christopher Marlowe's "Ignoto":

> I am not fashioned for these amorous times,
> To court thy beauty with lascivious rhymes:
> I cannot dally, caper, dance and sing,
> Oiling my saint with supple sonneting:
> I cannot cross my arms, or sigh, "Ah me,"
> "Ah me forlorn!" Egregious foppery!
> I cannot buss thy fill, play with thy hair,
> Swearing by Jove, "Thou art most debonnaire!"
> Not I, by cock! But I shall tell thee roundly,
> Hark in thine ear, zounds I can fuck thee soundly.

Though *Howl on Trial* centers on a particular poem, it is less a book about poetry than it is about a poem's encounter with history—history in the particular form of a society the poem not only places in question but actually insults: "Moloch the incomprehensible prison! Moloch the crossbone soulless jailhouse and Congress of sorrows! Moloch whose buildings are judgment! Moloch the vast stone of war! Moloch the stunned governments!" If such a book can emerge triumphant within the American judicial system, is Moloch as all embracing as he seems? The trial, as the editors of *Howl on Trial* know very well, gives reason for hope.

Howl on Trial opens with the assertion that "Fifty years after the trial it seems impossible to believe that anyone could have ever doubted the literary merit of *Howl and Other Poems*." That may be the way things appear to the talented people at 261 Columbus Avenue, but, despite "Howl"'s many, many adherents—its "howlers"—doubts about the "literary merit" of Ginsberg's work continue to be voiced, most recently by New Formalist writers such as David Mason. I don't agree with the naysayers but have to admit that there is something deliberately *annoying* about Ginsberg's poem, something which all its success has never succeeded in covering over. The poem continues to sting. *Howl on Trial* ignores that fact in order to pursue other matters—matters of considerable importance, to be sure, even matters of considerable personal importance to Allen Ginsberg, for whom free speech and censorship were burning issues. Bill Morgan is surely right when, in the concluding chapter, he insists that "The Censorship Battle Continues." But in making its case *Howl on Trial* is not quite fair to the amazing, violent, tender, excessive, *controversial* poem City Lights published on November 1, 1956.³

༄

"Howl" may be, as Jason Shinder has it, "the poem that changed America," but the event at Herbst Hall is an indication of how America can change "Howl." The poem is not only a thumbing of the nose at "propriety, moral 'value,' superficial 'maturity,'" but the product of a tremendous longing for the visionary, for what Ginsberg calls in "Model Texts: Inspirations Precursor to HOWL" the "breakthru to unobstructed Spirit," a condition which will redeem the "bad boy" aspect of his poem and give the writer access to another, more satisfying mode of "respectability." Ginsberg cites— and quotes from—Christopher Smart's "Jubilate Agno," Shelley's "Adonais" and "Ode to the West Wind," Apollinaire's "Zone," Kurt Schwitters' "Priimiititiii," Mayakovsky's "At the Top of My Voice," Lorca's *Poet in New York*, Hart Crane's "Atlantis," William Carlos Williams' "To Elsie," and of course Whitman's *Leaves of Grass*. From this point of view, the outcast becomes the poet-saint, the sage. In effect, the poet is saying, "I am not only not to be discarded, treated as dirt—*beaten down, destroyed*—I am at this moment *better than anyone*, and I can prove it by my words and by the precursor poets who come alive in the texture of my verse. I have transformed myself into the High Priest of your culture. Listen to the holiness of my utterance." (In his 1956 letter to Richard Eberhart, Ginsberg wrote, "I used to think I was mad to want to be a saint, but now what have I got to fear? People's opinions? Loss of a teaching job? I am living outside this context.")

"Howl" is indeed the "*radically* offensive" document David Gates claims it to be, but it is also the announcement of the creation of a poet—and the poet is, precisely, the redemption of the pariah. Ginsberg remarked in 1976 that "'Howl' is really about my mother," the formidable Naomi who died in the insane asylum and whose spirit animates his great poem, "Kaddish" ("More Explanations Twenty Years After"). Naomi's was definitely a mind "destroyed by madness," and she lurks behind the more public figure of Carl Solomon. In an interview with Lawrence Grobel, published in *Endangered Species: Writers Talk About Their Craft, Their Visions, Their Lives,* Ginsberg remarks, "'Howl' was actually written with [my mother] in mind":

> "Carl Solomon! I'm With You in Rockland" really is my mother and "I'm with you in Pilgrim State Hospital," in the sense of a release of feeling, an acknowledgement and release of maternal tenderness, which though thwarted still exists intact with me, or in anyone, probably. Tenderness toward mother, the only mother I have after all, whatever condition she was in. So "Howl" was actually an emotional reunion with my mother.

At the same time he remarks about his horror at actually seeing his mother:

> I sent her "Howl" at Pilgrim State Hospital, where she was in her last months before her stroke. She hadn't recognized me about a half year before when I visited. She thought I was a spy, actually. It was very disturbing—I wept. It seemed like the farthest limit of dehumanization and illness and madness, that she couldn't remember me.

The poet's letter to Eberhart insists that "I am saying that what seems 'mad' in America is our expression of natural ecstasy" but also admits to feelings "of sympathy and identification with the rejected, mystical, individual even 'mad.'" His ambivalent feelings about madness—cf. the hipster's exclamation, "crazy"—are at the very center of "Howl." The poem is an act of identification with the mother, but it is also an expression of the poet's horror at what his mother has become: trapped in the power of Moloch. "Howl" is simultaneously mad (really mad, like Naomi) and—a poem, an "expression of natural ecstasy." The power of the piece is that it inhabits both worlds and will not exchange one for the other:

Breakthroughs! over the river! flips and crucifixions!
gone down the flood! Highs! Epiphanies! Despairs!
Ten years' animal screams and suicides! Minds!
New loves! Mad generations! down on the rocks
of Time!

Remains To Be Seen

Robert Duncan: A Poet's Art

> So for me there is a question: Is there a me? I? What I do is that I pose a creative process
> in which I assemble me from surrounding facts including the body and so forth.
> —ROBERT DUNCAN[1]

"Robert would come to these parties, and if nothing else was going on, he could always draw. It was a form of play."

So said an artist friend of the poet Robert Duncan (1919-1988), whose graphic works are currently on display in a fascinating exhibition set up at two UC Berkeley locations: the Art Museum and the Bancroft Library.

"Play" is a central element in any description of Duncan, whose rich, dense, brilliant verse was at once a challenge and an inspiration to anyone who came into contact with it.

If we ask what "consciousness" is, we might answer that it is whatever, in our deep need for its representation, we may choose to make it be at any given moment. For Duncan, consciousness was bound up and intertwined with words like *childhood, magic, romance, primal*. "I am everywhere involved in religion," he once remarked with amusement, "but nowhere does my involvement produce a church."[2]

Acutely aware of all the artistic ramifications of Modernism—and constantly paying homage to them in his work—he nevertheless produced a poetry rooted in what Modernism always represented as its generic enemy: Romanticism. "I see always," he wrote in one of the poems of his great book, *The Opening of the Field* (1960), "the underside turning."

"Seeing" was by no means a simple thing for Duncan. A childhood accident he suffered at the age of three left him permanently cross-eyed, and his work refers on numerous occasions to his peculiarity of vision:

> being cross-eyed, I have been subject all my life, except for the first three years, to one
> of the states of presentational immediacy ... When I look at something, I see it double

and I can never tell which one is the real one—the one which I see with my left eye or the one that I see with my right eye. As a child I used to go forward and touch it.[3]

Indeed, "seeing" in the sense of "point of view" was also problematical for Duncan:

When a man's life becomes totally so informed that every bird and leaf speaks to him and every happening has meaning, he is considered to be *psychotic*. The shaman and the inspired poet, who take the universe to be alive, are brothers germane of the mystic and the paranoic. [4]

But it was not only Duncan's status as psychotic/shaman or as "cross-eyed bear" ("Gladly, the cross-eyed bear," he wrote, punning, in *The Opening of the Field*) or his advocacy of a Romantic esthetic which caused him problems. He was also, from the start, courageously committed to an explicitly homosexual Eros, speaking at one point of the search for "a homoerotic Christ."[5] His pioneering essay, "The Homosexual In Society," "the first discussion of homosexuality which included the frank avowal that the author was himself involved,"[6] appeared in Dwight MacDonald's journal, *Politics* in 1944 and was the direct cause of John Crowe Ransom's rejection of a previously-accepted poem of Duncan's for *The Kenyon Review*. "Blind lifelines," Duncan wrote in that essay, "—what Darwin illuminates as evolution—has its creative design, and in that process a man's sexuality is a natural factor in a biological economy larger and deeper than his own human will."[7]

Given such cross-currents (and there are more: I have yet to mention his lifelong interest in the occult, his adoptive parents having been ardent Theosophists, or the fact that his blood-mother died in giving birth to him), it is not surprising to discover that Duncan had difficulty in balancing everything against everything else, that the question of "unity" would be a major issue in his work. Pound's *Cantos* provided one of the solutions for this dilemma, but, at the same time, throughout his life, Duncan remained close to many painters—some of whose works he and his lover of nearly forty years, the artist Jess, collected and kept.

As Duncan was a kind of "Sunday painter," so Jess was a kind of "Sunday poet," and the interpenetration of these art forms, writing and painting, seems to have been an important aspect of the life they created together. This exhibit wisely includes work by Jess and various friends of the couple as well as by Robert, and the result is a fascinating, though necessarily partial look at a significant aspect of the artistic history of this region. "When I write by hand," Duncan remarked,

> I can feel the poem in my hand . . . The typewriter doesn't give me this kinesthetic feeling of the line: the kind of disequilibrium which you feel in the hand—the disequilibrium which produces the new line . . . I am a writer in the original sense of writing with my hand.[8]

"I can feel the poem in my hand." Duncan's implement for most of these works was not the brush but the wax crayon. Long before the concept of "the inner child" became fashionable, Duncan was aware of the aliveness of the child in his psyche. His drawings were in a way versions of what that child might do with a box of wax crayons. A crayon, unlike a brush, is held in the way that a pen is held, so Duncan's "drawing" might be regarded as a kind of "writing." Moreover, in the quotation he is speaking of "lines" of poetry, but he could just as easily be referring to "lines" of drawings. In some of the pieces, such as the extraordinary drawing for the play, *Faust Foutu*, words are actually part of the graphic design. Indeed, Duncan was always concerned with how his poems *looked* on the page; the visual was by no means an unimportant aspect of his poetry. In Jess's work, too, words, fragments of words, reviews, sentences, puns are part of the graphic design. One might say that, for both these artists, *writing was a form of drawing and drawing a form of writing*. This show, subtitled "A Poet's Art," is a demonstration of the deep connections between the two.

Duncan often referred to himself as a "derivative" poet, and his work naturally reflects not only personal enthusiasms (Jean Cocteau, for example) but the artistic currents of his time. He and Jess lived through the heroic age of Abstract Expressionism, and some of the crayon works are layered, color upon color, in the manner of Jess's teacher, the austere and brilliant Clyfford Still. Some of the work is figurative, some of it is abstract. Duncan once said that he "wanted to be made out of thousands of threads," that his "figure"' was "the Muslim rug which one spends a whole lifetime in tying,"[9] and the exhibit includes one of his designs for a rug as well as a rather gorgeous design for wallpaper.

But the primary effect of this show is that of a powerful intelligence moving from form to form. There is a striking drawing of a muscular male figure with an erection, and a marvelous George III who appears with mustache and tremendous hair-do wearing what appears to be an ill-fitting orange dress. In several of the pieces Duncan seems to be attempting to reconcile in a single image the frontal and side views of a face—no new motif in Modernist art but of particular interest here given the many currents of the poet's "multiphasic" personality as well as his difficulties in seeing. At the Bancroft there are marvelous decorated books and Duncan's beautiful calligraphy as well as the extraordinary collaboration between Robert and Jess, *A Book of Resemblances*, rightly described as "one of the most beautiful books of poetry produced in the last forty years."

A short essay can scarcely deal with the life which bursts from all these works. They are, in all senses of the phrase, *remains to be seen*, tokens of a career which is over but *not* over, which continues to challenge our assumptions and suppositions. "And I still find it miraculous," Duncan remarked once, "I don't know why, there's no way I qualify, I disqualify daily a million times . . . for being loved."[10] His complicated, rich works stand as instances of eroticism as collage, as the amazing connection between elements which look as though they could never connect at all.

"Drawingwise," Duncan remarked to a student once, ". . . your drawing looks like it was withdrawing, not going forward."[11] Duncan's drawings are never like that. They are reminders of an artist who once said, "The world of spirit is everything," and who praised Alfred North Whitehead because Whitehead thought of people "not as entities but as events."[12] To return to the opening quotation:

> So for me there is a question: Is there a me? I? What I do is that I pose a creative process in which I assemble me from surrounding facts including the body and so forth.

Duncan, like this show, was an event.

The Possibility Of Weldon Kees

Though he was featured at the John Natsoulas Gallery's 2002 Conference on the Beat Generation, Weldon Kees (1914-1955) was no "beatnik"; he was, however, part of the fabric of his time, as painter, poet, critic, fiction writer, composer, even entertainer. His very successful "Poets Follies" was a kind of poetry cabaret for which Kees composed songs and played piano. The poet's presumed suicide on July 18, 1955 (his car was discovered near the Golden Gate Bridge but the body was never found) gives his work a tragic dimension and propels him into myth. It was with this in mind that a number of us agreed to join a critical seminar on Kees held at the tenth annual West Chester University Poetry Conference.

Weldon Kees responded deeply to various currents, political (left wing/pacifist) and popular. He admired Fats Waller before Fats Waller was widely admired; he insisted that films were "art" at a time when they were regarded as mere "entertainment." (Film critic Pauline Kael was one of Kees' younger friends; they appeared together on Berkeley radio station KPFA.) One might call Kees a "poet noir," in some ways similar to Kenneth Fearing—a popular but equally paranoid, alcoholic poet whose work Kees read. Like Fearing's, Kees' poems are often frightening. Other influences include W.H. Auden and James Joyce: Kees wrote "Variations on a Theme by Joyce" ("The war is in words and the wood is the world"), and in "Five Villanelles" he criticizes a publisher who personally "turned down Joyce." Kees was admired by Kenneth Rexroth, who hosted the Six Gallery reading (though Kees died a few months before that reading took place). I think Kees' work, with its considerable bleakness, its sense of "a permanent and hopeless apocalypse" (in Rexroth's phrase), hovers between personal depression and an intense commentary on the world around him—surely a bleak, frightening, sometimes nostalgic world:

WHEN THE LEASE IS UP

Walk the horses down the hill
Through the darkening groves;
Pat their rumps and leave the stall;
Even the eyeless cat perceives
Things are not going well.

Fasten the lock on the drawingroom door,
Cover the tables with sheets:
This is the end of the swollen year
When even the sound of the rain repeats:
The lease is up, the time is near.

Pull the curtains to the sill,
Darken the rooms, cut all the wires.
Crush the embers as they fall
From the dying fires:
Things are not going well.

In *American Poetry in the Twentieth Century* Rexroth connects Kees to "a definite school of American verse—Robert Lowell, Theodore Roethke, Sylvia Plath, James Wright, John Berryman, and a number of others whom [critics] call the Confessional School, poets who have recorded profound psychological conflicts or mental breakdown . . . [For Kees] the horrors of *The Waste Land*, or W.H. Auden's ruined England in a new Dark Ages . . . were not literary conventions, but ever present reality, alive and malignant." Kees' considerable intelligence (the phrase "the mind" appears frequently in his work, and he praises "the mind / That moves towards meaning"), his interest in form, and his ability—which he shared with Fearing—to write at a level at which the personal is present only in an indirect way keep his poems from dissolving into mere self-pity, though self-pity is an aspect of many of them:

Much cry and little wool:
I have come back
As empty-handed as I went.

Poet Dana Gioia's essay, "The Loneliness of Weldon Kees" (in *Can Poetry Matter?*) is one of the best pieces ever written on Kees. Kees, Gioia writes,

> transformed the alienation and vacuity of contemporary life into lyric poetry. He does not offer readers comfort or escape. He did not transcend the problems of his century with a religious or political faith. He did not elude the vulgarization of public culture by immigrating to an aesthetic realm. What he offered was uncompromising honesty, the transforming shock of recognition. "All a poet can do today is warn" . . . He presented only the choices history offered his generation, and none of them were attractive.

In what remains of this essay, I want to examine a particular poem by Kees. The poem is not exactly "representative," but I think it goes to the heart of his enterprise. This is "To a Contemporary." It appears in the concluding section of *The Last Man* (1943).

To A Contemporary

J'ai plus de souvenirs que si j'avais mille ans.
—Baudelaire

Memories rich as Proust's or Baudelaire's are yours,
You think: snarled ravelings of doubt at evening scents
Of women, dazed with pleasure, whose white legs and arms
Once coiled with languor around you; arguments
With undistinguished friends, their bigotries each year
More fixed. Lamps in the mist that light strange faces fill
Your nights; your fingers drum upon the table as you stare,
Uncertain, at the floor. *Un vieux boudoir?* Impossible!
You frequently compare yourself to those whose memories
Are cruel, contemptible, like naked bone.

Yet, is there anything in this rank richness warm
Or permanent? At every climax, trapped, alone,
You seem to be a helpless passenger that drifts
On some frail boat; and with oblivious ease,
As from a distance, watch yourself
Disintegrate in foaming seas.

The quotation from Baudelaire is from one of the several poems Baudelaire called "Spleen"; the line may be translated as "I have more memories than if I had lived a thousand years." One of the meanings of "spleen"—an English word—is "excessive dejection or depression of spirits; gloominess and irritability; moroseness; melancholia" (*O.E.D.*). "In his mood of *spleen*," writes Baudelaire's biographer, Enid Starkie, "the poet imagines himself sitting in his lonely room, waiting for the work which does not come, and he fancies that he bears within himself all the dead memories of a thousand years, the dead hopes which are as many in number as the corpses piled up in a charnel-house, or those lying buried in a churchyard. Nothing, he thinks, can equal the dreariness of the long and empty days . . ." (*Baudelaire*).

Kees' poem goes from "Memories"—the first word—to "watch yourself / Disintegrate." Memory gives us the sense that we are a continuity of some sort; "disintegration" annihilates memory.

The opening line of "To a Contemporary" is more or less a version of the line quoted from Baudelaire—though the pronoun has shifted from I to you:

> Memories rich as Proust's or Baudelaire's are yours. . . .

But Kees' line is immediately undercut by the next phrase, "You *think*," which has the effect of a blunt *NOT*—just as the phrase "Memories *rich* as Proust's or Baudelaire's" transforms itself in the second section of the poem into "this *rank* richness."

Yet it is just possible that "you think" is not a commentary on the previous line but the beginning of a new movement: "You think . . . ," and the memories begin. The first "memory" is hardly encouraging, however: "snarled ravelings of doubt." Just as we begin to wonder about the nature of this "doubt," the poem shifts into eroticism: "evening scents / Of women, dazed with pleasure, whose white legs and arms / Once coiled with languor around you." The flow of the poem has survived "snarled ravelings of doubt," which strikes a discordant, enigmatic note, and is able to go on.

Yet the attractive eroticism is not continued. Instead of more eroticism, we get "arguments"—something closer to "war" than to "love." The pleasure-dazed women are replaced by "undistinguished friends, their bigotries each year / More fixed." At this point the poem has moved even further away from the idea of "rich memories." Indeed, in a sense it has stopped. The word "fixed" has a momentarily terminal effect upon it. Where can we go next?

Kees continues with a phrase, "Lamps in the mist," which gives us a moment of hope: light suggests order, even, here, the possibility of companionship. Yet the hope is only momentary: *these* lamps "light strange faces" which "fill your nights." We are not in the realm of companionship but in the realm of dream—possibly of nightmare or even hallucination. Suddenly the "you" of the poem is completely without its self-affirming, self-creating "memories." "Your fingers drum upon the table as you stare, / Uncertain, at the floor." Again the poem has ended. The "you" is not experiencing a rich memory but staring vacantly at the floor, nervously drumming his fingers on the table—in a state of uncertainty. We are a far cry from the grandeur of Baudelaire's line, "J'ai plus de souvenirs que si j'avais mille ans." But if English has failed us, why not try French? "Un vieux boudoir?"—"An old boudoir," another phrase from Baudelaire's poem. But this too is canceled out: "Impossible!" In the next line the opening word of the poem, "memories," appears again, but *these* memories are "cruel, contemptible," not something one would wish to keep in one's consciousness; rather, something one would prefer to forget. *These* memories are far from "rich"; they are "like naked bone," a phrase which suggests poverty, dire straits—the opposite of "rich."

Then there is a space, and the second section of the poem begins:

> Yet, is there anything in this rank richness warm
> Or permanent?

The opening word is "Yet," and its effect is to suggest that the first section really *did* in some way deal with rich memories, and that the poet has enumerated them. "Memories rich as Proust's or Baudelaire's are yours," *yet. . . .* This is of course not true, but it is not *completely* untrue. Kees has given us a sequence of what might pass for memories—and at least the erotic ones have some pleasurable elements, though the women's "white legs and arms" are not *presently* "coiled with languor around you" but were only "once" in that position.

Suppose Kees had written—leaving out the word "rank"—"Yet, is there anything in this richness warm / Or permanent?" The effect would be similar to what Elinor Wylie achieved in her sonnet sequence, "Wild Peaches." After a fine description of "brimming cornucopias," the poet suddenly turns and says,

> Down to the Puritan marrow of my bones
> There's something in this richness that I hate. . . .

Kees designation of the richness as "rank" complicates the statement even more and moves us away from a sentiment like Wylie's: the "rankness" of the richness makes it still another "Impossible." What we get now are classic Kees words: "trapped," "alone," "helpless"—words which propel us to the very center of this poet's bleak vision. If, like those dazed-with-pleasure women, we experience "climax," it is a climax which does not allow us to experience release—only feelings of entrapment, loneliness, helplessness.

Yet a kind of release does come.

Baudelaire writes in his essay "The Essence of Laughter" that there is "a permanent dualism in the human being," "a power of rapid self-division . . . of assisting as a . . . spectator at the phenomena of [one's] own ego": "an artist is only an artist on condition that he is a double man and that there is not one single phenomenon of his double nature of which he is ignorant." For Baudelaire, self-consciousness is a kind of fall in which the self splits apart— shifting from an unthinking, "innocent" entity into the grotesque and doubled man who is able to observe himself. Doubles also show up frequently in Kees—as in his poem, "Relating to Robinson."

At this point in "To a Contemporary," the poem's "you" explicitly becomes a doubled man—the "helpless passenger" but also the person who can "watch [himself]." Who is the "contemporary" to whom the poem is addressed? Who is the "you"? (James Reidel points out that Kees felt himself to be at a *distance* from his contemporaries: "I must say I feel too little sense of 'belonging' with my immediate contemporaries. . . .") With the appearance of the theme of doubleness it becomes clear that, whoever else the poem is about, the poem is also about Weldon Kees. Doubleness is a mirror in which— as Kees writes—you "watch yourself." Kees is simultaneously the "helpless passenger" on the frail boat and the observer. He does not identify himself *strongly* with the helpless, dying man but watches "as from a distance." Though he *is* the helpless man, he is not *fully* the helpless man—just as he is not fully the watcher. The poem allows Kees to maintain himself in a kind of balance, a kind of constant doubling as he moves from position to position. It was no accident that Unamuno's *Tragic Sense of Life* was found at Kee's bedside after his death. The world of the doubled man is the world of the fall—a world not of richness but, as Baudelaire would say, of *misère*, of poverty.

Yet look again at the concluding lines:

> and with oblivious ease,
> As from a distance, watch yourself
> Disintegrate in foaming seas.

Isn't there something beautiful in that image? Isn't there something attractive about the phrase "oblivious ease"—as if one were falling asleep? Does the phrase "foaming seas" perhaps recall Keats'

> magic casements, opening on the foam
> Of perilous seas, in faery lands forlorn?

Shelley's death by drowning—"a helpless passenger that drifts / On some frail boat"—may be partially operative here as well.

The burden of memory is the burden of the self, the burden of the carefully constructed ego. What a pleasure to watch all that pain of memory disintegrate, vanish—to be free of it. To disappear into the mother sea . . .

"To a Contemporary" is an evocation of certain kinds of French writing. It is an announcement that Kees is in the tradition of Proust and Baudelaire. At the same time, the poem's many negations suggest that Kees' poem is far from being a fully successful evocation of such writing: indeed, the poem suggests that Kees—who is also "you"—is hardly the equal of his illustrious predecessors. Baudelaire and Proust really had "rich memories." Indeed, Baudelaire produced marvelous Classical hexameters. Kees writes *loose* hexameters, and some of the lines aren't hexameters at all. Baudelaire wrote sonnets. "To a Contemporary"— divided into two parts like a sonnet—is a kind of *failed* sonnet in sixteen rather than fourteen lines. And its two concluding lines, beautiful as they are, are not hexameters. They are not even pentameters; they are mere tetrameters—the only ones in the poem.

"To a Contemporary" is a balancing act which plays among various contradictory, often interruptive modes. Assertions are constantly encountering their diametrical opposites. Kees is the helpless man who will die, yet he is also the man who watches and lives. The poem is a kind of field in which various fiercely oppositional elements come into contact but in which no choices are finally made. ("Watch yourself" can also mean "Be careful.")

I believe that, like this poem, Weldon Kees' work is the product of a consciousness which keeps itself alive by continually raising *possibilities*. Its creativity functions in a condition of *spleen*—"excessive dejection or depression of spirits; gloominess and irritability; moroseness; melancholia." But as long as no final choices are made, the poet lives. To choose one thing rather than another may mean to choose death. Kees' will to live keeps him in constant motion. Is he a poet, a painter, a songwriter, a story writer, a novelist, a critic, a playwright, a piano player? He is all of these and more. There is—forgive the pun—no single key to this artist's work: only *keys*.

Barry Singer

Black and Blue: The Life And Lyrics Of Andy Razaf

When people read poetry they can study the printed page, but each song lyric is hurled at them only once or twice in the course of an evening, and the audience has no chance to rehear or reread it. Thus, good lyrics should be simple, colloquial, rhymed, conversational lines. It is up to the lyric writer to take the few hundred words allotted him and use whatever ingenuity he has . . . Unlike good children, titles should be heard, not seen. I mean that listening to the argot in everyday conversation results in pay-dirt for lyric writers.
—IRA GERSHWIN, "Words and Music," *New York Times* 11/9/30

May God help the Alley, that street of deceit.
—ANDY RAZAF, "Flim-Flam Alley" (a poem)

Popular songs are where poetry goes when it tires of the stuffy atmosphere of Helicon. This is an essay about a lyricist.

⚭

In 1945, vaudevillian Harry Fox (1882-1959) sued the producers of the film, *The Dolly Sisters*, for representing him in the movie as a "lowly songwriter." Fox, the originator of the "Fox Trot," felt that such a representation was part of Rosie Dolly's "conspiracy to injure him." Once a prominent Broadway star, Fox had very little clout left in the entertainment industry at that time, and he lost the suit. But his accusation suggests the opinion early Broadway stars and vaudevillians had of the people who provided them with material. What if the "lowly songwriter" were, in addition, an African-American? What if he were not even a "songwriter" but merely a "lyricist," indeed, what Barry Singer calls "that never-before-considered commodity: a black lyricist"?

Singer's *Black and Blue* (Schirmer Books) is a wonderful consideration of the life and times of the African-American lyricist, Andy Razaf, who—

like his more famous composing partner, Thomas "Fats" Waller—was simultaneously triumphant and ill-starred. Razaf wrote songs everyone knows—"Ain't Misbehavin'," "Honeysuckle Rose"—yet, Singer points out, his "songs outlived his name." At the end of his life, writes Singer, "Andy Razaf was absolutely mystified at his continuing obscurity," his "utter anonymity": he was "a brilliant black man of words in an industry accustomed only to brilliant black men of music."

Both Andy Razaf and Fats Waller rose to prominence in the midst of a complex, immensely difficult situation: "the cutthroat and blatantly racist entertainment business of the [American] Twenties and Thirties." As a black entertainer, Waller was expected to communicate *Happy*; as a fat man, he was expected to communicate the same thing. (A radio announcer once referred to him as having the "jovial personality that is supposed to be one of the characteristics of the corpulent people.") Waller communicated *Happy*, but he also communicated *wild, exuberant, funny, desperate, self-destructive, brilliant, joyous, transgressive, free*—at times even *angry*. Andy Razaf, Waller's primary lyricist and "favorite poet next to Wordsworth," was an equally complex man.

Andy Razaf's song, "Memories of You" was written for *Blackbirds of 1930*—a show produced by Lew Leslie, a white man paradoxically known as the "black Ziegfeld" because of his elaborate productions featuring black entertainers. The song was conceived as a specialty number for the lyricist's "beautiful live-in paramour, Minto Cato": the music, composed by pianist Eubie Blake, was "tailored to display Cato's extraordinary three-octave vocal range":

> Why can't I forget like I should?
> Heaven knows I would if I could,
> But I just can't keep you off my mind.
> Tho' you've gone and love was in vain,
> All around me you still remain,
> Wonder why fate should be so unkind—
>
> Waking skies at sunrise,
> Every sunset too,
> Seems to be
> Bringing me
> Memories of you.
> Here and there,
> Ev'rywhere,

Scenes that we once knew,
And they all
Just recall
Memories of you.
How I wish I could forget those happy yesteryears
That have left a rosary of tears.
Your face beams
In my dreams
'Spite of all I do,
Ev'rything
Seems to bring
Memories of you.

The haunting "Memories of You" was immediately popular and rightly became a standard, a song pianist Willie "the Lion" Smith believed would live as long as music lived. Of course, one of the most important requirements of popular songs is that people should remember them; consequently, these songs often contain subtle mnemonic suggestions to the listener, hints that we should remember them. The most blatant example of this device is the opening line of the chorus of Herman Hupfeld's "As Time Goes By": "You must remember this. . . ." But there are many others, including Irving Berlin's "Remember" with its assertion, "You forgot to remember." Razaf's lyric—as colloquial and simple in its phrasing as anything by Berlin—deliberately plugs into that extremely intense energy source—memory as obsession: "Why can't I forget like I should? / Heaven knows I would if I could."

It may be that without self-pity we couldn't have popular songs. In our no-nonsense culture, self-pity is often frowned upon, but in popular songs it is released in immense quantities: songs allow us to express an emotion which in other contexts we might disapprove of, allow us—without ever insisting that we actually confront what we are doing—to "trouble deaf heaven with our bootless cries." Self-pity is an element in "Memories of You," as it is of innumerable popular songs. "Memories of You" is also structured in the usual way of popular songs: AABA, with the "bridge" or "release" a second melody which moves away from the primary melody only to return to it: melody; repeat melody; move away from melody; return to melody. The very structure of the song is a mini obsessive movement: a failed attempt to move away from an initial "statement"—an insistence on the power of "memory."

Andy Razaf's words are simple but effective. What particularly distinguishes the piece is a word occurring in the "release" section: the word "rosary." It's an amazing word to be showing up in a secular love lyric. When songwriters write the word "rosary," it is nearly always in the context of a religious (or quasi-religious) song: "My Mother's Rosary" or Razaf's own late song, "Precious Rosary." Barry Singer writes that "With origins rooted in the poetic voice of Scripture, the blues, lyrically, were folk poetry of a singular bipolarity—often religious in tone yet supremely secular in subject and spirit . . . [T]o master the art of blues lyric writing was to master an often contradictory, endlessly variable art. . . ." "Memories of You" is no blues, yet the word "rosary" momentarily thrusts the song into a realm which is indeed "religious in tone yet supremely secular in subject and spirit." Razaf might easily have written, "a legacy of tears" or even "a memory of tears." The phrase "rosary of tears" is at once supremely inappropriate and supremely appropriate. One suddenly realizes that the beads of a rosary—almost always black in color—are shaped like tears. Furthermore, a rosary is a circle: it is literally endless—like the "memories" Razaf is conjuring up.

In a piece written to be read at the funeral of the lyricist's close, immensely problematical friend and collaborator, Fats Waller, Razaf describes Waller as his "best friend" and goes on to say that Waller "has left the world a rosary of melodies that will keep his memory alive." Razaf again allows the sacred and the secular to meet in an extraordinary way, and the word rosary is again the focal point of the connection. Waller's songs (often written with Razaf's collaboration) are like the beads of a rosary: commonplace objects one comes across again and again but connected to memory (each bead of a rosary is a reminder of a prayer to be said) and charged at some level with divine power, though it is a divine power that deliberately chooses the most secular of secular areas in which to manifest. (One remembers that tap dancers frequently referred to the often recalcitrant left foot as "the church member.") Another song, "The Joint is Jumpin'"—a Waller/Razaf hymn to the Harlem rent party—is a magnificently exuberant, magnificently "low-down" performance piece. Like the later rhythm-and-blues, it is also a close relative—even a transmutation—of an extravagantly active prayer meeting: "Don't mind the hour," sings Waller,

> I'm in power.
> I got bail
> If you go to jail
> Let's keep the joint a-jumpin'!

Andreamen[en]tania Paul Razaf[in]keriefo (the letters in brackets are silent) was born in Washington, DC, in 1895. His grandfather, John Louis Waller—no relation to Fats—was an eminent black politician whose troubled career in some ways mirrored that of his grandson. A former slave, the brilliant John Louis was named American Consul to the African country of Madagascar on February 5, 1891, but by April, 1895, after a trial in Madagascar before a French military tribunal on trumped-up charges, he was languishing in a jail in French-controlled Marseilles. The French, writes Singer, "were determined to use . . . John Waller . . . as a final means for ending American influence in Madagascar." Barely supported by the United States government, Waller was accused—in the words of a Washington newspaper—of having "connived with the natives of Madagascar to overthrow French authority." Waller was eventually released and able to return to the United States, where he remained active and hopeful. He was, writes Singer, both "a towering role model" and "a chastening study in frustration" for his grandson. His "rise from freed slave to hyperactive political careerist, U.S. diplomatic service, and, finally, to ignominious eclipse in the years preceding and just following his grandson's birth, constitutes as extraordinary and evocative a life story as Andy Razaf's own." Razaf's mother, Jennie Maria, was John Louis Waller's daughter. At the age of fifteen she married Henri Razafkeriefo, royal nephew of Madagascar's Queen Ranavalona and a potential successor to the throne. Unfortunately, Queen Ranavalona ran afoul of French authority:

> [B]y the time Jennie Waller gave birth to their child in Washington, DC, in December, Henri Razafkeriefo was dead, murdered by France's invading Madagascar force . . . Jennie Razafkeriefo gave birth to Henri Razafkeriefo's son on December 15, 1895, eleven days before her own sixteenth birthday, naming the boy in the Madagascan fashion. . . .

The boy grew up in his grandfather's house, where many members of his immediate family wrote verse. "John Waller wrote light verse frequently," writes Barry Singer, "and [Andy's grandmother] Susan Waller wrote too, privately, for pleasure. [Andy's adored, demanding mother] Jennie Razafkeriefo quite fancied herself a legitimate poetess" and did in fact publish. Razaf himself claimed that his first original verse was written at the age of ten.

In 1911 Andrea's mother was supporting herself and her son as a stenographer. "Within the year," writes Barry Singer, "Jennie convinced [her son] to drop out of high school for a job that could help support them both":

It is not at all clear why Andrea Razafkeriefo decided to become a professional songwriter. "I was not positive at first that I could write songs," he conceded years later, "but I knew that I wanted to compose." He later acknowledged to an interviewer that as a boy he had in fact "hoped to confine [himself] to poetry," but recognizing that he "had to earn a livelihood in a more material way," had decided "to versify for music."

Razaf's first song lyric was written as early as 1909, a lyric that the 13-year-old audaciously sent to the very successful popular composer Charles K. Harris, writer of the song standard "After the Ball." Harris soon returned the submission, deigning to enclose with it a personal reply: "Dear Andrea—your lyrics show great merit but I would advise you to go into some other field."

In 1913—while he was working as an elevator boy—Razaf managed to get one of his songs, "Baltimo'," into a Shubert brothers review, *The Passing Show*, a production which also featured the work of another young songwriter, George Gershwin, born three years later than Razaf. The change of the lyricist's name from Razafkeriefo to Razaf was the suggestion of the *Passing Show*'s music publisher, James Kendis. Selling a song to the Shubert brothers was a considerable achievement for a seventeen-year-old composer, though the song was a "coon song," a song meant to be sung by whites in blackface. The rhythmic sophistication in "Baltimo'"—contrapuntal to the sound of a railroad train—is extremely impressive:

> When we pull in at that lovin'
> Station, station,
> On my knees, I'm goin' to bless
> Creation, creation,
> Listen, listen, engineer,
> Go like the devil, 'cause the track is clear,
> For goodness sakes
> Don't touch them brakes
> Till we get to Baltimo'.

In a later song Razaf would write,

> Swing low sweet rhythm,
> Rhythms of every kind,
> When I'm sad and weary,
> Rhythms ease my mind. . . .

But it wasn't "Baltimo'" that the young Razaf was aiming at. It was something far deeper than that: like the young George M. Cohan (1878-1942), who also injected rhythm and speed into his productions, Andy Razaf was aiming at nothing less than total success in an American context. In the America of his time—and the America of Cohan's time too—success and rhythm seemed at some level interchangeable. As the lyricist Ira Gershwin put it in "I Got Rhythm," the celebrated song he wrote with his brother George in 1930, "Who could ask for anything more?" Significantly, Fats Waller called his band "Fats Waller and His Rhythm." In an article published in 1926, George Gershwin insisted that "the successful jazz artist . . . should get the rhythm into his blood early in life":

> Acquisition of the jazz art in one's riper years is always difficult and sometimes impossible. One of our most distinguished American singers, who has made a profound study of jazz and who sings a great deal of it, has never been quite able to get the genuine rhythm of it.
> "Does Jazz Belong to Art?," *Singing*, July 1926

Andy Razaf—three years older than George Gershwin and nine years older than Thomas Waller—met his future partner in the early 1920s. In retrospect, writes Singer,

> The mismatched pairing . . . seems almost preordained. Waller was an extroverted, wildly carefree spirit just then discovering the fullness of his performing personality, as well as the great bacchanalian thirst that would stoke it. Razaf was an intense craftsman, equally charming and hardly shy but utterly temperate. Razaf's talent was no less effusive than Waller's . . . They were opposites who counterbalanced beautifully, their contemporaries later insisted . . . "During their years together," Waller's son Maurice later observed, "Andy's methodic planning and discipline served as a necessary balance for his partner's instability."

Singer goes on to observe, however, that the "equation was hardly so elementary":

> Beneath the surface . . . the two men were surprisingly similar. As impractical, for instance, as Waller undeniably could be, he also would prove far more worldly than his more business-wise but often artless partner. As levelheaded as Razaf was, the lyricist's sense of what was right and just could move him to behavior as volatile and sometimes self-destructive as that which would make his new partner so justly famous.

Both were mama's boys, dutifully bound in love to mother, and by marital devotion to exceedingly maternal spouses. This devotion did not, however, include for either man anything remotely resembling marital fidelity and neither perceived the slightest inconsistency in his respective conjugal juggling act. Lastly, both wrote quickly and hardly ever rewrote. For Fats Waller and for Andy Razaf, songwriting would be an act of spontaneous creation.

One of the greatest songs the pair produced (with Harry Brooks)—and one of the great songs of the twentieth century—gives Barry Singer his title: "(What Did I Do To Be So) Black and Blue." The song was written in 1929 for a show called *Hot Chocolates*, and the story of its genesis is itself an extraordinary one. Gangsters were immensely important factors in Harlem's economy during the 1920s, and *Hot Chocolates* was no exception. The brutal, notorious Dutch Schultz, "Beer Baron of the Bronx" (born Arthur Simon Flegenheimer in 1902; died, violently, in 1935) had money invested in *Hot Chocolates*. Schultz believed he knew what the show needed: "A funny number, he informed Razaf, something with a little 'colored girl' singing how tough it was to be colored." Razaf replied politely that he couldn't write a song like that. The next moment Razaf was pinned against a wall with Schultz's gun pointed at his head. He agreed to write the song, but it was hardly a "funny number." On opening night, Razaf had the misfortune to be standing next to Dutch Schultz when the song began. Terrified, Razaf believed that, were the song a failure, Dutch Schultz would kill him. At first the audience laughed, finding the song a "funny number." Then it stopped laughing. Finally the song ended, and there was silence. In that silence Razaf felt certain that his earthly days were over. Then the audience was standing, applauding, and crying out for a reprise. Dutch Schultz gave Razaf a well-deserved pat on the back.

"Black and Blue" was recorded by various people, including Edith Wilson, who introduced the song in *Hot Chocolates*. Perhaps the most riveting of all these recordings is the one Louis Armstrong made on July 22nd, 1929 for Okeh's "White" label rather than its "Race" label—a crossover hit for Armstrong:

> Out in the street
> Shufflin' feet
> Couples passin' two by two
> While here am I
> Left high and dry

Black, and 'cause I'm black I'm blue.
Browns and yellers [referring to the mixed race "high yellows"]
All have fellers,
Gentlemen prefer them light
Wish I could fade
Can't make the grade
Nothing but dark days in sight:

Cold empty bed
Springs hard as lead
Pains in my head
Feel like old Ned
What did I do
To be so black and blue?
No joys for me
No company
Even the mouse
Ran from my house
All my life thru
I've been so black and blue
I'm white inside
But that don't help my case
'Cause I can't hide
What is on my face
I'm so forlorn
Life's just a thorn
My heart is torn
Why was I born?
What did I do
To be so black and blue?

Just 'cause you're black
Folks think you lack
They laugh at you
And scorn you too
What did I do
To be so black and blue?
When you are near
They laugh and sneer

Set you aside
And you're denied
What did I do
To be so black and blue?
How sad I am
Each day I feel worse
My mark of Ham
Seems to be a curse
How will it end?
Ain't got a friend
My only sin
Is in
My skin
What did I do
To be so black and blue?

Popular music's self-pity is here raised to a sense of genuine suffering. What begins as the lament of a black woman who is "too dark" to be popular transforms itself into a lament for all black people: "My mark of Ham / Seems to be a curse." Singer remarks that Razaf sometimes manifested a rather disturbing sense of himself as victim; that sense here becomes not merely personal but historical. The casual early reference to "shufflin' feet" carries resonances of the extraordinarily successful Blake and Sissle show, *Shuffle Along* (1921: the first all-black Broadway hit). Black people were expected to "shuffle," and so they do in Razaf's song, but this particular black person, unable even to "shuffle along" with the rest, cries out painfully. Singer quotes Ralph Ellison's response to the song as Ellison wrote it in his classic novel, *Invisible Man* (1952):

> This familiar music . . . demanded action, the kind of which I was incapable . . . I sat on the chair's edge in a soaking sweat . . . It was exhausting—as though I had held my breath continuously for an hour under the terrifying serenity that comes from days of intense hunger . . . I had discovered unrecognized compulsions of my being— even though I could not answer "yes" to their promptings.

"A Porter's Love Song to a Chambermaid," written in 1930 with pianist James P. Johnson supplying the music, is, in a way, the opposite side of the coin. If "Black and Blue" is tragic and heartbreaking, "A Porter's Love Song" is light, funny, slightly surreal, optimistic. (No "pains in my head" in this song.) The revue for which the song was written was called "A Kitchen Mechanic's Revue." One thinks of the roughly contemporary *Threepenny Opera*, an "opera" supposedly written by beggars and priced at three pennies so that beggars could afford it. Razaf's proletariat revue featured "heroes of the mop and broom":

Tho' my position is of low degree
And all the others may look down on me,
I'll go smiling thru,
That's if I have you
I am the happiest of troubadours
Thinking of you while I'm massaging floors
At my leisure time
I made up this rhyme:

I will be the oil mop
If you'll be the oil
Then we both could mingle
Ev'ry time we toil
I will be the washboard
If you'll be the tub
Think of all the Mondays
We can rub-a-dub
I will be your shoebrush
If you'll be my shoe
Then I'd keep you bright, dear
Feeling good as new
If you'll be my razor
I will be your blade
That's a porter's love song
To a chambermaid.

I will be your dustpan
If you will be my broom
We could work together
All around the room
I will be your clothespin
Be my pulley line
We'll hang out together

Wouldn't that be fine?
I will be your dishpan
If you'll be my dish
We'll meet after meals, dear
What more could you wish?
I will be your window
Be my window shade,
That's a porter's love song
To a chambermaid

One can easily imagine the number being staged. This brilliant song plays upon the fact that *all* "positions" granted to black workers are "of low degree." That fact could be the cause of intense anger—and at times it was—but here it's simply accepted as a given. We know that neither the porter nor the chambermaid is likely to rise any higher in the social scale. Yet, the song suggests, love blossoms in "low degrees" as well as in high and causes the world around the singer (a world of washboards, shoebrushes, razors, dustpans, brooms) to come alive with metaphor. The very conditions of the porter's life are suddenly transformed by his joy. The concept of the "happy black man" is of course an aspect of this song, but the song deliberately takes that concept much further than is usually the case. It recognizes that the singer will probably spend his whole life "massaging floors." But if the world deliberately limits the jobs black people can have, it cannot limit their power of imagination—which is what the song is really about. "A Porter's Love Song to a Chambermaid" also carries a hint of the eroticism which is a major feature of Razaf's work. (Singer rightly describes some of "Honeysuckle Rose" as "filthy" and quotes "My Handy Man" in full: "He handles my front yard . . . /He sees that I get a nice, fresh piece every day / My man is such a handy man.") "A Porter's Love Song" deliberately conjures up a world of work—and then transcends it. I don't know of any song quite like it. It's simple and singable and funny, yet it's about how the erotic imagination transcends, literally, everything. For the porter, what he's singing is the Song of Songs.

Razaf's marvelous ability to evoke an entire milieu in simple language can also be found in the wonderful song, "Tan Manhattan," a song about Harlem, "where the South is north of Central Park." The song, never widely distributed, is beautifully performed by cabaret artist Bobby Short in his tribute album to Razaf, *Guess Who's Back in Town?* There is also a very endearing record of Razaf himself in his professional guise of "Crooning Andy Razaf" singing "A Porter's Love Song to a Chambermaid." Razaf's pleasant baritone, strict tempo and dreadful "crooning" is no match for the ebullient and rhythmically complex version recorded by Fats Waller in 1934.

Andy Razaf's professional anchor was not the Broadway stage, which was largely closed to him, but the immensely popular nightclubs of Harlem in the 1920s, a period when, Langston Hughes wrote, "the Negro was in vogue." "White people began to come to Harlem in droves," Hughes writes in *The Big Sea* (1940),

> For several years they packed the expensive Cotton Club on Lenox Avenue. But I was never there, because the Cotton Club was a Jim Crow club for gangsters and monied whites. They were not cordial to Negro patronage, unless you were a celebrity like Bojangles. So Harlem Negroes did not like the Cotton Club and never appreciated its Jim Crow policy in the very heart of their dark community. Nor did ordinary Negroes like the growing influx of whites toward Harlem after sundown, flooding the little cabarets and bars where formerly only colored people laughed and sang, and where now the strangers were given the best ringside tables to sit and stare at the Negro customers—like amusing animals in a zoo.
>
> The Negroes said: "We can't go downtown and sit and stare at you in your clubs. You won't even let us in your clubs." But they didn't say it out loud . . . So thousands of whites came to Harlem night after night, thinking the Negroes loved to have them there, and firmly believing that all Harlemites left their houses at sundown to sing and dance in cabarets, because most of the whites saw nothing but the cabarets, not the houses.

In his autobiography, *Of Minnie the Moocher & Me* (1976), Cab Calloway— who, like Duke Ellington, performed there—describes the ambiance of the gangster-operated Cotton Club:

> It was a huge room. The bandstand was a replica of a southern mansion, with large white columns and a backdrop painted with weeping willows and slave quarters. The band played on the veranda of the mansion, and in front of the veranda, down a few steps, was the dance floor, which was also used for the shows. The waiters were dressed in red tuxedos, like butlers in a southern mansion, and the tables were covered with red-and-white-checked gingham tablecloths. There were huge cut-crystal chandeliers, and the whole set was like the sleepy-time-down-South during slavery. Even the name, Cotton Club, was supposed to convey the southern feeling. I suppose the idea was to make whites who came to the club feel like they were being catered to and entertained by black slaves.

Calloway's book contains a delightful "Night-Club Map of Harlem," detailing the exact location of places like the Lafayette Theatre, where Fats Waller played organ, and Connie's Inn, the site of many Waller/Razaf productions. Near the corner of Lenox Avenue and 131st Street you can find "The Reefer Man": "Marahuana [*sic*] Cigarettes two for $25." Another prominent Harlem night spot was Small's Paradise, which, like Connie's Inn, was a "black and tan" establishment: a place where whites and blacks might mingle. Langston Hughes remarked that "a large part of the Harlem attraction for downtown New Yorkers lay in simply watching the colored customers amuse themselves." He adds,

> All of us [knew] that the gay and sparkling life of the so-called Negro Renaissance of the '20's was not so gay and sparkling beneath the surface. . . .

Barry Singer is particularly good in describing the crushing limitations placed upon black musical productions and in describing the horrible, complex situation in which both white and black musicians found themselves. Singer writes of "a hardening of perceptions, even a segregating of the form by white critics into a circumscribed theatrical ghetto narrowly defined by a few largely racist formulas derived primarily from *Shuffle Along* and *Shuffle Along*'s minstrel precursors":

> "Ambition" was the word that these critics dismissively wielded against any show that attempted to break free from these preconceptions, as neatly itemized by a reviewer for *Variety* in his negative assessment of *Chocolate Dandies'* efforts as early as 1924: "The absence of spirited stepping." Any "deliberate" attempts "to make the piece high-toned," such as a "leading woman" behaving "in action and manner" like a "prima donna," or a leading man utilizing "all the posing tricks of a soulful tenor in a Winter Garden musical comedy.—All of these pretensions toward white musical comedy . . . achieved at the expense of a genuine Negro spirit," leading to an evening of "white folks material, of which there is plenty . . . and not good darky entertainment, of which there is little enough for the best."
>
> Of course, in the wake of such brutal criticism, black musical creators soon steered clear of anything that might suggest white pretension in their Broadway work, continuing to rely on hoary, minstrel-evocative stereotypes, solidly grounded in Dixie. . . .

At the same time, Singer points out, "many white composers were penetrating Harlem nightlife . . . to the innermost low-down dives, in their passion for black music":

Lyricists like Dorothy Fields, Ted Koehler, even the young Lorenz Hart and Ira Gershwin . . . studied closely the slangy, impudent lyric argot of black music. This attention was enormously flattering to Harlem's black songwriters. James P. Johnson, Willie "the Lion" Smith, and young Thomas "Fats" Waller would all be terrifically proud, for example, when Gershwin invited them to the party following his "Rhapsody in Blue" premiere at a very fashionable Park Avenue hotel. Yet inherent in this studious attention were the seeds of usurpation. Black songwriters were never encouraged by Tin Pan Alley nor even permitted to attempt songs in supposed "white" style. Thus, when in time Gershwin, Arlen, McHugh, Koehler, and Fields at last mastered music and lyric writing in the black style, they inevitably, however unintentionally, begat the disenfranchisement of the very black music makers whom they venerated. Calculatingly or not, Harlem's white musician admirers were all party to this ruthless cycle. That is why, with Gershwin's delightful "Rhapsody in Blue" as a misinterpreted beacon, the marketing value of the word "jazz," from a strictly commercial songwriting perspective, continued to be pried away from black musicians by Tin Pan Alley in the name of [bandleader Paul] Whiteman and [George] Gershwin. . . .

Razaf himself wrote, "The white boys absorbed what [we] knew and now they don't want us anymore. Every so-called new music form that the whites create, like 'swing' and 'jazz,' is a steal from Negro syncopation or is based on Negro dances and Negro mannerism." Deliberately distancing himself from the people from whom he had learned, George Gershwin wrote in *Theatre Magazine* in 1925, "Jazz is not Negro but American. It is the spontaneous expression of the nervous energy of modern American life." The composer's "Rhapsody in Blue" had been written and performed the previous year. If jazz were to be made "respectable," it had to be carefully removed from its African-American roots. There would be room, later, for acknowledgment, but the first order of the day was denial. This same story was of course repeated in the history of rock and roll—a musical phenomenon which put not only Andy Razaf but people like Cole Porter and Irving Berlin entirely out of business.

With the death of Fats Waller in 1943—the composer was thirty-nine years old—Andy Razaf's career was to all extents and purposes over, though he lived until 1973 and continued to write. Singer traces the frustration and occasional triumphs of Razaf's later life. Razaf had contracted syphilis in his early days, and from 1951 until his death the disease caused him enormous pain and even paralysis. Within two years of Razaf's death the black musical was briefly back in vogue and caused what Singer calls Razaf's "repeated rediscovery." Though Razaf was never given anything like the financial remuneration which was his due—he and Waller probably wrote "I Can't Give You Anything But Love, Baby," which was credited to Jimmy McHugh and Dorothy Fields—the money he did receive through his songs kept him afloat during his later years, when Tin Pan Alley—"Flim-Flam Alley," in Razaf's poem—passed him by. Barry Singer writes of Andy Razaf's "relative failure," his "long-term failure as a commercial songwriter." Another way to put it is the phrase President Jimmy Carter used when asked about the failure of one of the U.S. attempts to rescue hostages in Iran: "Failure?" said Carter hastily, "I wouldn't say it was a failure. I would say it was a limited success." "Limited success" was all that the America of his time held out to the immensely talented Andy Razaf.

One of the problems with biography is that the biographer rarely has as good a mind as his subject. Often, therefore, the subject is made over into the lesser image of the biographer. Barry Singer's *Black and Blue* teems with the author's knowledge of the period and with his genuine passion for his subject, who is presented in the light of an extremely complex historical moment. Singer tells us that he was initially discouraged in his attempt:

> "You can't never put it back together," one veteran Harlem musician had bluntly insisted to me, early on. "It's too jumbled, the history, too fragmented. Nobody never told it straight—even as it was happening, we was inventing it. And don't think that was no accident neither."

Singer gives the right answer: "Yet the urge to reconstruct is uncontainable." *Black and Blue* tells us things we need to know and tells them in a way that pays homage to the realities of a period which has already faded into myth and legend. It would be wonderful if a collection of Andy Razaf's lyrics would appear, as collections of the lyrics of Cole Porter, Lorenz Hart, Irving Berlin, and Ira Gershwin have already appeared. That would be a book worth seeing. "You can call me 'The Dreamer,'" wrote Andy Razaf,

> I don't care if you do.

Unassimilable

The Complete Poems of Kenneth Rexroth

> I have seen no more evident monstrosity and miracle in the world than myself.
> —MONTAIGNE

> I starve under capitalism, and I would starve under a dictatorship of the proletariat
> for the same reasons. After all I am interested in perpetual revolution in a sense
> other than Trotsky's—the constant raising into relevance of ignored values. Poetry
> has for its mission in society the reduction of what the Society of Jesus named
> "invincible ignorance," and the true poet is as much to be feared by the proletariat
> as by the bourgeoisie.
> —KENNETH REXROTH (1931),
>   quoted in Linda Hamalian, *A Life of Kenneth Rexroth* (1991)

Copper Canyon Press has just released Kenneth Rexroth's *Complete Poems*.
It's a most welcome volume, carefully and lovingly edited by poet Sam Hamill
and Bradford Morrow, Rexroth's literary executor. It contains even more
work than the New Directions volumes, *The Collected Shorter Poems of Kenneth
Rexroth* (1966) and *The Collected Longer Poems of Kenneth Rexroth* (1968).
Though born in South Bend, Indiana, Rexroth (1905-1982) was at the
absolute center of the San Francisco Renaissance. His poetry, his poetry
readings—often to jazz accompaniment—his radio broadcasts, his lively
newspaper columns, his considerable body of essays, and his even more
considerable personal brilliance and charisma made him a force to be reckoned
with on the West Coast. "I came to California in 1927," Rexroth told David
Meltzer in a 1969 interview collected in *The San Francisco Poets*:

> The day I got into town, San Francisco's leading poet, California's leading poet,
> killed himself, George Sterling. He pretty much represented the California scene in
> those days . . . The San Francisco literary world was dominated by people to whom
> the native son and daughter thing was all important, although most of them were
> not native sons and daughters . . .

It's hard to believe now, with all the tremendous activity that has been in San Francisco, that San Francisco, when we came there to live, was very much of a backwater town . . . We met people who would say to you, "Who do you think is California's leading writer?" And you would say, "Gertrude Stein." They would say, "Who is that?" And then they would say, "Oh, yes!" They knew her, you see, her brother was in society on the Peninsula, but they didn't know she wrote . . . We just didn't have any competition. It was like Picasso dropping back into the world of Trollope.

Though San Francisco was definitely a cultural backwater, Rexroth frequently insisted that one of the city's chief attractions was the fact that it was "the only city in the United States which was not settled overland by the westward-spreading puritan tradition."

It's easy to forget that work by Kenneth Rexroth was included in Louis Zukofsky's famous 1931 "Objectivist" issue of *Poetry* (Chicago). In a letter to Zukofsky—whose work Rexroth admired for a time—Rexroth confesses that in writing this kind of poetry, "The most diverse influences have arisen to name the ideas on my page, from Proclus to Bradley or Royce, from Stoicism to the 'organic philosophy.' I really had no idea my brain contained such a horde."

Rexroth did not continue to write in the style published under the banner of "Objectivism," and he is not even mentioned in Michael Heller's *Conviction's Net of Branches: Essays on the Objectivist Poets and Poetry* (1985). Nonetheless, he remained sympathetic to that early work and referred to it, not as "Objectivist" but as "Cubist" poetry. "Cubism" in poetry, writes Rexroth in *Pierre Reverdy: Selected Poems*,

is the conscious, deliberate dissociation and recombination of elements into a new artistic entity made self-sufficient by its rigorous architecture. This is quite different from the free association of the Surrealists and the combination of unconscious utterance and political nihilism of Dada . . . Only Walter Conrad Arensberg in his last poems, Gertrude Stein in *Tender Buttons* and a very few other pieces, much of the work of the young Yvor Winters and others of his generation of Chicago Modernists, Laura Riding's best work and my own poems later collected in *The Art of Worldly Wisdom* could be said to show the deliberate practice of the principles of creative construction which guided Juan Gris or Pierre Reverdy.

He goes on to assert that T.S. Eliot in *The Waste Land*

works . . . with fragmented and recombined arguments; Pierre Reverdy with dismembered propositions from which subject, operator and object have been wrenched free and restructured into an invisible or subliminal discourse which owes its cogency to its own strict, complex and secret logic.

Poetry such as this attempts not just a new syntax of the word. Its revolution is aimed at the syntax of the mind itself. Its restructuring of experience is purposive, not dreamlike, and hence it possesses an uncanniness fundamentally different in kind from the most haunted utterances of the Surrealist or Symbolist unconscious. Contrary to what we are taught, it appears first in the ultimate expressions of Neo-Symbolism in Mallarmé, . . . above all in his hieratic metaphysical ritual, *Un Coup de dés.*

Rexroth was deeply aware of his friend Yvor Winters' rejection of this kind of verse as "the deliberate courting of madness." Yet, "when the ordinary materials of poetry are broken up, recombined in structures radically different from those we assume to be the result of causal, or of what we have come to accept as logical sequence, and then an abnormally focused attention is invited to their apprehension, they are given an intense significance, . . . they seem to assume an unanalyzable transcendental claim":

We still know almost nothing about how the mind works in states of rapture nor why the disjunction, the ecstasis, of self and experience should produce a whole range of peculiar nervous responses . . . We are dealing with a self-induced, or naturally and mysteriously come-by, creative state from which two of the most fundamental human activities diverge, the aesthetic and the mystic act. The creative matrix is the same in both . . . [I]f poetic vision is refined until it is sufficiently piercing and sufficiently tensile, it cuts through the reality it has reorganized to an existential transcendence.

Finally, Rexroth argues that

The revolution of the sensibility that began with Baudelaire became in the latter work of Mallarmé a thoroughgoing syntactical revolution in the language because it was realized that the logical structure of the Indo-European languages was an inadequate vehicle for so profound a change in the sensibility. In actual fact, although Apollinaire is usually considered the watershed of modern poetry, no single poem of his represents as thoroughgoing a change in method as Mallarmé's.

Reverdy, Rexroth insists, "has certainly been the leading influence on my own work—incomparably more than anyone in English or American."

What kind of poetry did Rexroth's "restructuring of the mind"—his attempt to cut "through the reality it has reorganized to an existential transcendence"—produce? "A Prolegomenon to a Theodicy" (1925-1927) is perhaps the finest of Rexroth's Cubist poems. The title suggests its religious orientation—as does the apocalyptic tone of its concluding pages:

> The bell
> Too softly and too slowly tolled
> And the first wave was snow
> The second ice
> The third fire
> The fourth blood
> The fifth adders
> The sixth smother
> The seventh foul stink
> And unnumbered beasts swam in the sea
> Some feather footed
> Some devoid of any feet
> And phosphorescent breath
> The enduring bell
> The wash of wave . . .
>
> Some lay with their knees partly drawn up
> Some lay on their sides
> Some lay stretched at full length
> Some lay on their backs
> Some were stooping
> Some held their heads bent down
> Some drew up their legs
> Some embraced
> Some kicked out with arms and legs
> Some were kneeling
> Some stood and inhaled deep breaths
> Some crawled
> Some walked
> Some felt about in the dark
> Some arose
> Some gazed, sitting still

That is Gertrude Stein filtered through a religious sensibility—Gertrude Stein as the Last Judgment—and its rhythms and repetitions had an effect on the much later "Thou Shalt Not Kill" (1953), a brilliant poem written in memory of Dylan Thomas:

> They are stoning Stephen,
> They are casting him forth from every city in the world.
> Under the Welcome sign,
> Under the Rotary emblem,
> On the highway in the suburbs,
> His body lies under the hurling stones.
> He was full of faith and power.
> He did great wonders among the people.
> They could not stand against his wisdom.
> They could not bear the spirit with which he spoke.

But "Thou Shalt Not Kill" is something of an anomaly in Rexroth's later work. Compare the lines from "Prolegomenon" to these from *In What Hour* (1940). In these latter lines, Rexroth achieved the tone that would characterize much of what he would do throughout the rest of his career:

> The great geometrical winter constellations
> Lift up over the Sierra Nevada,
> I walk under the stars, my feet on the known round earth.
> My eyes following the lights of an airplane,
> Red and green, growling deep into the Hyades.
> The note of the engine rises, shrill, faint,
> Finally inaudible, and the lights go out
> In the southeast haze beneath the feet of Orion.
> As the sound departs I am chilled and grow sick
> With the thought that has come over me.
> ("Requiem for the Spanish Dead")

In his excellent book, *The Relevance of Rexroth* (1990), Ken Knabb quotes Rexroth on "the Social Lie or the Great Fraud—to know that the 'official version of anything is most likely false and that all authority is based on fraud.'" The following quotations are all from Rexroth:

Every day all states do things which, if they were the acts of individuals, would lead to summary arrest and often execution . . . What is called 'growing up,' 'getting a little common sense,' is largely the learning of techniques for outwitting the more destructive forces at large in the social order. The mature man lives quietly, does good privately, assumes personal responsibility for his actions, treats others with friendliness and courtesy, finds mischief boring and keeps out of it.

∽

An appreciable number of Americans really do believe the Great Fraud of the mass culture, what the French call the *hallucination publicitaire*. They only know what they read in the papers. They think it is really like the movies . . . The art of being civilized is the art of learning to read between the lies.

∽

Most of the real difficulty of communication comes from social convention, from a vast conspiracy to agree to accept the world as something it really isn't at all.

Linda Hamalian's warts-and-not-quite-all biography of Rexroth is proof that Rexroth the man often had difficulty living up to his own vision of "maturity." (Even his admirers speak of the toll taken on him by "paranoia.") But Rexroth's railing against "the Great Fraud" is surely an indication of one of his deepest convictions. Though, like Jack Kerouac, he retained throughout his life a relationship with Roman Catholicism and died a Catholic—and maintained a considerable interest in Buddhism as well—in these quotations he seems like nothing so much as a secular version of a fire-and-brimstone Protestant raging against the wickedness and unreality of the world. Rexroth never lost his religious sensibility and his desire to break through to "an existential transcendence"—nor the sense of fierce dualism which gave rise to that desire—but they were replaced to some degree by the practice of what he called "the art of being civilized." (The word "civilized" is one of the most important words in his *oeuvre*.) Rexroth's shift of esthetic tone was a shift to another mode of religiosity. The desire to "restructure the mind" became the basis not only of a change in poetic strategy but of what we now call an "alternative life-style." Rexroth liked to begin his poetry readings by asking, "Well, what would you like tonight—sex, mysticism or revolution?" and was delighted when a woman in the audience responded, "What's the

difference?" More and more, erotic love—not politics, poetry or religion—
seemed, if properly performed, the instrument of social change:

> We slept naked
> On top of the covers and woke
> In the chilly dawn and crept
> Between the warm sheets and made love
> In the morning you said
> "It snowed last night on the mountain"
> High up on the blue black diorite
> Faint orange streaks of snow
> In the ruddy dawn
> I said
> "It has been snowing for months
> All over Canada and Alaska
> And Minnesota and Michigan
> Right now wet snow is falling
> In the morning streets of Chicago
> Bit by bit they are making over the world
> Even in Mexico even for us"
> ("Gradualism")[1]

Rexroth produced a number of long poems throughout his life, beginning
with "The Homestead Called Damascus," which the author claimed was
"written before I was twenty years old." In its opening lines he makes a bold
reference to a phrase in James Joyce's *Ulysses*: "the ineluctable modality of the
visible." Allowing his religious sensibilities full play, Rexroth turns Joyce's
phrase into "the 'ineluctable modality' of the *in*visible":

> Heaven is full of definite stars
> And crowded with modest angels, robed
> In tubular, neuter folds of pink and blue.
> Their feet tread doubtless on that utter
> Hollowness, with never a question
> Of the "ineluctable modality"
> Of the invisible; busy, orderly,
> Content to ignore the coal pockets
> In the galaxy, dark nebulae,
> And black broken windows into space.

Youthful minds may fret infinity,
Moistly disheveled, poking in odd
Corners for unsampled vocations
Of the spirit, while the flesh is strong.
Experience sinks its roots in space—
Euclidean, warped, or otherwise.
The will constructs rhomboids, nonagons,
And paragons in time to suit each taste.
Or, if the will, then circumstance.
History demands satisfaction,
And never lacks, with or without help
From the subjects of its curious science.

The problem with this dense medium—slightly reminiscent of Hart Crane—is that over the course of a long poem, it is utterly unreadable. (Harriet Monroe, editor of *Poetry*, dismissed "The Homestead Called Damascus" as "a lot of talky talk.")

Many people have commented on the wide range of Rexroth's erudition—in many languages—but if he had a single "precursor" poet, it would have to have been Ezra Pound. Rexroth was far from Pound politically, but there is so much about Rexroth that reminds you of Pound: translations from the Chinese and Japanese, an intense interest in the troubadours (many of whom Pound had translated), a commitment to free verse and the long poem, the denunciation of the present day, even the intensely hectoring tone of much of the work, which insisted that the poet's opinions about society were intensely meaningful. Indeed, even Rexroth's interest in poetry and jazz was a kind of extension of Pound's admiration of the troubadours—poets whom Pound associated with the Homeric singer. Jazz poetry, wrote Rexroth, "returns poetry to music and to public entertainment as it was in the days of Homer or the troubadours." Like Pound, Rexroth collected a group of younger writers whom he both pushed forward and "educated." "We were all brought up on Daddy Rexroth's reading list," remarked Robert Duncan. "The amount of labor and confusion he saved younger people was immense," said poet-critic Thomas Parkinson. Like Pound, Rexroth had a deep distrust of "the academy," calling universities "fog factories." And like Pound, Rexroth took to the radio—Berkeley independent station, KPFA-FM—to expound his theories.[2]

Rexroth opened his *Collected Shorter Poems* with these lines, quietly attributed to "Anonymous Provençal":

When the nightingale cries
All night and all day,
I have my sweetheart
Under the flower
Till the watch from the tower
Cries, "Lovers, rise!
The dawn comes and the bright day."

The lines deliberately recall Ezra Pound's famous tour-de-force, "Alba" (Dawn), a poem Pound placed at the beginning of his own translations from the Provençal:

When the nightingale to his mate
Sings day-long and night late
My love and I keep state
In bower
In flower,
'Till the watchman on the tower
Cry:
"Up! Thou rascal, Rise,
I see the white
    Light
    And the night
      Flies."

Initially one wonders why Rexroth would place his rather pedestrian rendering of the poem against Pound's obviously brilliant, obviously superior version. (Pound even gives an equivalent of troubadour rhyming—a practice Rexroth does not follow either here or in his translations of Reverdy.) The answer is that Rexroth's poem is making a rather subtle point. What is "brilliant" for one person, after all, may be merely "flashy" for another. There is a problem with Pound's poem: it centers in the concluding word, "Flies." Obviously, Pound means the word as a verb: he is talking about the night "flying" away. Yet, from a syntactic point of view, it is possible that the word could be a noun: that is, Pound could be talking about creatures, "night flies." He isn't, of course, but the ambiguity—the inexactness—remains. Rexroth's version is more pedestrian than Pound's in every way, but it is also more exact. Pound needs "flies" for his rhyme—he couldn't use "And the night is flying away," for example—but the meaning of his poem suffers because of it. (Pound might have written "And the night / Dies"—but the poem might well have died along with it.)

Ezra Pound is a particularly important figure for Kenneth Rexroth because the *Cantos* represents a way of dealing with the genius-poet's "diverse influences," his "horde" of references. The problem for Pound was to find some form in which it was possible to exhibit the multiplicity of his imaginative constructs without falling into utter chaos—the shapelessness that is the poet-sculptor's deepest enemy. When Pound is successful in doing this—as he is in Canto LXXIV or Canto 99—the effect is nothing less than thrilling: it is as if the mind's sense of its own infinity had momentarily found a home. (Pound of course had his doubts as to whether he could achieve the same effect in the *Cantos* as a whole.) Rexroth's problem was to do what Pound did without sounding like Pound. In addition, there was the problem of "obscurity": Pound's *Cantos* were notoriously difficult to understand. If, as a young man, Rexroth thought that "literary Cubism was the future of American poetry," Ken Knabb points out that as Rexroth began to actually produce such poetry he began to realize that—despite the fact that "the current language of society [has] been debauched by the exploitative uses to which it [has] been put, and . . . it [is] necessary to find gaps in the structure of communication which [are] still fluent and through which the mind of the reader [can] be assaulted"—it was necessary for him to function in more accessible forms if he wanted to have an audience.

The Dragon and the Unicorn (1944-1950), is one of Rexroth's solutions to the problem of the long poem. It begins with a rather problematical reference to an incident in the life of Christ:

> "And what is love?" said Pilate,
> And washed his hands.

(Pilate in fact asked, "What is truth?" See John 18:38.)

The poem then moves into an "accessible," fairly straightforward travelogue—an anecdotal mode, often quite beautifully written, which Rexroth maintains throughout the poem, though always with interruptions:

> All night long
> The white snow falls on the white
> Peaks through the quiet darkness.
> The overland express train
> Drives through the night, through the snow.

In the morning the land slopes
To the Atlantic, the sky
Is thicker, Spring stirs, smelling
Like old wet wood, new life speaks
In pale green fringes of marsh
Marigolds on the edges
Of the mountain snow drifts.

Against this language—always interesting, full of wit and stories, close to Rexroth's celebrated conversation—is another, more problematical, more abstract language, a language of philosophical distinctions:

It is doubtful if the world
Presents itself in any
Important aspects under
The forms of serial time
And atomic space. It is
True that the intellect has
Come to be conditioned by them,
But important experience
Comes to us in freedom and
Is realized as value,
And the intellect alone
Can know nothing of freedom
And value because it is
Concerned with the necessary
And they are by definition
Unnecessitated. Love
Of course is the ultimate
Mode of free evaluation.
Perfect love casts out knowledge.

The poem, like much of the work of the troubadours, is the interplay between these two uses of language, abstract and particular, philosophical and anecdotal. Though the philosophical passages are far from "accessible"— and are clearly necessary to the poem—they can be skipped by the reader who finds them tedious. For the reader who is philosophically equal to them, they are there in all their glorious abstraction; but for other readers there are stories, jokes, and they are often quite good stories and jokes:

> The author of *Le Rideau levé*,
> Approached as a colleague by
> Sade in prison, repulsed him
> Succinctly, "Mon Sieur, je ne suis
> Pas ici pour avoir donné des
> Confits empoisonnés aux femmes
> De chambre." The existentialistes
> Don't like him very much.
>
> (The French is "Sir, I am not / here for having given
> / poisoned preserves to / chambermaids.")

Pound of course is capable of stories and jokes as well, but Rexroth carries Pound's techniques further—and, unlike Pound or Olson, he does not move the words of his poem around the page. There are no disturbing "field techniques" in Rexroth: the left-hand margin is always returned to.

The Dragon and the Unicorn is a triumph of Rexroth's determination to write a poem which could be read by anyone but which does not simplify his complex sense of the world. There remains a problem, however. The passage quoted above indicates Rexroth's antipathy to the "existentialistes," with their powerful sense of alienation. In his introduction to the *Collected Longer Poems*, Rexroth writes that "It is easy to overcome alienation—the net of the cash nexus can simply be stepped out of, but only by the self actualizing man":

> But everyone is self actualizing and can realize it by the simplest act—the self unselving itself, the only act that is actual act . . . I hope I have made it clear that the self does not do this by an act of will, by sheer assertion. He who would save his life must lose it.

Discussing Cubist poetry's "unanalyzable transcendental claim" Rexroth alludes to "certain projected physical responses" which accompany "the person undergoing the poetic experience, whether poet or reader":

> Vertigo, rapture, transport, crystalline and plangent sounds, shattered and refracted light, indefinite depths, weightlessness, piercing odors and tastes, and synthesizing these sensations and affects, an all-consuming clarity. These are the phenomena that often attend what theologians call natural mysticism. They can be found especially in the poetry of St. Mechtild of Magdeburg and St. Hildegarde of Bingen, great favorites of the psychologists who have written on this subject, but they are equally prominent in the poetry of Sappho or Henry Vaughan or the prose of Jacob Boehme, as well as in many modern poets.

It is important to note here that Rexroth does not understand "mysticism" to be an experience beyond words: rather, it can be embodied in the poetry of writers such as Pierre Reverdy. At the same time, Rexroth insists that such poetry—the work of the "self actualizing man"—involves "the self unselving itself": "He who would save his life must lose it." Rexroth is right to insist that mysticism *as a literary technique* is a very important way of approaching a good many modern poets. At the same time, however, his own poetry is a case of the self's *in*ability to "unselve itself." His is not a poetry of unselving but of fierce ego assertion, of judgment; it is an attempt—by no means always successful—to embody wisdom:

> Why this sudden outburst of
> Homosexuality?
> The American mass culture
> Has identified the normal
> Sex relation with the stuffing
> Of an omnivorous and
> Insensate vagina with
> Highly perishable and
> Expensive objects of non
> Utility. Useless value
> Has replaced use value and has
> Been linked with sex satisfaction.
> Since every young American
> Male knows that very soon the State
> Is going to take him out and
> Murder him very nastily,
> He is inclined to withdraw from
> The activities prescribed for him
> In the advertising pages.
> Since it is physically
> Impossible to realize
> The fullness of love except
> Between a man and woman,
> This is at best a sort of
> Marking time before execution.
> For similar reasons, children
> In the highschools take heroin.

That passage is a poetry of statement—of extremely dubious statement. We are much more likely to find Rexroth's verse "beautiful" if we at least tentatively agree with his opinions. Here, in his benighted insistence that "it is physically / Impossible to realize / The fullness of love except / Between a man and woman," he is as offensive as Pound on the Jews. Opinions, often debatable ones, come fast and furiously throughout *The Dragon and the Unicorn*:

> Lawrence, Lawrence, what a lot
> Of hogwash you have fathered.
> Etruscan art is just plain bad.
> It is the commercial art
> Of mercenary provincials,
> On a par with Australian
> Magazine covers. Where it is
> Good at all, it was done by Greeks.

We can see more clearly what is disturbing in Rexroth's conception if we turn to another follower of Pound's, Charles Olson. Though Olson was equally noted for his ego-assertion—he could be as dogmatic as Rexroth—he nevertheless kept himself rooted in what he understood to be "Negative Capability," a concept which comes from the Romantic poet John Keats. In a letter to his brothers George and Thomas (December 21, 1817), Keats explains Negative Capability in this way:

> that is, when a man is capable of being in uncertainties, mysteries, doubts, without any irritable reaching after fact and reason—Coleridge, for instance, would let go by a fine isolated verisimilitude caught from the Penetralium of mystery, from being incapable of remaining content with half-knowledge.

In another letter—to Richard Woodhouse (October 27, 1818)—Keats asserts that "the poetical character . . . is not itself—it has no self—it is everything and nothing":

> It has as much delight in conceiving an Iago as an Imogen.
>   A poet is the most unpoetical of anything in existence; because he has no identity—he is continually infor[ming]—and filling some other body.

In the central sections of Olson's famous poem, "The Kingfishers," the pronoun and the concept "I" simply disappear from the poem, though they return with a vengeance in the concluding section. One can sense something of the same thing happening in this short piece from Olson's *Maximus Poems IV, V, VI*:

MAXIMUS, MARCH 1961-2

by the way into the woods

Indian   otter

"Lake"   ponds   orient

show me   (exhibit

myself)

In a way similar to Mallarmé's *Un Coup de dés*, the spaces around the words allow for multiple meanings (the word "orient," for example, might be a verb or a noun) and, while one has a sense of an intense experience happening—indeed, an experience which "shows me myself"—one does not have a sense of the individuality of the person doing the experiencing. The poem is in this sense the opposite of a "dramatic monologue." (In *A Guide to* The Maximus Poems *of Charles Olson* George F. Butterick tells us that "Olson spoke of this poem as resulting from or having to do with a revelatory experience made possible . . . through the consciousness-expanding drug, psilocybin, a synthetic form of the Sacred Mushroom of the Mexican Indians—which he experienced a few weeks earlier, in February 1961, in an experiment conducted by drug researcher Timothy Leary." Similarly, Rexroth remarks in the introduction to his Reverdy translations that "At the present moment [1969] the quest of such experiences [of natural mysticism] by way of hallucinogenic drugs is immensely fashionable.")

"Negative Capability" implies the disappearance of the poet as ego, as self. Despite Rexroth's theme of "unselving," there is little "Negative Capability" in his work.[3] In "Remembering Rexroth" (*Poetry Flash*, January, 1992), Morgan Gibson correctly observes that Rexroth always "had an extraordinary conviction of being right." At times—as in the passages quoted above—this makes for boring, even annoying writing. At other times, however, it is Rexroth's great strength:

For Eli Jacobson
December 1952

There are few of us now, soon
There will be none. We were comrades
Together, we believed we
Would see with our own eyes the new
World where man was no longer
Wolf to man, but men and women
Were all brothers and lovers
Together. We will not see it.
We will not see it, none of us.
It is farther off than we thought.
In our young days we believed
That as we grew old and fell
Out of rank, new recruits, young
And with the wisdom of youth,
Would take our places and they
Surely would grow old in the
Golden Age. They have not come.
They will not come. There are not
Many of us left. Once we
Marched in closed ranks, today each
Of us fights off the enemy,
A lonely isolated guerrilla.
All this has happened before,
Many times. It does not matter.
We were comrades together,
Life was good for us. It is
Good to be brave—nothing is
Better. Food tastes better. Wine
Is more brilliant. Girls are more
Beautiful. The sky is bluer
For the brave—for the brave and
Happy comrades and for the
Lonely brave retreating warriors.
You had a good life. Even all
Its sorrows and defeats and
Disillusionments were good,

Met with courage and a gay heart.
You are gone and we are that
Much more alone. We are one fewer,
Soon we shall be none. We know now
We have failed for a long time.
And we do not care. We few will
Remember as long as we can,
Our children may remember,
Some day the world will remember.
Then they will say, "They lived in
The days of the good comrades.
It must have been wonderful
To have been alive then, though it
Is very beautiful now."
We will be remembered, all
Of us, always, by all men,
In the good days now so far away.
In the good days never come,
We will not know. We will not care.
Our lives were the best. We were the
Happiest men alive in our day.

That poem is as much a poetry of statement—and of the ego—as the passage I quoted from *The Dragon and the Unicorn*, yet it is, as Ken Knabb and others have pointed out, enormously moving. Perhaps the deepest element of Rexroth's verse is its nostalgia, its sense of elegy. There are few poets who can touch him in this regard:

At the door of my thatched hut,
Buried deep in the forested mountains,
The wind in the ancient ginko tree
Sounds like the rustle of brocaded silk.
("Erinnerung" from "Imitations of the Chinese,"
1974: the title means "Remembrance," "Memory")

"Colors of things gone dead," he wrote in an early poem, "of dear moments lost in tragedy." Time, the great theme of elegies, is a subject Rexroth returns to again and again—the word "gone" echoes throughout his work—as is the notion that value is to be found only in *this* world ecstatically apprehended:

> The order of the universe
> Is only a reflection
> Of the human will and reason . . .
> The great principles and forces
> That move the world . . . have order
> Only as a reflection
> Of the courage, loyalty,
> Love, and honesty of men.
> By themselves they are cruel
> And utterly frivolous.
> The man who yields to them goes mad.
> ("They Say This Isn't A Poem")

Rexroth faced the challenge of Pound and of "that revolution of the sensibility that began with Baudelaire" in a brave and often brilliant way. He is rightly praised for the depth and beauty of his nature poetry. The American West, writes Linda Hamalian in her essay, "Rediscovering Community: Rexroth and the Whitman Tradition," created in Rexroth "a pervading, comforting conviction that no artistic accomplishment could ever match this landscape" and aroused in him "a sense of a sacramental presence in all things. . . ." He was extraordinarily erudite, but he could use his erudition in a playful manner. He translated lines by William Carlos Williams—the great advocate of "the American language"—into Latin ("De Fera Dormita"): suddenly Williams sounds like Catullus! And in a poem addressed to Williams, Rexroth defined the poet as "one who creates / Sacramental relationships / That last always." In his later years Rexroth placed much of his hope for change not in "poetry" but in song. Song, he insisted, gets to the root of the matter by presenting "an alternative kind of human being" ("Back to the Sources of Literature"):

The real thing about your [David Meltzer's] stuff, or Joni Mitchell's stuff . . . is that it involves and presents a pattern of human relationships which is unassimilable by the society. What the songs speak of cannot be assimilated. I mean, here is a love song . . . but the kind of love it sings of can't exist in this society. The song gets out like a bit of radioactive cobalt. It just foments subversion around itself as long as it is available . . .

The whole problem is to find works of art which remain permanently unassimilable and permanently corruptive . . . The songs of Shakespeare are permanently indigestible and permanently subversive.
(Interview, *The San Francisco Poets*)

If Rexroth was not capable of the lyrical heights of his friend, Robert Duncan (Duncan's "Such is the Sickness of Many a Good Thing" is one of the most beautiful and musical examples of free verse ever written), he was certainly capable of considerable depth, insight, and passion.

This last perhaps made him a rather difficult person, despite his charm. In his introduction to the *Complete Poems,* co-editor Sam Hamill writes, "Although apparently incapable of monogamy, [Rexroth] nevertheless believed in marriage as the highest sacrament." Rexroth's biographer, the unforgiving Linda Hamalian, makes the point in a somewhat fiercer way: "He saw no contradiction between his longing for a stable, profound relationship with one woman and his predisposition to screw anyone within reach." Despite the fact that Rexroth encouraged and attracted many prominent women writers, who admired him as well, he could refer to them at times as "writresses." (Cf. "waitresses.") Used after his own desert, remarked Shakespeare, which of us would 'scape whipping? Rexroth was both monstrosity and miracle, and he deserves considerably better than he has received.

☙

In 1992 Morgan Gibson wrote, "The point of many of [Rexroth's] allusions may be clear, but the processes of his imaginative thinking are not so easily grasped. More, not less, explication of his work is needed." Donald K. Gutierrez's *Revolutionary Rexroth* appeared in 1986 and his *"The Holiness of the Real": The Short Verse of Kenneth Rexroth* ten years later, but apart from such efforts there has been very little. Gibson may be right about the "clarity" of Rexroth's myriad allusions, but a guide to the allusions—like the guides to Pound's and Olson's poetry—would be a very useful volume. *The Dragon and the Unicorn* quietly quotes from Eugene V. Debs, for example, and Rexroth re-writes St. Augustine's "Love God and do what you will" as "Love and do what you will."

Kenneth Rexroth saw himself as a member of an international community. Currently even his sympathetic critics tend to regard him as a regional (California) writer, albeit one of genius. One review of the *Complete Poems* bore the headline, "A poet transformed by California / Kenneth Rexroth collection shows how state worked its magic on him."[4] Rexroth might well have regarded such a designation as another example of the provincialism—"the native son and daughter thing"—he battled all his life. In writing this essay I myself have said nothing of his fine translations or, to use Ken Knabb's word, of the continuing "relevance" of his social conscience: subjects for another paper. In 1969 Rexroth—always the anarchist—told David Meltzer,

> What happened with Vietnam, and the Russian-Chinese split, was that the movement again fell into the hands of people who were representing other people's foreign offices. American radicals are placed in the ridiculous position of supporting the foreign policies of Ho Chi Minh, or Chairman Mao, or Fidel Castro, of Tito, or Israel. That may be better than Stalin, but it is still an army, it is still a foreign office, it is still a state . . . You know! Here's a Negro in San Francisco and he is running around in African clothes and he's talking about the glories of the Congo or Nigeria or Ghana or whatever side he has taken. Why? What for? It is just another state. It is the same old shit come back. . . . [5]

In addition to this *Complete Poems* and a handful of books still in print, Ken Knabb's Bureau of Public Secrets website has a considerable amount of Rexroth material: http://www.bopsecrets.org. You can also find information about Rexroth at the Modern American Poetry site: http://www.english. uiuc.edu/maps/poets/m_r/rexroth/rexroth.htm.

Contemporaries

Slam

Look at me now and here I am.
—GERTRUDE STEIN

My wife Adelle and I hosted the Seattle Teen Slam Team at our home recently. They were in town to compete in the National Teen Poetry Slam Championships, which were held at the Regency Theater on Earth Day— Saturday, April 22, 2000. The trip was arranged by Paul Nelson, who is a poetry dynamo in the Seattle area: hosting readings, putting poetry on the radio, getting poets paid for their efforts, writing excellent poetry of his own. Check out his web sites: http://www.inpeoria.org and http://www.splab.org. Joining Paul *chez moi* was the team: Nicole Bade, Angela Dy, Rafi Soifer, Ben Warden; the alternate, Nordica Friedrich; the team manager, Shea Kauffman; and the team's coaches, Paula Friedrich and Tim Sanders. We found beds for some, but many lay happily sleeping-bagged on our living room rug.

There were many events involved in this three-day "National Youth Poetry Festival." The organizers write,

> Now in its third year, the National Youth Poetry Slam Festival first kicked off in Hartford, Connecticut as an off-shoot of the adult slam. But due to the rising number of poetry programs for youths nationwide, last year in Albuquerque, New Mexico, The Youth Slam became its own event. An entire festival that celebrates and embraces the creativity of today's teenagers, Brave New Voices 2000 has more young poets coming together from across the globe than ever before.

Adelle and I attended the "grand slam finals" at the Grand Ballroom at the Regency Building in San Francisco. It was an extraordinary event. I saw "slam queen" Ariana Waynes, a "National Poetry Slam Champ 1999," in the audience, though she didn't read or judge. (I keep thinking of her, unfairly no doubt, as "Buffy the Poetry Slayer.") The competitive aspects of the event were deliberately downplayed—the judges frequently acted more like a cheering section than like judges—and the mood was enormously upbeat. It was "You'll shout when it hits you, yes indeed," as the old spiritual put it. And if you didn't shout, the mc complained that you were insufficiently responsive: "I can't heeear you!" The main mc for the event was Saul Williams, featured in Marc Levin's 1998 film, *Slam*. Standing ovations were frequent. You felt a little as though you were in church, a large church. And in fact a donation basket was passed through the audience at one point. (This despite the fact that people had paid to get in, as they do not in a church.) When the basket came round, Nelson nudged me and said, "If you didn't know you were in church before, you know it now."

The Seattle team did very well: everyone spoke effectively, and their material was thoughtful and well-written; Bade and Soifer performed a riveting multi-voiced piece dealing with what we in Berkeley call "the Battle of Seattle." But, as Nelson put it, "the hip-hop stylings of Berkeley/Oakland won over the capacity crowd at the Regency Theater."

There were many assertions of the superior virtues of youth and suggestions that youth would change the world. "Youth Speaks," read the logo, ". . . because the next generation can speak for itself." To belong to this group all you had to be was—young. I couldn't help thinking of the "exclusiveness" of the old Pepsi Generation ad: "If you're living you belong." We don't want any dead ones! (Pushing sixty, I also remembered the aged Falstaff's inclusion of himself in the phrase "we youth.") The content of the poetry, usually memorized, was often reminiscent of high school assemblies—situations in which the point is to allow a young person to present him or herself to an audience but, at the same time, to quietly insist that what the person says must be "uplifting" or "inspiring" according to local conceptions of what is uplifting and inspiring: in short, say it, but make it dead. The poetry tended to be deeply involved with ego assertion—as in "I am Hamlet the Dane!"— rather than ego examination, though of course any writing involves some ego examination.

Among the non-teenagers reading at the Regency event was Beau Sia, whose presentation was one of the highlights of the evening. This is the poem he put on the cover of his book, *a night without armor II: the revenge* (for sale at the event). On the cover the poem looks like a piece of graffiti:

I DON'T CARE WHAT YOU THINK
ABOUT THE WAY I WRITE
I DIE ON THE PAGE
EVERY TIME. WHAT
DO YOU KNOW
ABOUT PUSH-UPS?
TRUE LOVE?
PRESSURE?
AT NIGHT I LIE
IN MY QUEEN-SIZE
BED ALONE. DREAMING
ABOUT IGNOBLE
THINGS. I AM NOT
FANCY. I AM NOT SPECIAL
I AM BETTER THAN YOU.
I AM ALONE. I AM THE
PRODUCT.

The number of I's in that poem is characteristic of much of the emotional push of slam poetry. Gertrude Stein nailed it many years ago when she wrote, "Look at me now and here I am." Much of Sia's poem is a statement of pretty straight, not-too-thoughtful adolescent angst—or at least what our culture usually puts forth as adolescent angst. For males of my generation, such angst was embodied by writers like Thomas Wolfe and J.D. Salinger, movies like *Rebel Without a Cause*, and figures such as James Dean and Elvis Presley. It's easy enough to recognize: "I AM NOT / FANCY. I AM NOT SPECIAL / I AM BETTER THAN YOU. / I AM ALONE."

But if Sia gives us adolescence in a readily-packaged, easily-recognizable form, he also gives us little surprises which jolt us and force us to recognize that we are dealing with something far more genuine here. When he writes, "I DIE ON THE PAGE / EVERY TIME. WHAT / DO YOU KNOW ABOUT . . ." we expect the next word to be "ME," but in fact it's "PUSH-UPS." Similarly, the word "PRODUCT" at the end of the poem is completely unexpected. Sia is giving the adolescent audience what it believes it wants— a mirror of what it believes it's like—but, at the same time, he is ahead of the audience, moving it into a genuine experience of language.

It is perhaps too much to ask of real teenagers to display such consciousness. It's enough that they should enter into the rituals of poetry, enough that they should write verse that people can understand and care for, enough that they should learn to perform in ways that interest and captivate. And captivating they were. It was wonderful to hear the discussions in my living room—not discussions of TV or clothing but of poetry. It was also wonderful to see the performers in action—to see what they had learned about presenting a poem. As for the poetry, most of it was relatively conventional. Much involved popular political positions such as the difficulties of women in our society. Displays of "emotional honesty" were valued: one very young slammer shouted out to a girl who had ignored him, "You are my first love!" The crowd loved it. It was also a good idea to sound as African-American as possible, whether or not you actually were African-American. Sheer energy of sound (whether or not the words were intelligible) was also applauded—appropriately enough to a poetry gathering, where the sound of the poem is always a factor. Indeed, there were Bosnian teenagers reading in Bosnian, though they didn't compete. And a group of young women from London. The work I heard was obviously rooted in current musical forms—people danced to some of the poems—but it was also rooted in the poetries of many ancient cultures. Didn't the Homeric singers memorize their poems just like the slammers?

A friend whispered to me that there was nothing very "literary" about this work. If she meant that there were few allusions in the manner of, say, Ezra Pound, she was quite correct. But the *form* of these presentations was entirely literary. No matter how ignorant of the history of poetry any individual poet may have been, no matter how few actual poems he or she may have read, that poet functioned within a working definition of what constituted a poem, and it was a fairly conventional definition. The poem was short, frequently narrative, it issued out of the often-asserted "I," etc. There was not a single poem which placed such poetry— or poetry itself—in question, no single moment which genuinely astonished and forced us to review our conception of what might constitute the art. There was, in short, nothing stunningly original. On the other hand, there was nothing really bad, either. The worst acts had something endearing about them, just as those high-school assemblies often did, and the four hours passed quickly.

While staying at my home, Seattle coach Paula L. Friedrich gave me a copy of her chapbook, *Exotic Plants* (direct inquiries to seaslam@rocketmail.com or call 206-366-2280). Friedrich is a graduate of the Creative Writing/Poetry program at Oberlin and has represented Seattle on three National Poetry Slam teams. She is also Board President of the Seattle Poetry Slam and performs with the ensemble, *A Slip of the Tongue*.

Though I didn't hear her read, I was aware that she has been extremely involved in slam, and I was curious about her book. Questions like "Is it really poetry?" "Does it communicate on the page?" seem to me, frankly, of little consequence, but here was a book by someone deeply involved in slam. What was it like?

Exotic Plants is divided into three sections, "Confessions I Would not Make to a God," "Medusa's Diner," and "Taking Apart Tinkerbell." It is roughly chronological, beginning with a poem dealing with the author's childhood and ending with a poem about the adult poet living in Seattle. *Exotic Plants* may betray its slam roots by the frequent appearance of the pronoun "I," which appears perhaps more than any other word in the book. Like the work I heard at the slam, Friedrich's book has nothing in it that can be called "experimental."

The word "Confessions" suggests the focus of the first section, "Confessions I Would not Make to a God". These poems are indeed "confessional," with echoes of Plath and others:

> I am up the cherry tree
> with my new, blue dress on.
>
> Grandma Omi will make *Kirschentorte*,
> and say *meine Susse*, my sweetie,
> like she always does.
>
> Daddy bought wooden paddles with a rubber ball
> to bang around outside the apartment
> until my brother and I rang the bell and said
> *ich mocte ins Haus gehen bitte*,
> door buzzed through the speaker   *ja, ja.*

Apart from the odd placement of the comma after "new"—perhaps a typo—this is competent, carefully-written verse, but it is little more than that. It is also a *kind* of poem we have seen and heard very, very often. A sub-text of this kind of writing is always, "See, I am writing a poem: this is like other poems you've read—so you can recognize it—but it is also different because it has my particular subject matter, my life." Unfortunately, the particularities of the life are not sufficiently present to lift the poem into something really memorable. For the most part it is—a poem, not bad, but one of many. The concluding lines—particularly

"Little hearts that drop from my hands"—move towards something more genuinely touching:

> I wanted the cherries
> from the tree in Germany.
> Little hearts that drop from my hands
> to my dress, which
> Omi will wash today.

Friedrich's poems—like successful slam poetry in general?—often have a "twist" at the end which makes you reconsider everything. This is also true of Beau Sia's work. If your poem is going to be judged, you will want to have a strong ending—something which will ring in the judges' ears as you close.

Friedrich's confessional section explores childhood experience, the Family Romance ("the young girls who like their fathers so much, you know, / they never get married . . . "), ethnicity ("Mark of the Mongol"), religion and sex, youthful friendship; it concludes in Seattle, where the poet now lives. The themes are familiar—which is fine if you've never experienced them—but they are hardly examples of Pound's directive to "make it new." As I suggested earlier, these poems are competently written but not spectacular; they have the feeling of apprenticeship—as if Friedrich were learning her trade through them.

The poems in the concluding two sections include several references to myths—which is not something I heard in the slam—and the poet at times takes on various personae, though the assertion of the "I" remains a theme:

> I am Eurydice teasing you into hell.
>
> Your slumber mutters from the mattress.
>
> I baptize the precipice,   you slide. . . .

There are also comic poems ("Lego Woman") and fanciful ones ("If M.C. Escher Were My Lover, / We'd Never Have Time for Pizza"). For me, by far the finest poem in the book was the concluding one, "Persephone." Friedrich's placement of the poem suggests that she understands its strength: a slam poet is aware of the need for a good ending.

In the light, my nails are bloody from too many pomegranate
seeds.
I guzzle milk like moonbeams; turn blinds for the amaryllis,
swing children onto my hips, squeeze snot from their nostrils,
watch them grow.

Mother, I transplanted my roots to a water-drenched city.
You would rip them if you could face
                            some rapacious, stinking god
with a spear.

But when the sun is done with the exposition of all dark
corners,
I screw my face into question marks,
exclamation points,   our fingers dragons or whales
we darken sidewalks,   tides;

sleep until two becomes one.

Feel free to fly here,
                    after three.

Everything in this breakthrough poem seems magical and enigmatic. For the
first time in the book we come face to face with mystery. The I is of course
present, but it seems to open itself into a darkness which we find nowhere
else in *Exotic Plants*. Here, autobiographical and mythic elements touch: the
"water-drenched city" is obviously Seattle, but the moon and blood suggest
archetypal feminine experience. Persephone of course lives half of the year in
hell, underground—and she has been "raped." The poem is not exactly
"accessible," but it stays with us for a long time, nudging us into an awareness
which is never specific but constantly alive. What do the concluding lines
mean? Are they an assertion of freedom ("Feel free to fly here") followed by
the assertion of a limitation: "after three"? The poem is like—in Keats' terms—
a sudden influx of Negative Capability after a book full of the Egotistical
Sublime, and it brings us perhaps to another insight about slam. Slam is a
wonderful way to experience the rituals and observances of poetry and to see
oneself as participating in those rituals. But poetry needs to *transcend* its
rituals. It is possible that every feeling of individual freedom eventually
transforms itself into a burden from which, once again, we need to be freed.

Slam gave the teenagers who visited me something they will always remember—and which I will always remember; but perhaps it is finally something they need to leave behind. Poetry is frequently represented as winged. "Feel free to fly here," writes Friedrich: Freedom. But there is also the qualification, "After three": Limitation. Friedrich's concluding poem transcends not only the limitations of her book but probably of slam poetry as well. It will be interesting to see what becomes of her, and it.

S.A.Y. Poetry, a CD of the Seattle Slam Finalists, is available for purchase. Contact:

It Plays in Peoria Productions
14 S. Division
Auburn, WA 980015318
www.splab.org
888-735-MEAT
www.inpeoria.org
253-735-6328

In addition, David Yanofsky has made a documentary film about slam. It's called *Poetic License*. You can get information about it at www.poetic license.org.

&

Some Further Comments, 2007

A few excerpts from the above essay appear in *The Spoken Word Revolution Redux* (Sourcebooks, 2007). Thinking about the excerpts brought me back once again to slam poetry.

Though I am a performance poet who has given hundreds of poetry readings, I have a problem with "slam poetry" and "spoken word poetry." Such poetry seems to me little more than the assertion of the "ego": this is what *I* think, these are *my* feelings. I think the popularity of spoken word is partly due to that fact. Americans like to think of themselves as "individuals" and feel that "self-expression" if properly presented is a good thing: after all, everyone is different, we all have individual feelings and they should be expressed. It seems to me that the problem with that formulation is basically that it isn't true—which is why so many "individuals" end up saying exactly the same things! The "ego" of "individuality" is the ego generated by mass culture; it isn't real. From a political point of view, that fictional ego is very useful: one man, one vote. But from the point of view of self-contemplation, it is false. I wrote this in the introduction to my *Greatest Hits 1974-2004* (Pudding House):

> I can't get it out of my head that, though I may be "unique," I am not an "individual." The word "individual" comes from the Latin *individuus*—indivisible, something which can no longer be "divided." If I think of myself as a political entity, then I am happy to be *individuus*: the rights of the individual are everywhere to be respected. If I think of myself as a thinking/feeling entity, however, I am something very different from that: I am not at all *individuus*; I am as divided as I can be. This collection of *Greatest Hits 1974-2004* is a testimony to ways in which that perception (obsession) has followed me throughout my life.

One of the questions my work raises is how you can present spoken poetry, performed poetry which is *not* an assertion of the ego—which remains true to an understanding of selfhood as multiple. At one point, L=A=N=G=U=A=G=E poets claimed that *all* spoken work was an assertion of the ego; to arrive at any kind of "multiplicity" you had to turn away from "performance" and concentrate on the silence of "writing." I don't think these poets were right about that, but I can see why they said it—and see it particularly clearly in the phenomena of "spoken word" and "slam."

Adrienne Rich

The School Among The Ruins: Poems 2000-2004

> How I've hated speaking "as a woman"
> for mere continuation
> when the broken is what I saw.
> —ADRIENNE RICH, "Terza Rima," *Fox: Poems 1998-2000*

The School Among the Ruins: Poems 2000-2004 (W.W. Norton) is Adrienne Rich's most recent volume. It follows *Midnight Salvage: Poems 1995-1998* (1999) and *Fox: Poems 1998-2000* (2001). None of these volumes is an attempt to produce an individual "masterpiece"; each is a kind of way-station in an ongoing engagement with poetic language. "By 1956," Rich writes in "Blood, Bread, and Poetry" (*Arts of the Possible*, 2001), "I had begun dating each of my poems by year. I did this because I was finished with the idea of a poem as a single, encapsulated event, a work of art complete in itself":

> I knew my life was changing, my work was changing, and I needed to indicate to readers my sense of being engaged in a long, continuing process. It seems to me now that this was an oblique political statement . . . It was a declaration that placed poetry in a historical continuity, not above or outside history.

Rich describes herself as "a writer in a country where native-born fascistic tendencies, allied to the practices of 'free' marketing, have been trying to eviscerate language of meaning" ("Arts of the Possible," *Arts of the Possible*). As a poet, she says in "Blood, Bread, and Poetry," she feels "more and more urgently the dynamic between poetry as language and poetry as a kind of action, probing, burning, stripping, placing itself in dialogue with others out beyond the individual self." Poetic language connects us "with all that is not simply white chauvinist/male supremacist/straight/puritanical—with what is 'dark,' 'effeminate,' 'inverted,' 'primitive,' 'volatile,' 'sinister'"; it constitutes "writing . . . that may not be male, or white, or heterosexual, or middle-class."

In her earliest encounters with poetry, Rich writes, "my . . . mind did not shut down for the sake of consistency"; later she came to realize that poetry "reasserts the claim to a complex historical and cultural identity, the selves who are both of the past and of tomorrow." "We are," she insists, "trying to build a political and cultural movement in the heart of capitalism"; at the same time she confesses to "the fragmentation I suffer in myself." In reading Simone de Beauvoir and James Baldwin, Rich writes, "I began to taste the concrete reality of being unfree, how continuous and permeating and corrosive a condition it is, and how it is maintained through culture as much as through the use of force."

What kind of writing is contained in *The School Among the Ruins*? Does the title refer metaphorically to poetry, which, Rich says, is "a kind of teaching" ("Blood, Bread Poetry")? How does her complex vision of poetry connect to the actual poems she produces? In what way does her poetry assert "freedom" and not merely the ruminations of the individual self—or, worse, the ruminations of late Capitalism?

To begin with, Rich's poems are by no means conventionally "clear." The book opens with "Centaur's Requiem":

> your hooves drawn together underbelly
> shoulders in mud   your mane
> of wisp and soil deporting all the horse of you
>
> your longhaired neck
> eyes   jaw yes   and ears
> unforgivably human on such a creature
> unforgivably what you are
> deposited in the grit-kicked field of a champion
>
> tender neck and nostrils   teacher   water-lily suction-spot
> what you were   marvelous   we could not stand
>
> Night drops   an awaited storm
> driving in to wreck your path
> Foam on your hide like flowers
> where you fell   or fall   desire

The poem is a puzzle piece which remains resonant—indeed, becomes *more* resonant—as one considers it, but never fully declares its "meaning." A "centaur" is of course a creature from Classical mythology; the creature has the head, trunk and arms of a man and the body and legs of a horse. (The notion of such a creature may have arisen from an imperfect perception of men riding horses.) Since the poem is a "requiem," this centaur must be dead—yet the poet seems to feel "desire," tenderness towards it. The poem resembles Rilke's "Archaic Torso of Apollo," with its famous concluding line, "*Du mußt dein Leben ändern*" ("You must change your life"), so it is possible that Rich is looking at a statue of a centaur, perhaps one that has sunk into the mud of the "grit-kicked field" in which she encounters it. Certainly the notion of "change" is as central to her consciousness as it was to Rilke's.

In any case, the creature is, or has been, "marvelous"—an entity which seems to connect us to some realm of authenticity. Further—in a book whose title poem involves a "school" and teachers—Rich calls the centaur a "teacher." *Why does the centaur have long hair?* Is this poem an oblique lament for the sixties or for the seventies—for a time of power? "The movements of the 1960s and the 1970s in the United States," Rich writes in "Arts of the Possible" (1997), "were openings out of apertures previously sealed, into collective imagination and hope . . . They have been relentlessly trivialized, derided, and demonized by the Right and by what's now known as the political center":

> I've been struck by the presumption, endlessly issuing from the media, in academic discourse, and from liberal as well as conservative platforms, that the questions raised by Marxism, socialism, and communism must inexorably be identified with their use and abuse by certain repressively authoritarian regimes of the twentieth century: therefore they are henceforth to be non-questions.

Is the centaur—still potent even in death—an emblem of "Marxism, socialism, and communism"? "Capitalism," Rich goes on, "vulgarizes and reduces complex relations to a banal iconography." What kind of "iconography" are we dealing with here? Is this a political poem? Is it a lament for a time in which "marvelous" creatures such as centaurs were freely imagined by humankind? Is it a lament for poetic fictions? And why does the creature cause desire? Isn't Rich known to be a lesbian feminist? Why should she feel desire for a creature which is part man and part horse?

The questions I am raising here are not, in Rich's term, "non-questions" and they are not questions which can be easily or definitively answered—not something which can be handled by the evening news. Rich's language deliberately moves us into a realm in which nothing is certain but which opens us to the process of *questioning*. In Capitalist society, Rich asserts, "everything . . . tends toward becoming a *thing* until people can speak only in terms of the *thing*, the inert and always obsolescent commodity" ("Arts of the Possible"). The centaur is a *thing* and it may be "obsolescent," but it is not a commodity: it is a linguistic—or "poetic"—fiction; while it can be speculated about, it cannot in any way be bought. Indeed, its "being" is pure speculation: no one any more believes that centaurs "really" exist in any form except poetic fictions, speculations, "possibilities."

It is Rich's great perception to realize that *speculation itself is political*—that "questioning" in a society in which "distinctions fade and subtleties vanish" ("Arts of the Possible") is a political act. Her poem does not assert that Capitalist society is a bad thing; instead, it thrusts us into a realm in which questions, ideas—thought—arise. Further: it speculates about something which *had* power and which might yet be involved in some sort of resurgence. Like "Marxism, socialism, and communism," the centaur is really nothing but a bundle of ideas, a myth. Can one "kill" a myth? The poem is fragmentary, incomplete—Rich refers to her own feelings of fragmentation—but it *points towards* a wholeness which it cannot manifest. It stands, as Rich says, not as a piece of merchandise but as something "unforgivably human."

The School Among the Ruins is full of poetry like that—a poetry of questioning and of struggle rather than what Rich calls "the sweetly flowing measures of my earlier books" ("Blood, Bread, and Poetry"), which is not to say that the book is necessarily difficult or "obscure." There are a number of love poems in it, poems in which the poet turns away from heavy political questions to indulge herself in the sweetness of sentiment:

> There's a beat in my head
> song of my country
>
> called Happiness, U.S.A.
> Drowns out bouzouki
>
> drowns out world and fusion
> with its *Get—get—get*
>
> into your happiness before
> *happiness pulls away . . .*
>
> break out of that style
> give me your smile
> awhile
> ("This Evening Let's"—a very amusing title)

There is also a fine tribute to French poet Guillaume Apollinaire and French songwriter Georges Brassens, "After Apollinaire & Brassens":

> what flows under the Seine
> Mississippi Jordan Tigris
> Elbe Amazon Indus Nile
>
> and all the tributaries
> who knows where song goes
> now and from whom
> toward what longings

(Rich's volume, *Midnight Salvage* has a beautiful, partial translation of Brassens' song, "Chanson pour l'Auvergnat.")[1]

One can follow themes of home ("and home no simple matter"— "Dislocations: Seven Scenarios"), innocence ("can I say it was not I   listed as Innocence / betrayed you"—"Equinox"), and words ("the power to hurl words is a weapon," "a word can be crushed like a goblet underfoot"— "Transparencies") throughout *The School Among the Ruins*. There are also themes of change ("and we remain or not but not remain / as now we think we are"—"As finally by wind or grass"), of self-criticism (*"Kid, you always / took yourself so hard!"*—"To Have Written the Truth"; "Cut the harping . . . / You're human, porous like all the rest"—"Tendril") and of old age ("Palms flung upward: 'What now?' / Hand slicing the air or across the throat. / A long wave to the departing"—"Screen Door"). The phrase "not here yet" repeats. There is a play on the etymology of the word "conversion": "You need to *turn yourself around* / face in another direction"—"Ritual Acts," my italics). The title poem is an extremely powerful statement of the immense human cost of bombing other countries ("One: I don't know where your mother / is Two: I don't know / why they are trying to hurt us"): "Great falling light of summer," Rich asks, "will you last / longer than schooltime?"

Perhaps the finest sequence of the volume—and the volume has far more "sequences" than it has "individual poems"—is "USonian Journals 2000." The term "Usonian," Rich explains, is "the term used by Frank Lloyd Wright for his prairie-inspired architecture. Here it means *of the United States of North America.*" This section is in prose, but it is no less powerful for that. It touches on a subject dear to Rich's heart—the nature of the oral:

Imagine written language that walks away from human conversation. A written literature, back turned to oral traditions, estranged from music and body. So what might reanimate, rearticulate, becomes less and less available.[2]

In her attempt to write "the history of the dispossessed" ("Blood, Bread, and Poetry"), Adrienne Rich is not attempting a chronicle of events so much as she is attempting to *transform* the dispossessed: "We need to begin changing the questions," she writes ("Arts of the Possible"). *The School Among the Ruins* is a book full of questions, and it concludes not with an "answer" but with still another question: "Not for her but still for someone?"

This is the beginning of the final stanza of "Tendril," the poem in which that line occurs:

> She had wanted to find meaning in the past but the future drove
> a vagrant tank a rogue bulldozer
>
> rearranging the past in a blip
> coherence smashed into vestige

This experience of "coherence smashed," of "the broken," is a fundamental one for Adrienne Rich. She is fond of quoting a passage from James Baldwin: "Any real change implies the breakup of the world as one has always known it, the loss of all that gave one an identity, the end of safety." If chaos, incoherence, "the end of safety" is painful—the word Rich uses to describe her experience of it is "suffer"—it is also alive with possibilities. Her poetry is a constant affirmation of what Maria Mazziotti Gillan and Jennifer Gillan call "the unsettling of America": "the constant erecting, blurring, breaking, clarifying, and crossing of boundaries that are a consequence of the complex intersections among peoples, cultures, and languages within national borders, which themselves are revised constantly" (*Unsettling America*). The study of history is not the study of a series of events whose meanings are fixed by executive decree but the study of events whose intensity has erupted into possibility—into *questions*. The capacity to write poetry, Rich says, is "the capacity to hook syllables together in a way that [heats] the blood." How does that heat—that alchemy—happen?

> one syllable then another
> gropes upward
> one stroke laid on another

sound from one throat then another
never in the making
making beauty or sense

always mis-taken, draft, roughed-in
only to be struck out
is blurt is roughed-up
hot keeps body
in leaden hour
simmering
("Tell Me")

Poetry is indeed "the school among the ruins" of Western history. But it is a school whose "teaching" is a curriculum of questions—and what is questioned is precisely the curriculum: "Can [I] say," Rich asks in one poem, "I was mistaken?" ("Equinox") The following beautiful lines, like Adrienne Rich's work as a whole, are this poet's answer to Robert Graves' famous assertion (made in his poem, "To Juan at the Winter Solstice" and echoing the scholarship of *The White Goddess*, 1947), "There is one story and one story only." Rich's lines are a miniature *ars poetica*:

There is the story of the mind's
temperature neither cold nor celibate
Ardent The story of
not one thing only
("There is No One Story and One Story Only")

And again:

No you can't go home yet
but you aren't lost
this is our school
("The School Among the Ruins")

Shadow of the Vampire

Nosferatu as Literature: Vampires, Vamps, and Volupté

> What I try to convey is his tremendous *stillness* and the way it combines with his savagery to produce a hypnotic power. And with Dracula there is something else. The loneliness of evil. . . .
> —CHRISTOPHER LEE on the role of Dracula,
>   quoted in the Signet Classic edition of Stoker's novel

> . . . *et nous faisons horreur aux petits enfants que nous voulons aimer!*
> . . . and we cause horror in the children we want to love!
> —CHARLES BAUDELAIRE, "Le Désespoir de la Vielle" ("The Despair of the Old Woman")

> *Là, tout n'est qu'ordre et beauté / Luxe, calme et volupté.*
> There, there is nothing but order and beauty / Sumptuousness, calm, and sensual delight.
> —CHARLES BAUDELAIRE, "L'Invitation au Voyage" ("Invitation to the Voyage")

1.

Along with his new book of poetry, *Interrogations at Noon*, Dana Gioia recently published the libretto to *Nosferatu* (Graywolf Press, 2001), an opera he wrote in collaboration with composer Alva Henderson. The libretto is based on F. W. Murnau's classic 1922 silent film, *Nosferatu*, which was itself based on Bram Stoker's classic 1897 novel, *Dracula*. Murnau had to change the title— "Nosferatu" means "The Undead"—because of copyright restrictions on "Dracula."

Gioia's book contains, in addition to the libretto, an interesting, instructive foreword by Anne Williams, "Listening to the Children of the Night: The Vampire and Romantic Mythology," as well as Gioia's own essay—a typically challenging one—"Sotto Voce: Notes on the Libretto as a Literary Form." For this New Formalist poet, the opera libretto is still another—form.

Clearly, the best way to experience this libretto is to see it performed. In this essay, however, I want to concentrate on the purely literary aspects of *Nosferatu*. Gioia tells us that he "resolved to write poetry that would be equally interesting on the page and on the stage—though perhaps in different ways." "For me," Gioia writes,

> the primary appeal of opera lay in its ritual elements. Music allows the audience to experience the words not intellectually but physically, emotionally, and indeed unconsciously. Under such conditions I could explore very different ways of writing than I might use on the page.

2.

In her foreword to *Nosferatu*, Anne Williams rightly emphasizes the theme of the Byronic *homme*—rather than *femme*—*fatal*, the male "vamp":

> Byron was perfecting a new archetype, the Byronic hero, or *homme fatal*. Like Milton's Satan, who first appears in *Paradise Lost* (1671) as an "archangel ruin'd," this character is thoroughly paradoxical. He is a man of action, yet also capable of intense passion and feminine sensitivity. Milton's Satan was tortured by remorse for the rebel angels who had followed him into battle with God and then into Hell, but Byron's Giaours and Conrads and Laras are tortured by romantic love. The object of their passion is always the unattainable woman they are fated to destroy . . . The vampire enters English literature in the distinguished company of a Byronic hero: indeed, as his dark double . . . The vampire is also always doomed to kill the thing he loves.

Williams goes on to write about Coleridge's *Christabel* (1797), Dr. John Polidori (Byron's friend and author of *The Vampyre*, 1818, the first vampire novel in English), Sheridan LeFanu's novella, *Carmilla* (1872), and Heinrich Marschner's opera, *Der Vampyr* (1828), based on Polidori's book. One wishes that she had extended her scope even further. The Dracula myth moves simultaneously in a number of directions and crosses over boundaries of "high" and "low" culture. It is at once expressive of genuine cultural problems and something we regard as high camp.

Ms. Williams mentions both Byron and Milton, but she does not mention the extremely important figure of Charles Baudelaire, in whose work the "vampire" is *both* the woman and the poet himself ("Je suis de mon coeur le vampire"—"I am the vampire of my heart," "L'Héautontimorouménos"). Baudelaire's *Les Fleurs du Mal* was first published in 1857. The Satanic theme is clearly present in "Les Litanies de Satan" ("Litanies of Satan") with its refrain, "Ô Satan, prends pitié de ma longue misère" ("O Satan, take pity on my long wretchedness").

"Litanies of Satan"—in which the poet prays to Satan as savior rather than to Jesus—is one of the first indications of the important conception of the poet as "maudit"—damned. Stéphane Mallarmé, who read Baudelaire with great care, wrote in his essay, "Crise de vers" ("Crisis of Verse," 1897): "Je dis: une fleur! Et . . . musicalement se lève . . . l'absente de tous bouquets" ("I say: a flower! And . . . musically there arises . . . the one that is absent from all bouquets"). When God says "flower," a flower appears—just as when God says, "Let there be light," light appears. When the poet says "flower," there appears precisely "l'absente de tous bouquets"—the flower that *isn't* there. God's realm is the realm of Truth and Being. The poet's realm is the realm of Non Being, Absence, Fiction—the realm of Satan. From this point of view, the poet speaks not from the area of light—Baudelaire was no poet laureate—but from the area of darkness, even the area of (in all the senses of the word) "obscurity." If bliss is present all, it appears as something longed for and distant: "Là, tout n'est qu'ordre et beauté / Luxe, calme, et volupté."

Ms. Williams also does not mention the way the Dracula theme works itself out in art. It was through the influence of a painting by Philip Burne Jones—Rudyard Kipling's cousin—that that immensely popular poet produced "The Vampire":

> A fool there was and he made his prayer
> (Even as you and I!)
> To a rag and a bone and a hank of hair
> (We called her the woman who did not care)
> But the fool he called her his lady fair
> (Even as you and I!).

And the painter Edvard Munch described his painting, "The Vampire" in prose that might have been written by Bram Stoker:

> And he lay his head against her breast—he felt the blood rush in her veins—he listened to her heartbeat—He buried his face in her lap—he felt two burning lips in the back of his neck—it gave him a freezing sensation through his body—a freezing lust—Then he pressed her forcefully toward him.

Oscar Wilde's play, *Salome* (1893) belongs in this list of vampires too—as do Aubrey Beardsley's hilarious, disturbing illustrations to Wilde's play. Walter

Pater's famous description in *The Renaissance* (1873) of the *Mona Lisa* also should be mentioned: "She is older than the rocks among which she sits; like the vampire, she has been dead many times, and learned the secrets of the grave . . . "—especially since Yeats used that passage, refashioned as free verse, to open his edition of *The Oxford Book of Modern Poetry* (1937). Indeed, Yeats himself has vampire figures:

> Herodias' daughters have returned again,
> A sudden blast of dusty wind and after
> Thunder of feet, tumult of images,
> Their purpose in the labyrinth of the wind. . . .
> ("Nineteen Hundred and Nineteen")

If from some points of view the maleness of the vampire is important, from other points of view it is not. In all cases, a diseased or "improper" (even "kinky") sexuality is working itself out and in all cases the vampire combines male and female elements: the female vampire is dominant and murderous rather than submissive and satisfying; the male vampire has a feminine "frailty." The vampire is at once a powerfully subversive image and comfortingly mainstream. Anne Rice has emphasized some of the vampire's homoerotic elements; Mel Brooks' witty title, *Dracula: Dead and Loving It* suggests some of its paradoxes. The popular television programs, *Buffy, the Vampire Slayer* and its spin-off, *Angel* emphasize the myth's connections to notions of American adolescent angst with its alienation and its sense of suffering.

In addition, some sort of religious element is always present in the vampire story. In Stoker's novel, Dracula (the name means "dragon" in Romanian) represents the forces of darkness, antiquity and superstition, as opposed to Dr. Van Helsing, who represents the forces of modern science, rationality and illumination. There are also suggestions of the Wandering Jew about the vampire: the infected Mina cries out, "Unclean! Unclean! Even the Almighty shuns my polluted flesh! I must bear this mark of shame upon my forehead until the Judgment Day." Somewhat surprisingly, Dracula is also represented as of limited intelligence: he is described in Van Helsing's fractured English as having a "child-brain that lie in [the] tomb for centuries, that grow not yet to our stature, and that do only work selfish and therefore small." One remembers Carlyle's cry from *Sartor Resartus* (1833): "Close thy Byron; open thy Goethe"—another attempt to turn from "selfishness" to a generous awareness of others.

For the Protestant imagination, the figure of Milton's Satan easily slides over into the figure of the Pope as Anti-Christ. One of the most famous moments in Tod Browning's 1931 film, *Dracula* is when Bela Lugosi says, "I never drink . . . wine." We of course know that Dracula "drinks" blood. This deliberate association of blood with wine is of course also a feature of the Catholic Mass: "For this is my Body, and this is my Blood." With his terrible rituals, Count Dracula is a kind of evil priest—a distorted and darkly fearful version of Catholicism: he is the "Pope" of a bad religion— even, when he becomes a "bat," a sort of *Un*-Holy Spirit, an *un*-dove. (The "Godfather," Don Corleone, has some of these characteristics as well: not for nothing did Francis Ford Coppola go on to make his own version of *Dracula*.) Yet Dracula's suffering and nineteenth-century erotic glamour give us ample opportunity for (in The Rolling Stones' resonant phrase) "sympathy for the devil." Like Baudelaire's "Old Woman," the vampire causes horror in the very people he wishes to love—often one of the predicaments of the adolescent in the midst of hormonal changes.

It is in such a thought climate that this paradoxical, totally mythical figure exists. He represents the "outsider" on all levels. For the most part, the vampire fails to achieve what he wishes to achieve—yet he achieves something. Though he may die at the end of the story, he is nevertheless back to haunt us in the next film or book; he remains a *powerful* "outsider," even a *popular* outsider, a thoroughly assimilated "unassimilable"—an "individual" in extremis. He is often an immigrant, someone from another country—and that is important in Gioia's conception. Despite his Old World background, however, the vampire is usually to be found in modern urban settings: indeed, it is primarily in modern urban settings that he appears as a threat. In an essay on "Cinema, Instrument of Poetry" Luis Buñuel quotes Engels: the filmmaker "will have accomplished his task honorably when, through a faithful depiction of authentic social relations, he will have destroyed the conventional representation of the nature of these relations, shaken the optimism of the bourgeois world and obliged the [viewer] to question the permanence of the existing order. . . ." That is precisely what the figure of the vampire does—though his ultimate destruction also represents the triumph of the bourgeois world. Like Satan, he is the "dark" version of Jesus. What does he want? Power, of course. (Gioia's Nosferatu says, "I've come to conquer—to make a new domain. . . .") But, as Williams points out, also "what else?—control of the women."

3.

F.W. Murnau's 1922 film, *Nosferatu*—remade as *Nosferatu the Vampyre* by Werner Herzog in 1979—is described in the credits as "adapted from Bram Stoker's *Dracula*." In the hands of Murnau and script writer, Henrik Galeen, a number of changes were made to Stoker's story. The locale is changed from London, England to Bremen, Germany, and the book's Mina Harker is changed to Nina Harker. More importantly, Dracula loses a great many of his Byronic overtones to become a figure of pure horror: "the terrible figure of NOSFERATU . . . hunched, with claw-like hands at the ready. . . ." (The film is subtitled "Eine Symphonie des Grauens"—"A Symphony of Horror.") As played by Max Schreck, this "Dracula" seems an embodiment of hunger or of that "loneliness" Christopher Lee speaks of. The fact that this figure of terror also sports, according to the script, "a large hooked nose" suggests not only the Wandering Jew but an all-too-common anti-Semitic stereotype.

In Stoker's novel, Mina is a victim of the vampire; she is saved through the efforts of Dr. Van Helsing and others. In Murnau's film, Van Helsing's role is minimized and Nina is both victim and savior—at the cost of her life:

> Only a woman can break his frightful spell—a woman pure in heart—who will offer her blood freely to Nosferatu and . . . will keep the vampire by her side until after the cock has crowed.

Though Murnau allows Nina to die in the arms of her husband, Nosferatu and Nina become a "couple" in a way that they do not in Stoker's novel. Nina's self-sacrifice releases Bremen from the terrible plague which Dracula's presence has inflicted on it. This is the film script's version of some of the film's concluding moments:

> NINA'S face expresses a horrible fascination and attraction, as the shadow of NOSFERATU'S hand creeps up across the white of her dress until it rests over her heart. Suddenly the shadow of the hand grips into a fist; NINA'S face is thrown back in a convulsion of pain, and then her expression relaxes . . .
> NOSFERATU stands still, drinking at NINA'S throat.
> A cock crows in the dawn light.
> NOSFERATU raises his face slowly and deliberately from the throat of his victim and turns to look towards the window . . .

NOSFERATU rises slowly to his full height; he turns slowly towards the window; holds his left hand to his chest as he staggers to get away from the light coming through the window.

NOSFERATU stumbles, as the bright beams of the sun streaming in the window strike him. His right hand goes across to shield his face; he turns about, faces left, and then his image begins to disappear. White smoke rises from a sunlit patch on the bedroom floor . . .

TITLE: "*And at that moment, as if by a miracle, the sick no longer died, and the stifling shadow of the vampire vanished with the morning sun.*"[1]

Like Murnau, Gioia changes the location of the story. In his version, *Nosferatu* is set "in the Baltic seaport of Wisborg in the mid-nineteenth century." He also changes the names of his characters. His Cast of Characters is worth quoting in full:

ELLEN HUTTER, *a young woman*
ERIC HUTTER, *her husband*
COUNT ORLOCK, *later called* NOSFERATU, *a Hungarian nobleman*
HEINRICH SKULLER, *a businessman*
DR. FRANZ HARDING, *a specialist in nervous diseases*
SERVANTS
MONKS
TOWNSPEOPLE
MADMEN
ASYLUM GUARDS[2]

Gioia's Dracula (called Orlock in the First Act, Nosferatu in the Second) is not the horrific monster of Murnau's film. When we first see him he is "a tall, thin man in his late sixties." When he appears in the Second Act—after feeding on the crew of the ship which brings him to Wisborg—he is "now much younger and more vital than before."

Money is an issue in Gioia's libretto as it is not in Murnau's film. Eric's employer, Skuller—who, we learn later, is in league with Nosferatu—points out that the young man's wife Ellen requires looking after, "and that takes money." He tells Eric of "A wealthy nobleman in Hungary—/ Count Orlock is his name":

I've bought a place for him on speculation.
I've put my capital at risk. But if
We sell the house to him, there will be profit!

Ironies abound in Skuller's speeches: the Count "needs to get away and find new life"; he is "eager to do business." Skuller advises the young man not to despise "the safety and freedom that money buys. / Unless you provide, [Ellen] may be lost." Such sentiments are echoed a few moments later, when the scientist, Dr. Franz Harding, remarks about Ellen,

> She's buried every day
> Beneath the unpaid bills, expenses, worry.
> Her husband has no work. He barely has
> Money enough to feed the two of them.

Eric confesses that he aches "with desire. / I twist in its thorns":

> I am still a starving child
> Standing in the dark,
> Staring through a window
> At a feast I cannot taste,
> Watching the bright faces
> Blessed with affection
> I cannot share.

These are the first of many moments in the play when language we would associate with the vampire is spoken by others—particularly by Eric and Ellen. The doctor's reference to Ellen's being "buried every day" suggests Nosferatu, who must sleep in his coffin. Throughout the play, our awareness of Nosferatu causes "ordinary" statements to take on a resonance which they would not "ordinarily" have: our awareness of the myth and its implications charges language with an intensity of meaning which the immediate circumstances would not justify in themselves. In effect, language is becoming constantly symbolic—though exactly what it symbolizes is not yet clearly grasped by the characters. This dream-like quality, in which words release themselves from their immediate circumstances in order to signify in various directions, is one of the strengths of this libretto, which is constantly moving us away from the ordinary into "another" realm. "Ellen's Dream" is a particularly resonant instance of this technique; its conclusion suggests the celebration of a Black Mass:

> The room was a chapel lit by candles,
> But the cross had been broken in two.

> The priest held a chalice of blood in his hands,
> And on the altar—was you.

Gioia produces a serviceable blank verse for most of the expository passages and various song forms for the arias. The beauty and artificiality of these forms are part of what draws us into the magical area of the myth which is being created moment by moment. If Eric is able to say things like "I am an agent selling property. / I deal with the nobility," he also says things like

> Flesh of my flesh, heart of my heart,
> Nothing on earth can keep us apart.
> No place so remote, no journey so far,
> That I will not be wherever you are.

> You are the shadow striding beside me.

This duet is titled "The Lovers' Vow." But the phrase "You are the shadow striding beside me" suggests Nosferatu, who is often referred to as a "shadow." Like the vampire—who relies primarily on rhetoric—the poet must "draw us in" through his use of language. (A moment later Eric and Ellen sing about "Blood of my blood. . . .")

Perhaps the finest of Gioia's arias is "Nosferatu's Nocturne"—a haunting piece which brings to mind some of the best of W.H. Auden's theatrical lyrics:

> I am the image that darkens your glass,
> The shadow that falls wherever you pass.
> I am the dream you cannot forget,
> The face you remember without having met.

> I am the truth that must not be spoken,
> The midnight vow that cannot be broken.
> I am the bell that tolls out the hours.
> I am the fire that warms and devours.

> I am the hunger that you have denied,
> The ache of desire piercing your side.
> I am the sin you have never confessed,
> The forbidden hand caressing your breast.

> You've heard me inside you speak in your dreams,
> Sigh in the ocean, whisper in streams.
> I am the future you crave and you fear.
> You know what I bring. Now I am here.[3]

In Murnau's wonderfully paranoiac film, Nosferatu is the embodiment of some powerful, ancient principle of evil: he is horrible and he is hungry—a nightmare figure. But he is not "inside" the heroine. In Gioia's version of the story, Nosferatu retains some of this quality, but, at the same time, he tends to be the "shadow" side of the characters themselves—the side they cannot fully acknowledge. In destroying Nosferatu for the sake of her husband and the town, Ellen is certainly acting heroically—but she is also affirming the power of repression. There is no question of "integrating" her dark side—which is the course most therapists would suggest: her dark side must be totally destroyed, even at the cost of Ellen's own life. In Murnau's film, the heroine learns how to destroy the vampire by reading a book; in Gioia's libretto, Skuller—Nosferatu's servant—somewhat implausibly *explains* to her how to do it. Once she determines to kill Nosferatu, Ellen says,

> What is there left to choose except my death?
> Why should the darkness not be brought to light?

The second line is particularly apt. Much of Gioia's work is a deliberate confrontation with "the dark"—which is precisely what Ellen must do as well. (The *word* "dark" haunts this poet, appearing in his works again and again.) In Ellen's speech, "darkness"—Nosferatu—is "brought to light," revealed. At the same time, however, "light" is what destroys the vampire, turns him into, literally, nothing. In a sense, light causes an overly "exposed," overly "present" darkness to turn into—darkness: light thus not only "reveals" something; it causes it to vanish entirely—which is in fact what darkness does. Is light—consciousness—a mode of revelation? Or is it a weapon? Is light at some level indistinguishable from darkness? What the sun does to the "darkness" of night, the dawn does to the vampire. At some level he is nothing but a bad dream which vanishes as we wake.

4.

Anne Williams is surely right when she asserts that *Nosferatu* gave Gioia "the opportunity to return the myth of the vampire to its Byronic roots." Gioia's vampire is clearly more Byronic than Murnau's. But by insisting that the vampire is an aspect of everyone's life—their "dark" side—Gioia further humanizes the character. This is how Murnau handles Nosferatu's death:

> NOSFERATU rises slowly to his full height; he turns slowly towards the window; holds his left hand to his chest as he staggers to get away from the light coming through the window.
> NOSFERATU stumbles, as the bright beams of the sun streaming in the window strike him. His right hand goes across to shield his face; he turns about, faces left, and then his image begins to disappear. White smoke rises from a sunlit patch on the bedroom floor . . .

This is how Gioia handles it:

> *[Ellen] collapses, dead. Nosferatu stands transfixed by the light. He starts to turn away but deliberately turns back to face the window and is slowly destroyed. Moments later Harding and Marthe enter the room and stare in bewildered terror at Ellen's body.*

In Murnau, Nosferatu "staggers to get away from the light coming through the window." In Gioia's version, Nosferatu "deliberately turns back to face the window and is slowly destroyed." In effect, the rejected lover allows himself to be destroyed: if Ellen is dead, he must die too.

Gioia himself points to the personal dimensions of *Nosferatu*. "As a child," he says, "I loved horror movies, which I knew mostly from television":

> Always obsessive about my passions, I read all the movie books in the library and bought—to my parents' horror—each new issue of *Famous Monsters of Filmland*. These sources soon led me to German silent horror and fantasy films like Fritz Lang's *Metropolis* (1926) and Murnau's *Nosferatu* (1922), both of which I managed to see at age twelve. (Los Angeles offers advantages to juvenile film buffs.) *Nosferatu*, therefore, was a part of my working-class, Latin-Catholic childhood and not my university years, and I first watched it as a horror movie and not a classic of German Expressionist cinema. Perhaps for that reason working on the libretto touched other childhood memories of religion, family, and poverty. Memories of my beautiful Aunt Felice dying of cancer, the *Salve Regina* being recited at the end of

our parochial school's daily morning Mass, and the constant family worries about money intermingled naturally with my first sighting of Max Schreck's shadow climbing the stairway towards his shuddering victim. I had never written about any of these early experiences before. But the new form invited new subjects, and I could disguise my life as part of someone else's story since the underlying myth was big enough to hold it all.

Like a vampire—like F. W. Murnau—the young Gioia caused his parents to experience "horror." His personal life could be "disguised" in the Dracula myth—just as, he asserts, the audience of opera can "disguise" its own subjectivity in the characters it sees:

> [The] special lyric intensity [of opera] explains why people so often cry at the opera, even at the performances of works they have known for years. For a few moments they have become the character on the stage. That imaginary figure's sufferings have become their own.

Yet when dealing with the thoroughly Symbolist world of myth, the personal is only one of many dimensions. *Nosferatu* definitely has implications for the current practice of poetry—our own "crise de vers," as Mallarmé would say—but not only for poetry. An increase in the visibility of the Latin or Hispanic elements of American culture means an increase in the visibility of Catholicism—an issue in *Nosferatu*—and Gioia himself points out the relevance of the Dracula myth to the imagination of AIDS, often referred to as a "plague." (When Nosferatu arrives in Wisborg, so does the plague.) At the same time, the libretto has a nineteenth-century quality about it—not so far from Wilde's *Salome*: it thrusts us into the "darkness" of immense sexual repression, the role of women, rivalry, warfare, love, hunger, money, religion, the family—the entire panoply of what for this poet are deeply ambiguous subjects. "I like writing poems that have a surface which executes one shape and a sub-text which executes another," he says in *The Irish Review*.

Indeed, Gioia's essay, "Sotto Voce," is full of interesting, perhaps not fully conscious parallels between opera, poetry and—Nosferatu. "Poetry," Gioia writes, "is a lonely art form."[4] I have quoted Christopher Lee on the essential loneliness of the Dracula character. (In a sense, Dracula, like a librettist, is looking for "the excitement of collaboration.") Opera, writes Gioia, "remains a foreign art form." The Count, too, is "foreign"—as is his "art form." "For me," Gioia goes on, "the primary appeal of opera lay in its ritual elements." Ritual is a feature of Dracula as well. Indeed, in Gioia theater has a tendency to move towards the specific ritual of the Catholic Mass: *Nosferatu* quotes in full the great prayer, *Salve Regina* (Hail, Holy Queen), part of the liturgy, as well as the Medieval Latin poem, *Dies Irae*—Day of Wrath. Gioia told me that he deliberately included references to each of the seven sacraments in his libretto. There are also suggestions of the Black Mass. In the libretto, he writes, "the poetic text exists not to survive as words but to be transformed into another medium. Sometimes that transformation is violent." It is precisely such a "violent transformation" into another "medium" that Dracula attempts to enact upon his victims. And finally, Gioia tells us that the composer and librettist of an American opera must face "indifference, contempt, or at best condescension." So too the vampire. Gioia's mythic material is not only alive with all of the meanings of the Dracula legend: it is in addition an emblem of opera itself. To put it another way, the libretto is vibrant with the poet's active self-consciousness. Like the writer who decides to read his work aloud—to "perform" it—*Nosferatu* gives "voice" to what was initially utterly silent, a film without sound. One could easily write a separate essay on the implications of Gioia's use of the libretto as a form of "performance poetry."

In "Sotto Voce" Gioia writes

> What opera excels at is presenting peak moments of human emotion. While the structure of opera is narrative, its power is lyric . . . it can represent the full emotional intensity of a specific moment. . . .

And in "Bourgeois in Bohemia," an essay on T.S. Eliot:

> Neither [Wallace Stevens nor T.S. Eliot] would abandon his middle-class morality for art. But the Muse demanded sacrifice, and they offered their youth, their marriages, their friendships, even, all evidence suggests, their sexuality. No Americans ever wrote greater poems.

In this latter passage Gioia is asserting that the road to the longed-for is through "sacrifice": "they offered their youth, their marriages, their friendships, even, all evidence suggests, their sexuality." At the "peak moment" of *Nosferatu,* both Ellen and Nosferatu sacrifice themselves: the moment of their union is also the moment in which they give up everything—even their existence.

Liebestod is of course an ancient theme, in opera and elsewhere. But the theme takes on a special quality here. These lovers are sacrificing themselves for someone else: Ellen for her husband and the town, Nosferatu for Ellen. In a Catholic context, self-sacrifice always calls to mind the figure of Jesus. In a way, it is not "the shadow of the vampire" that hangs over this play so much as it is the shadow of the *imitatio Christi*, the "imitation of Christ."

The "peak moment" of *Nosferatu* is a moment of liberation—as all such moments are. But what is liberated is the realization of Christ as vampire. "Sacrifice" ought to lead to some mode of resurrection. Here, instead, it leads to death. While it is true that Ellen's sacrifice "saves" her husband and the town from Nosferatu's plague—and so there is some point to it—it is not her husband and the town that we want to have saved: it is Ellen. The conclusion of Murnau's film makes much of the positive aspects of the heroine's sacrifice:

> TITLE: *"And at that moment, as if by a miracle, the sick no longer died, and the stifling shadow of the vampire vanished with the morning sun."*

Gioia's libretto ends in a much starker manner:

> *[Ellen] collapses, dead . . . Moments later Harding and Marthe enter the room and stare in bewildered terror at Ellen's body.*

Gioia's *Nosferatu* is an assertion, from a man who may be a Catholic atheist, of the simultaneous value and destructiveness of the *imitatio Christi*—which is also in Gioia's symbolizing imagination the life of poetry. The sacred is affirmed by *Nosferatu,* but it is presented as being at least as murderous as it is restorative. In "Bourgeois in Bohemia" Gioia quotes T.S. Eliot's response to the news that a young man has dedicated his life to poetry. Eliot remarks, "He's getting ready for a sad life." "Can Poetry Matter?" indeed! Gioia's new book of poetry, *Interrogations at Noon,* begins with an attack on the poet's very instrument, words:

> The world does not need words. It articulates itself
> in sunlight, leaves, and shadows. The stones on the path
> are no less real for lying uncatalogued and uncounted.
> The fluent leaves speak only the dialect of pure being.
> The kiss is still fully itself though no words were spoken.
> ("Words")

Nosferatu is a deliberate affront to what Gioia calls in his introduction to Robert McDowell's *The Diviners* "our sentimental, upbeat age." It is an assertion, as he says in that essay, of "the contradictory impulses at the center of the human heart." At the same time, however, *Nosferatu* is an opera—an example of an art which deliberately combines music, drama, and poetry, an art which is, to use a word Gioia uses, "integrative." We do not walk out of the theater feeling that we have confronted the horrific contradictions of human nature. Rather, we feel released, purified even. *Though the "material" of Gioia's work is violently contradictory—good vs. evil, light vs. darkness—its mode is persistently "integrative."* "Poetry," Gioia writes in *The Irish Review*,

> comes from a point in our past when we understood our own experience without separating our minds from our bodies, our logic from intuition and imagination . . . The poet's role remains primitive—namely to reflect existence truthfully as we experience it individually, which is to say, holistically . . . What 'taste' is . . . is an integrative faculty that all artists and readers consciously train and develop across their lifetimes; it integrates the intellect, emotions, imagination, intuition and the senses. Critical methodologies tend to be primarily analytical and consequently they are unable to grapple with the complex, holistic nature of poetry.

Gioia's assertions about "the new narrative"—"The new narrative must tell a memorable story in language that constantly delivers a lyric *frisson*"—and about opera—"While the structure of opera is narrative, its power is lyric"—are really assertions about the need for myth. It is only through a mythological construction that "the contradictory impulses at the center of the human heart" can be expressed, and the myth that is closest to Gioia's hand is the myth of Catholicism. Dracula is that myth turned round and darkened. There is a line in one of the poems in *Interrogations at Noon*, "A California Requiem," which is almost a description of the concluding scene of *Nosferatu*: "We are," Gioia writes, "like shadows the bright noon erases." Our lives are brief, fleeting, shadow-like. Yet the beauty of the "holistic" mythological construction, which combines the personal with the impersonal, the lyric with the narrative, gives us a tentative, problematical, fragile "immortality." In the world of art—if not in life—"toute énormité fleurit comme une fleur": "every outrage blossoms like a flower."[5]

The Achievement Of Dana Gioia

A talk delivered at the West Chester University Poetry Conference, June 2004

The title of this talk, "The Achievement of Dana Gioia," sounds a little as though Dana Gioia's "achievement" were over, finished. We usually deal with the "achievement" of dead writers such as Robert Frost or T.S. Eliot. Perhaps we should say instead, "The *Continuing* Achievement of Dana Gioia"; perhaps even—since he is still a young man—the possible *future* achievement of Dana Gioia.

Since childhood, Dana Gioia has been an achiever. "In my childhood milieu," he writes in his essay, "Lonely Impulse of Delight"—the title is from Yeats' "An Irish Airman Foresees His Death"—

> reading was associated with self-improvement. I suppose this uplifting motive played some role in my intellectual pursuits, but my insatiable appetite for books came mostly from curiosity and pleasure. I liked to read. I liked to study and investigate subjects that interested me . . . My interests changed and developed year by year.

He describes himself lying in bed and reading while his brother slept:

> Once we were in bed, [my parents] never forced us to turn off the lights—one of their countless kindnesses. Consequently, every night I read in bed, often for hours. When I remember my childhood reading, I see myself in Sears and Roebuck pajamas propped up under the covers devouring *The Circus of Dr. Lao*, *The Time Machine* or *The Lost World* while my younger brother Ted sleeps in the twin bed beside me. I usually kept the next book I planned to read on my nightstand—not so much as an incentive to finish my current selection but simply to provide anticipatory pleasure.

One thinks of him, not only as a child but as an adult, as continually *awake*, at the service of a consciousness (embodied initially in books) which is always prodding him to one more thought, one more new idea. "Even as a young boy," he writes, "I had trouble falling asleep."

Dana Gioia is the only member of the Bush administration consistently to receive good press—even ecstatic press—and that in itself is no mean "achievement." His enormous energy and his boundless sense of creative possibility—his sense of *play*—matched with his good sense, his practicality, have made him a magnificent chair of the National Endowment for the Arts. We all know this and are grateful. That too is an achievement. It is also of some importance that, though he is no priest, a public intellectual of Gioia's stature is speaking to a predominantly Protestant country from the point of view of Catholicism—not from the ordinary sense of Catholicism, perhaps, but from the point of view of Catholicism nonetheless. Hispanics, Italians, the Irish—all are predominantly Catholic people, and it is their voices that we can find echoed in his. Even further, he is a Westerner speaking to a country in which the principle sources of power—both cultural and political—tend to reside in the East: "I am Latin," he writes in "Fallen Western Star,"

(Italian, Mexican, and American Indian) without a drop of British blood in my veins, but English is my tongue. It belongs to me as much as to any member of the House of Lords. The classics of English—Shakespeare, Milton, Pope, and Keats—are my classics. The myths and images of its literature are native to my imagination. And yet this rich literary past often stands at one remove from the experiential reality of the West. Our seasons, climate, landscape, natural life, and history are alien to the world-views of both England and New England. Spanish—not French—colors our regional accent. The world looks and feels different in California from the way it does in Massachusetts or Manchester—not only the natural landscape but also the urban one. There is no use listening for a nightingale among the scrub oaks and chaparral. Our challenge is not only to find the right words to describe our experience but also to discover the right images, myths, and characters. We must describe a reality that has never been fully captured in English.

Gioia is also famous for his criticism, which is always articulate, provocative, intelligent, and passionately conceived. His essay—and then later the book—*Can Poetry Matter?* was a kind of trumpet blast of a new sensibility which had many important things to say and which—amazingly—was defending rhyme and meter in an intelligent, even compelling way. When recently I was putting together a collection of my essays, I discovered that almost all my best pieces referred to Gioia in some way. I didn't always agree with him, of course, but the effect he had on my thought was clearly far-reaching and profound. One could write a long essay on Gioia the critic. But, as is often the case with poet/critics, Gioia's criticism arises out of issues which inform his poetry. It is Dana Gioia the poet—the man of ideas who is also the man of emotions—that I wish to speak of today. Gioia's criticism is of considerable cultural importance—and it is beautifully written—but it is in poetry that his deepest achievement lies. In talking about his poetry I will move perhaps overly freely in and around various of Dana Gioia's books. I assume that most people in this room are familiar with them.

I once remarked upon the number of times the word "dark" appears in Dana Gioia's poetry; it is almost omnipresent. One finds it for example in the concluding lines of "Insomnia":

> The terrible clarity this moment brings,
> the useless insight, the unbroken dark.

Elegy and loss are important themes in this poet's work, but have you noticed how often violence enters Dana Gioia's poetry? His most recent book of poetry, *Interrogations at Noon*, has these lines via Seneca:

> Now, servants of the underworld, begin!
> Let my voice shake the deepest pit of hell
> And wake the Furies, daughters of the Night.
> Come to me sisters, with your hair aflame,
> With savage claws. Inflict your punishments.

And the concluding two stanzas of his brilliant poem, "The Homecoming," from *The Gods of Winter* are first, an ecstatic affirmation of violence—a giving in to it—and second, a disillusioned movement away from it. The word "dark" appears in the first stanza; the word "darkness" appears in the second. Interestingly, the first phrase of the first stanza, "I felt a sudden tremor of delight," comes close to Gioia's description of his childhood reading as "a lonely impulse of delight." (The books read by the protagonist of "The Homecoming" as a young man are essentially the same books Gioia read as a young man.)

"The Homecoming" is a dramatic monologue spoken by a man who has just escaped from prison; at the conclusion of the poem, the man murders his foster mother. His reaction to the murder is,

> I felt a sudden tremor of delight,
> a happiness that went beyond my body

as if the walls around me had collapsed,
and a small dark room where I had been confined
had been amazingly transformed by light.
Radiant and invincible, I knew
I was the source of energy, and all
the jails and sheriffs could not hold me back.
I had been strong enough. And I was free.

But as I stood there gloating, gradually
the darkness and the walls closed in again.
Sensing the power melting from my arms,
I realized the energy I felt
was just adrenaline—the phoney high
that violence unleashes in your blood.
I saw her body lying on the floor
and knew that we would always be together.
All I could do was wait for the police.
I had come home, and there was no escape.

The second stanza, beginning "But as I stood there gloating," is a point-by-point refutation of the first stanza. If "I was free" in the first stanza, in the second "there was no escape." If "I was the source of energy" in the first stanza, in the second stanza "the energy I felt / was just adrenaline—the phoney high / that violence unleashes in your blood."

Gioia clearly wishes us to feel that the protagonist's experience of "Radiance" and "invincibility" is a false form of true mystical experience: that it "was just adrenaline." Yet don't the lines as we initially experience them feel like a genuine evocation of a mystical state?

I felt a sudden tremor of delight,
a happiness that went beyond my body
as if the walls around me had collapsed,
and a small dark room where I had been confined
had been amazingly transformed by light.
Radiant and invincible, I knew
I was the source of energy, and all
the jails and sheriffs could not hold me back.
I had been strong enough. And I was free.

True, it is violence which causes this feeling of radiance and invincibility, but isn't there something about that passage which is utterly convincing? Aren't all mystical states temporary? Doesn't even the highest of mystical states involve a rush of "adrenaline"? Gioia writes in "A Lonely Impulse of Delight" that he "found spiritual sustenance . . . in *The Lives of the Saints*, especially in its vivid accounts of legendary hermits and martyrs."

What is the theme of violence doing in the consciousness of this most gentle of men, whom I have never once heard raise his voice in anger? Freudian notions of "repression" and the violence with which repressed contents sometimes announce themselves are of course relevant here. Like Freud, Gioia understands the mind to be a deeply divided entity. "I like writing poems that have a surface which executes one shape and a sub-text which executes another," he writes in *The Irish Review*. From this point of view, the "I" who says "I was free" represents deep-seated desires which the protagonist has suppressed and which are "let out"—freed—in a cathartic moment; this "I" is "Mister Hyde." But there is more to it than that. That we live in a violent nation and in an extremely violent historical period will come as no surprise to anyone in this audience, and in part the violence of Gioia's poems is an expression of this greater societal violence. (As a child, Gioia says, he lived in a "violent" neighborhood.)

But I would suggest that the violence we encounter in Gioia's poetry goes beyond Freudian or sociological categories. *It is the violence of thought itself.* Imagination, feelings of radiance and invincibility, announce themselves to Gioia in a profoundly disturbing, alienating way. They thrust him *out*, away from community, into what he calls in "A Lonely Impulse of Delight" "odd behavior," "secrecy," "the pattern of a double life," into behavior which is—as he writes—"clearly excessive, indeed almost shameful": "Not able to control this passion," he says, "I needed to hide it." This is his poem, "Country Wife"—the title perhaps echoes Frost's "The Hill Wife"—from *Daily Horoscope*. Each stanza of the poem is a triolet:

> She makes her way through the dark trees
> Down to the lake to be alone.
> Following their voices on the breeze,
> She makes her way. Through the dark trees
> The distant stars are all she sees.
> They cannot light the way she's gone.
> She makes her way through the dark trees
> Down to the lake to be alone.

> The night reflected on the lake,
> The fire of stars changed into water.
> She cannot see the winds that break
> The night reflected on the lake
> But knows they motion for her sake.
> These are the choices they have brought her:
> The night reflected on the lake,
> The fire of stars changed into water.

In the famous crossing-the-Alps passage of Wordsworth's *The Prelude*, Imagination is first seen as a negative force:

> Imagination—here the Power so called
> Through sad incompetence of human speech,
> That awful Power rose from the mind's abyss
> Like an unfathered vapour that enwraps,
> At once, some lonely traveler. I was lost. . . .

But the force's "strength / Of usurpation" transforms itself into sheer vision:

> The light of sense
> Goes out, but with a flash that has revealed
> The invisible world . . .
> Our destiny, our being's heart and home,
> Is with infinitude, and only there . . .

The great "achievement" of Dana Gioia's early life must have been the tempering of this impulse, the discovery of ways in which this ambiguous, violent, sleep-preventing wildness of consciousness could be used to good purpose, "the fire of stars changed into water." As "The Homecoming" demonstrates, "energy" is a violence which may result in the most appalling events. Yet, as Blake says—and as Gioia's poetry often demonstrates—energy is also eternal delight. Words are a place in which this violence—this power of imagination—can find a home, yet, as Gioia writes in *Interrogations at Noon*, "So much of what we live goes on inside," "The world does not need words." *Form* is a tempering device, and if Gioia is a formalist, he is a formalist whose stanzas burst with a Romantic understanding of consciousness and the poet's role. He opens *Interrogations at Noon* with a quotation from Flaubert:

> Human speech is like a cracked kettle on which we beat crude rhythms for bears to dance to, while we long to make music that will melt the stars.

One of the great tenets of American Puritanism is the notion that choosing is an unqualified good: it is what affirms us as human. (The great poem of Puritanism, Milton's *Paradise Lost*, is all about a *wrong choice*.) Dana Gioia's work is alive with choices which are *not quite* made—or, if made, made in the context of elegy rather than triumph, so that the thing chosen against retains some power. His work is a way of giving "local habitation and a name" to forces which exist in pure darkness and which simultaneously energize and threaten; indeed, the poet's task is precisely to retain the energy and to diminish the threat.

In Gioia's work there is always a secret world which intrudes itself upon the daylight world of ordinary consciousness. In "A Lonely Impulse of Delight" he asserts that "every true reader has a secret life, which is . . . intense, complex, and important . . . Our inner lives are as rich and real as our outer lives, even if they remain mostly unknowable to others." And he writes in the beautiful concluding poem of *Interrogations at Noon*,

> What we conceal
> Is always more than what we dare confide.
> Think of the letters that we write our dead.

Dana Gioia's energies extend in an extraordinary number of directions, and his poetry often circles around the notion of rediscovery—even, at times, of resurrection. Yet the elegiac is always at work as well. One sometimes wonders why a man named Joy writes poems of such sadness. At the core of his work are not only themes of the Romantic Imagination or violence or "the contradictory impulses at the center of the human heart"; at the core of his work are what Virgil called "lacrimae rerum," "the tears of things." Gioia's Nosferatu is a villain, yes, but he is also the secret hero of the play. And like everything else—like us—he vanishes. It is Dana Gioia's achievement to tell us these things in a way which is profound, funny, compelling, and always—like violence—provocative. He gives us the "fire" not as it is in itself but as it is reflected in the deep water of a poet's consciousness.

Annie Finch

Calendars, Centering and Decentering

The word rhythm ("flow") is applied to all the arts and to nature; meter ("measure") is a more specific term applied only to poetry. Aristotle said, "Meter is sections of rhythm." Meter, like "time" in music, is exact rhythm.

The meter of a poem is determined by the kind of metrical "foot" and by the number of feet in a line. A metrical foot is a unit of measure made up of accented and unaccented syllables.

—Jotted down in my childhood

∽

Trochee trips from long to short.
From long to long in solemn sort
Slow spondee stalks; strong foot! Yet ill able
Ever to come up with dactyl trisyllable.
Iambics march from short to long—
With a leap and a bound the swift anapaests throng.
—SAMUEL TAYLOR COLERIDGE, "Metrical Feet: Lesson for a Boy"

1.

Recently, poet Annie Finch put out a call for "poems in any non-iambic meters—anapests, sapphics, trochees, cretics, dactyls, amphibrachs, alcaics, or others." Only a short time ago, such a call would have been greeted with bewildered questions about what exactly anapests, sapphics, trochees, cretics, dactyls, amphibrachs (my favorite), and alcaics were. At this point, I'm sure Finch has received a flood of submissions. Her classic book, *The Ghost of Meter* (1993), is no doubt partly responsible for this situation.

Annie Finch's work on metrics is so interesting, illuminating and complex that it threatens to eclipse her considerable accomplishments as a poet. On the other hand, it is scarcely possible to talk about her poetry without talking about her poetics, which functions as a matrix out of which the poems emerge. In another poet, a poem like "Caribou Kitchen" might pass as somewhat rhythmical free verse—especially since Finch provides us with no end rhymes to guide our understanding of the rhythm:

> Most things have vanished
> while we were talking
> (the dents in a pitcher
> gleam by the gas lamp),
> but nothing is lost
> (cups in far corners).
> Arms still lean
> over the table
> (shadows on the oilcloth).

Yet notice the number of dactylic feet (stressed syllable followed by two unstressed syllables) in the poem: "Most things have," "gleam by the," "cups in far," "over the." The poem, like many others in *Calendars* (Tupelo Press, 2003), is structured around two "voices"[1] : one of the voices remarks in a somewhat abstract way, "Most things have vanished / while we were talking / but nothing is lost"; the other voice, in parentheses, notices only particulars ("dents in a pitcher," "the gas lamp," "cups in far corners"). The tension between these voices is to some degree resolved when the abstract voice illustrates its point by noting a particular—"Arms still lean / over the table"—while the other voice notes the "shadows" of those arms "on the oilcloth." Thesis/antithesis/synthesis.

The poem's title probably refers to a kitchen in the Cariboo Mountains, a part of the Rocky Mountains in southwest Canada. Yet "caribou" (reindeer) is by etymology "pawer," "scratcher," by virtue of the animal's digging in the snow to find food. We might dig a little as well.

In *The Ghost of Meter* Finch associates dactyls with "a feminized alternate system . . . something quieter, less established, more authentic"; with a "direct spirituality that is so quiet it is almost inaccessible"; with the "beautiful but inaccessible"; with "vagueness, night and the unspeakable"; with "the archetypal feminine rhythm of the sea" (this last, though prose, is a line that might be scanned). Finch opposes dactyls or triple rhythms to "iambic pentameter," the English heroic line—the meter of Shakespeare's plays. An "iamb" is an unstressed syllable followed by a stressed syllable, a "rising" rhythm; "pentameter" indicates five of these per line. Iambic pentameter, she argues, connotes "traditional literary sanctity," "traditional patriarchal conventions," "the normal conventional human supports." She even goes so far as to refer to "the fatal stupefaction" of iambic pentameter. Finch's own work involves the search for "a [non-iambic] countermeter that is more oriented toward human experience." With this in mind, look at the poem again.

The first two lines are made up of a dactyl followed by a trochee (stressed syllable followed by unstressed)—a "falling" rhythm. The next line is similar, especially since "the" can be read as an "extra" syllable, and "gleam by the gas lamp" brings us back to a strict dactyl/trochee combination. The phase "but nothing is lost" concludes the thought and, appropriately, ends on a stressed syllable. (The "rising" rhythm here is qualified by the falling rhythm of the next line.) The surprise of the poem, the moment when it "turns," is in the next line, which barely resembles any other line in the poem. "Arms still lean" is made up of three stressed syllables—and, for a moment, from the point of view of rhythm, we have absolutely no idea where the poem may go.

Where it goes is back to beginning: "over the table" echoes the dactyl/trochee combination of the opening lines. The poem then ends with a perfectly regular trochaic tetrameter (four stresses). The "meaning" of the poem, the interplay between the two voices and its resolution, is reasonably straightforward. Yet, throughout the poem, the insistent play of the rhythm suggests something more. What are those dactyls, hinting of "vagueness, night and the unspeakable," doing there? What world beyond the safety of the kitchen do they suggest? Is it a world in which things *are* lost—as opposed to the kitchen? Is it a place in which wild animals like caribou forage for food? What does the word "shadows" have to do with the word "gleam"—or with the word "vanished"? Indeed, the concluding line, which I read as a perfectly regular trochaic tetrameter, might be read as still another dactyl/trochee combination if we observe the old-fashioned verse practice of eliding the "e" in "the" with the vowel which follows it. The line would then be "shadows on th'oilcloth"—clumsy perhaps but regular. Even without the elision—and despite the fact that it seems to be regular—the line oddly, and disturbingly, echoes the lines preceding it. The specific action of the poem and its meaning are one thing; but there is another area, equally meaningful but hidden, problematical, "dark"—one might call it "rhythm"—and this latter is perhaps the environing circumstance out of which the poem's specific oppositions arise. In the world of rhythm a line like "Most things have vanished" and a line like "cups in far corners" echo one another, though in the world of explicit meaning they tend towards opposition. One might say that Finch's poem simultaneously generates oppositions, attempts to resolve them—and attempts as well to move beyond them.

2.

A "calendar" marks time—indeed, it *measures* time and so has a "metrical" function—and Finch carefully dates the poems in *Calendars*. "Caribou Kitchen," written in 1970, is the earliest. "Watching the Oregon Whale" (2000), quoted here in full, is the most recent:

> A hard gray wave, her fin, walks out on the water
> that thickens to open and then parts open, around her.
>
> Measured by her delved water, I follow her fill
> into and out of green light in the depth she has spun
>
> through the twenty-six fathoms of her silent orison,
> then sink with her till she rises, lulled with the krill.
>
> Beads of salt spray stop me, like metal crying.
> Her cupped face breathes its spouts, like a jewel-wet prong.
>
> In a cormorant's barnacle path, I trail her, spun
> down through my life in the making of her difference,
>
> fixing my mouth, with the offerings of silence,
> on her dark whale-road where all green partings run,
>
> where ocean's hidden bodies twist fathoms around her,
> making her green-fed hunger grow fertile as water.

I don't know whether Finch has read D.H. Lawrence's famous poem, "Whales Weep Not!," but it's interesting to compare Lawrence's poem to "Watching the Oregon Whale." Not surprisingly, Lawrence focuses on mating, "dark rainbow bliss in the sea." These are some lines from "Whales Weep Not!":

And they rock and they rock, through the sensual ageless ages
on the depths of the seven seas,
and through the salt they reel with drunk delight
and in the tropics tremble they with love
and roll with massive, strong desire, like gods.
Then the great bull lies up against his bride
in the blue deep of the sea
as mountain pressing on mountain, in the zest of life;
and out of the inward roaring of the inner red ocean of whale blood
the long tip reaches strong, intense, like a maelstrom-tip, and comes to rest
in the clasp and the soft, wild clutch of a she-whale's fathomless
      body.

And over the bridge of the whale's strong phallus, linking the wonder of whales
the burning archangels under the sea keep passing, back and forth,
keep passing archangels of bliss
from him to her, from her to him, great Cherubim. . . .

Lawrence's poem is deeply phallic—"over the bridge of the whale's strong phallus, linking the wonder of whales"—but its phallocentrism does not represent the male member as a weapon, which is the way the phallus is commonly represented in our culture: "This is my rifle / This is my gun / This is for fighting / This is for fun." (Ironically, that doggerel vulgarity is strict dactylic/trochaic—very similar to Finch's.) In Lawrence, the phallus—which, if we disregard the opening word, is imaged here in nearly exact dactylic heptameter (seven stresses)—is understood as a "bridge," a "rainbow," and it stands at the center of a communal vision. "Whales Weep Not!" is an image of an ancient community of whales, not of a single whale or even of a couple: "And they rock and they rock, through the sensual ageless ages."

Now, iambic pentameter has a powerful association not only with phallocentricity—with patriarchy—but with war. Unrhymed iambic pentameter—blank verse—was invented by the 16th-century poet Henry Howard, Earl of Surrey, for the specific purpose of translating the *Aeneid*, a poem which begins with one of the most famous dactyls in Western poetry: *Arma virumque cano* ("Arms and the man I sing")—hardly the kind of dactyl Finch has in mind. Iambic pentameter was designed to be the English equivalent to Virgil's dactylic hexameters (themselves the equivalents to Homer's dactylic hexameters). It is part of a tradition of Western poetry which, again and again, is a profound celebration of war. The line I have just quoted from "Whales Weep Not" is strictly pentameter—five stresses—but it is *not* iambic. Very likely influenced by Whitman's dactyls (as in "Out of the Cradle Endlessly Rocking"), Lawrence is producing a perfectly regular pentameter line full of triple rhythms—in this case, anapests (two unstressed syllables followed by a stressed syllable). As Coleridge accurately points out in "Metrical Feet," you can "march" to iambic pentameter—even to a relatively peaceful version of it: "The curfew tolls the knell of parting day." Triple rhythms give us something closer to a dance—again as Coleridge suggests: "With a leap and a bound the swift anapests throng." (In *The Ghost of Meter* Finch describes the anapest as a "bridge" between the iamb and the dactyl: "anapestic rhythm," she writes, is "a rising rhythm like the iamb but a triple rhythm like the dactyl" and so "has a bridging function.")

Lawrence's rhythms are an attempt to convey the dance-like movements of the whales as he imagines them under the water. The line lengths vary ("in the clasp and the soft, wild clutch of a she-whale's fathomless body" is anapestic hexameter) but triple rhythms clearly predominate. Lawrence is imagining a patriarchy—but it is a patriarchy which makes love, not war. (There is a moment when the whales are threatened: then the "bull-whales gather their women and whale-calves in a ring . . . and range themselves like great fierce Seraphim facing the threat"—but there is never any question of imperial conquest. Melville's *Moby Dick* is an obvious influence on Lawrence's poem— Lawrence wrote a book on *Classic American Literature*—but these whales are at some distance from Melville's "killer.")

Finch's poem begins with something she can see—she is "whale watching" in Oregon:

> A hard gray wave, her fin, walks out on the water
> that thickens to open and then parts open, around her.

The whale is definitely female, but there is just a hint of an androgynous phallic power in that "fin" ("a hard gray wave")—especially since "the water . . . thickens to open and then parts open." The theme of fertility—hinted at in "Caribou Kitchen"—is important here as well: the word "green" repeats ("green light," "green partings," "green-fed hunger") and the poem concludes with the phrase "fertile as water." For a poet as concerned with metrics as Finch is, the word "measured" is important as well. Finch herself is "measured" by the whale's "delved water"—the "depths" to which the creature is capable of descending—and suddenly finds herself following, led on by the beckoning of a "green light":

> I follow her fill
> into and out of green light in the depth she has spun
> through the twenty-six fathoms of her silent orison,
> then sink with her till she rises. . . .

The whale's descent into the depths is understood as a "silent" prayer—an "orison." (Inevitably, one thinks of Hamlet's line to Ophelia: "Nymph, in thy orisons, be all my sins remembered": in Shakespeare too, the word is associated with a female figure.) Suddenly the poet's reverie is interrupted by "beads of salt spray," which awaken her to her separateness from the whale. In the very next moment, however, she becomes "a cormorant" and follows the whale in that form:

> I trail her, spun
> down through my life in the making of her difference,
>
> fixing my mouth, with the offerings of silence,
> on her dark whale-road. . . .

Though Finch is acutely aware of her "difference" from the whale, she is nonetheless "spun / down through" her own life—and, interestingly, it is not her eyes but her "mouth" which is fixed "on [the] dark whale-road." The phrase "offerings of silence" deliberately echoes the phrase "silent orison": the poet's words—still not formed, still "silent"—and the whale's action of diving into the depths are both "offerings," "prayers." The poem closes with a vision of the depths of the sea,

> where ocean's hidden bodies twist fathoms around her,
> making her green-fed hunger grow fertile as water.

One thinks, as both parallel and contrast, "Full fathom five thy father lies. . . ."

The whale's falling and rising, rising and falling is not unlike the spirals and repetitions of triple feet in a poet's line. It is not in the least like a "march." The poem's lines, however, are nonetheless pentameter—five stresses in each. Furthermore, the poem is—surprisingly—a sonnet, though it is arranged in couplets and oddly rhymed: aa bc cb dd ce ed aa—returning in a circular way to its beginning at the conclusion. In her introduction to *A Formal Feeling Comes: Poems in Form by Contemporary Women*, Finch writes, "A number of contributors, sensitive to the gender implications of form, write in historically powerful poetic forms in order to transform them and claim some of their strength. Rita Dove, for example, describes her chosen form (the sonnet) as 'stultifying,' but hears voices in it that are 'sing[ing] in their chains.'" It is such a "transformed" sonnet that Finch has produced here—fourteen rhyming pentameter lines.

The "traditional" sonnet is a poem about love. Written by a man, it often addresses an idealized woman, sometimes referred to as a "goddess." In Finch's poem we are aware that the speaker is a woman—presumably Finch herself—and, if it is a love poem, it is only a love poem in a sense. In "Coherent Decentering: Towards a New Model of the Poetic Self" (published in *Beyond Confession*, ed. David Graham and Kate Sontag), Finch writes, "As a woman, I knew too much about how it feels to be something—nightingale, urn, woman—that is an object in other people's eyes." As a woman, Finch might well be the object of a male sonnet. Here, she is turning the tables—but only to a degree. Unlike Elizabeth Barrett Browning—who wrote sonnets to her husband—Finch is writing a sonnet to a creature. Moreover, the creature is not seen—as it is in Lawrence's poem—as part of a community but as an isolated figure, not unlike the "solitary" bird to which Whitman addresses "Out of the Cradle Endlessly Rocking." The poet and the object the poet sees become the poles of the poem, and the poem is entirely about their interaction and their problematical similarity/dissimilarity. What does the whale, brilliantly alive in "the archetypal feminine rhythm of the sea," signify?

In "Poetry and the Goddess," a fascinating, still unpublished paper, Finch writes that "In Goddess-oriented spirituality, the attitude towards the body is the opposite to that in mainstream Judeo-Christianity: dirt, blood, sex, soul, earth, death, animal are not to be transcended but are direct embodiments of the immanent Goddess":

> In a poetics of thea-logy as opposed to theology, connections of shape and identity within and between poems are not accidental or annoying, but crucial. For one thing, a strong skeleton of pattern and coherence, from this perspective, gives more freedom for the self to lose its egoistic identity.

It is precisely in the area of form that "the self" loses "its egoistic identity" and becomes, as Finch puts it in "Coherent Decentering," a "decentered self." On the level of content, "Watching the Oregon Whale" deliberately maintains the distance between the poet and the whale. We never lose the sense of the pronoun "I"—which remains separate from the "she/her" of the whale. But as mythologized entity—as "embodiment of the immanent Goddess"—the whale-as-deity *includes* the poet, who, looking to find the "goddess within," finds it "without," in a whale. An "orison"—a prayer—is something which is repeated over and over again for centuries in the same form and often in the same place. So too a formal poem recognizes the fact that others have spoken in this particular way. Though the poet's eyes keep her at a distance from the whale, her mouth "fixes" itself on the "dark whale-road." In the *speaking* of a "traditional" form the poet merges with others. (Interestingly, the poem ends with an "oral" image: "her green-fed hunger."[3] Finch often writes of the poem's "body": here we have "where ocean's hidden bodies twist fathoms around her." It is the only moment in the poem where we are given a sense of the whale's community.)

Annie Finch is rightly associated with formalism. But she insists on an enormous amount of freedom within her formalism: her lines are rarely exactly the same. The opening line of "Watching the Oregon Whale" begins with three iambics—"A hard gray wave, her fin." That is followed by a single stress ("walks") and then a dactyl ("out on the") and a trochee ("water"). The line can also be read as four iambics and an anapest, with an extra unstressed syllable, but Finch's emphasis on dactyls gives them a special character in her work, and anapests have a tendency to turn into their opposite: dactyls. Certainly the poem is filled with triple rhythms ("In a cormorant's barnacle path, I trail her, spun," "then sink with her till she rises, lulled with the krill"). Whatever the interplay of the various feet—Finch favors "metrical diversity" not only among poems but within them[2]—the poem is definitely "non-iambic," and the concluding line settles into a predominantly dactylic form: dactyl, trochee, dactyl, dactyl, trochee. "Meter," Finch writes in *A Formal Feeling Comes,*

> led me into—and out of—my own labyrinths [one thinks of the whale and the ocean depths in "Watching the Oregon Whale"] when I could no longer "think of anything to say" in free verse. I was raised to feel that form was illicit, and experiments in form still feel to me like forays into the outlawed wilderness. Because of the excitement this generates, and because of the absorbing challenges of formal poetic craft, communion with form can distract me, so that the poem comes out by itself.

If on the one hand Finch insists upon "dactylic rhythm as an alternative to [iambic] pentameter," on the other hand she recognizes "the persistent power of the pentameter to order experience." In her important essay on T.S. Eliot in *The Ghost of Meter* she offers a "reconciliation" between dactyls and iambics. Finch is a formalist who has been through the experience of free verse and who is trying to redefine "traditional" forms in a way which will allow her to function in what amounts to an unprecedented fashion. Her mind has a strong "oppositional" cast—a very "Western," even "patriarchal" trait—which leads her to think in terms of antitheses or "opposing forces," as she says in the paradoxically-titled "Coherent Decentering": iamb vs. dactyl, male vs. female forms, self vs. no-self. At the same time, however, she writes in that same essay of her fervent belief in "the falseness and unnecessariness of the subject-object distinction," a distinction which in fact she affirms as much as she denies. In "Coherent Decentering," the poet's father tells her,

> That idea you have of being separate from the world is a habit. It's just an illusion! It's a way you have of thinking *about* experience, and it gets in the way of true experience. It's not necessary for the self to be separate.[4]

Finch comments, "Already I knew he was right, because of my quiet hours in nature I had felt the consciousness of a rock, a berry, a leaf just as I felt my own consciousness . . . The more I thought about these themes, the more I found myself writing poems that turn object into subject . . . and poems that turn subject into object. . . ." *Both* subject and object may be transcended in the realm of "rhythm" and metrics—rhythm and metrics can be seen as the primary materia out of which various subjects and objects emerge—but Finch has a tendency to identify her rhythm and metrics with "a *feminized* alternate system . . . something quieter, less established, more authentic" (my italics), so rhythm and metrics become part of a polarization, an attempt to *avoid* iambic pentameter. At other times, of course, rhythm is understood, like the ocean itself, as the "mother" of everything, including iambic pentameter. "The Goddess is not simply present in everything," Finch writes in "Poetry and the Goddess," The Goddess *is* everything." It is out of such fruitful, unresolved tensions, such "opposing forces"—"fertile as water"—that her poems arise.

Indeed, the poems can be seen, like the whale's appearance and disappearance, as extraordinarily complex balancing acts. Finch writes that "dactylic passages . . . carry compelling connotations of the unconscious, the body, female energy, and the power of nature" ("Dactylic Meter: A Many-Sounding Sea," *An Exaltation of Forms*—again associating the dactyl with the ocean), but she also writes of "the irrationality and loss of control traditionally associated with triple meters" (*The Ghost of Meter*). Finch is not only *using* meter, she is *mythologizing* it. The words "dactyl" and "Goddess" are more or less interchangeable ways of naming a power which seems to reside at the very center of this poet's consciousness, and her essay, "Coherent Decentering" is an attempt to deal with both the positive and negative aspects of that power. The essay is haunted by "the incoherent worldview that is a *sine qua non* of much contemporary avant-garde poetics." Through "syntactic coherence," Finch hopes to achieve a "counterpoise of energies that incorporates, as all balance does, opposing forces: center and circumference (to use Dickinson's terms), coherence and incoherence, boundary and core." In this passage Finch has managed to neutralize the charged word "incoherence" by placing it in a list which also includes a generalizing statement about "balance," the words "coherence," "boundary," and "core," and a literary reference to a revered precursor. But fears are not to be quelled so easily, and "silence" is one of the most frequently repeated words in *Calendars*. The penultimate poem of the book concludes (in free verse),

> Something's waiting to run out on us.
> The mist
> and creak
> of wines is due
> when we run out of dusk.

If Finch is heir to the modernist perception of multiplicity—"the multiplicity of patterned and formal structures," "the complex fertility and multiply-detailed generosity of the Earth" ("Poetry and the Goddess")—she is also heir to modernist anxieties (explicit in both Pound and Eliot) that the work fails to "cohere," that it is a disunity, a madness expressing "irrationality and loss of control."[5] Behind such fears is the fear that the poet's self, like the work, also fails to "cohere." *"The 'I' is not unified,"* she writes in "Coherent Decentering" (my italics).

Finch insists in "Poetry and the Goddess" that "my . . . motivation for writing in form . . . is a positive force," but her conception of form clearly has a considerable dark side. The issue is complicated by the poet's own strong tendency to see things in "oppositional" rather than "multiple" terms. Though her essay on "T.S. Eliot and the Metrical Crisis of the Early Twentieth Century" is an attempt to show the ultimate compatibility of iambic pentameter and "dactylic rhythm," she is acutely aware that "the harmony of coexisting meters and voices pulls apart," and the overall impression left by *The Ghost of Meter* is not one of harmony but of opposition. Indeed, the book postulates a history in which one poetic foot, the dactyl, is constantly at war with another foot, the iamb (particularly in its pentameter form). Where is "the multiplicity of patterned and formal structures" in this scheme? I am not saying that Finch is being in any way hypocritical or even self-deceiving. It is precisely her powerful desire to remain open to her own consciousness that involves her in so much complexity, contradiction, and richness of perception.

3.

Annie Finch suggests, accurately and often brilliantly, that triple rhythms are associated with "the feminine," and her perception brings her to a number of very interesting readings of male poets. Nowhere does she mention, however, that triple rhythm is also explicitly (and widely) associated with comic verse. It isn't difficult to find examples:

> When you're lying awake with a dismal headache,
>   and repose is taboo'd by anxiety,
> I conceive you may use any language you choose
>   to indulge in, without impropriety;
> For your brain is on fire—the bedclothes conspire
>   of usual slumber to plunder you:
> First your counterpane goes, and uncovers your toes,
>   and your sheet slips demurely from under you.
> —W.S. GILBERT, "Nightmare"

⁊

> "What do you paint, when you paint a wall?"
> Said John D.'s grandson Nelson.
> "Do you paint just anything there at all?
> "Will there be any doves, or a tree in fall?
> "Or a hunting scene, like an English hall?"
> "I paint what I see," said Rivera.
> —E.B. WHITE, "I Paint What I See"

⁊

> Oh to be Machiavellian, oh to be unscrupulous,
>   Oh to be glib!
> Oh to be ever prepared with a plausible fib!
> —OGDEN NASH, "Golly, How Truth Will Out"

Even

> When I was a windy boy and a bit
> And the black spit of the chapel fold,
> (Sighed the old ram rod, dying of women),
> I tiptoed shy in the gooseberry wood,
> The rude owl cried like a telltale tit,
> I skipped in a blush as the big girls rolled
> Ninepin down on the donkeys' common,
> And on seesaw sunday nights I wooed
> Whoever I would with my wicked eyes. . . .
> —DYLAN THOMAS, "Lament"

though Thomas is also capable of wonderfully magical triple rhythms, as here, in a passage clearly associated with "the feminine":

> Never and never, my girl riding far and near
> In the land of the hearthstone tales, and spelled asleep,
> Fear or believe that the wolf in a sheepwhite hood
> Loping and bleating roughly and blithely shall leap,
> > My dear, my dear,
> Out of a lair in the flocked leaves in the dew dipped year
> To eat your heart in the house in the rosy wood.
> ("In Country Sleep")

Annie Finch is her own person, but her work reminds me a little of the work of Adelaide Crapsey, an American poet who died of tuberculosis in 1914 at the age of thirty-six. At her death, Crapsey had completed two-thirds of her *Analysis of English Metrics*, described by Jean Webster in the 1915 *Vassar Miscellany* as "an exhaustive scientific thesis relating to accent . . . which, years before, she had planned to accomplish as her serious life work":

> Though her mind was intensely preoccupied with the technical and analytical aspects of prosody, still the creative, artistic side of her nature was so spontaneously alive, that she accomplished a very considerable volume of original poetry—almost as a by-product of her study in metrics.

Finch's poetry is no "by-product of her study in metrics," but one senses in her work the spirit of such half-forgotten, fiercely non-modernist writers as

Crapsey or Sara Teasdale. These lines, by Crapsey—the inventor of the cinquain—sound eerily like Finch:

Grain Field

Scarlet the poppies
Blue the corn-flowers,
Golden the wheat.
Gold for The Eternal:
Blue for Our Lady:
Red for the five
Wounds of her Son.

Jesus the "Son" is present here, but God the Father—except for a vague reference to "The Eternal," an elided phrase—is not, and the "Lady" of Crapsey's imagination is deeply connected, like Finch's Goddess, to the earth: poppies, cornflowers, wheat. "The Goddess," writes Finch, "is not simply present in everything. The Goddess *is* everything . . . she is the world." (Finch speaks, amusingly if extravagantly, of "free verse monotheism.") Like Finch's, Crapsey's poem is full of dactyls, triple rhythms, feminine endings, with each of the concluding lines resolving itself in a single stressed syllable. Like Finch, Crapsey is Goddess-based and decidedly non-iambic.

Annie Finch is perhaps the *revenge* of writers like Adelaide Crapsey. One hears them both with fascination and renewed interest. "The decentered self is like the head of Medusa," writes Finch in "Coherent Decentering": "If you try to look at it directly, you will turn to stone and be thrown right back into the egotistical Self. By contrast, coherent decentering uses language's common syntactic capacities to create the *experience* of the decentered self for the reader, rather than depicting it."

Filled with "opposing forces"—and coherently incoherent—Annie Finch's poetry seduces and changes.

Diane di Prima

Recollections Of My Life As A Woman: The New York Years

I am not in the flame, I am the flame
—DIANE DI PRIMA, "Canticle of St. Joan"

The following quotation is one of the central perceptions of Diane di Prima's long-awaited, riveting memoir, *Recollections of My Life as a Woman: The New York Years* (Viking, 2001). The perception is linked to various incidents in di Prima's life—particularly to her taking peyote and to her clandestine love affair with the married LeRoi Jones (Amiri Baraka):

> These new poems of mine ["The Jungle," "The Ballroom," "The Party," "The Beach," "Lord Jim," "The Yeoman of the Guard," "Blackout"], with their longer lines and almost deadly certainty, had already begun before Roi knocked on my door. They had begun with my first peyote trip, and with the vast permission I had found in Jimmy Waring's "composition classes." But now, as my emotional life came to a strong, though temporary, focus—this new work, too, came to a fruition: a powerful voice found its way through me and into the world. The first of many voices that would speak through me, now that I no longer sought to control the poem.
>
> *For isn't it not that we "find our voice" as poetry teachers are so fond of saying, but rather that voices find us, and perhaps we welcome them? Is not poetry a dance from possession to possession—"obsession" in the full sense the word had in nineteenth-century magick? We are "ridden" as by the gods.*

The perception is all the stronger because it seems to move in a direction opposite to the primary direction of di Prima's life: the assertion of her will— a word which is often capitalized in this book. Indeed, the word "control"— present in the above quotation—echoes throughout *Recollections of my Life as a Woman*, as in the author's assertion that her "struggle for control over my own life had been an epic one" or "what I heard from lovers, was that I was a controlling or castrating bitch." One feels at times that perhaps the worst thing that can happen to di Prima is something occurring "against her will." Yet the poem "comes to fruition" as something *outside* the poet's "control"—outside her "will." One thinks of a remark Stanley Fish makes in his recent book, *How Milton Works*: Milton, writes Fish, "longs to be absorbed by a power greater than he." At the same time, Milton "experiences absorption as a threat . . . to his very being." Di Prima's statement is an assertion of a truth which is at some distance from what "poetry teachers are so fond of saying." If it contradicts those teachers—and even contradicts some aspects of di Prima's own experience—so be it: that is the nature of "truth."

There is no doubt that *Recollections of my Life as a Woman* stirs up strong feelings. A woman friend of mine attended a reading di Prima was giving to publicize the book. Di Prima read the following passage:

> When Billie [Holiday] was coming to Carnegie Hall there was no way I could have gone. No way to afford it. But I had a friend, a kind of acquaintance on the fringe of the scene, a woman named Joan McCarthy who liked us all very much and would invite us over to eat steak and talk. She was a woman who was not like any of us at all, she held a straight job, had no imagination, nothing in her mind or conversation flew, and we were always fondly exasperated or outright angry when we left her house. I think she was glamorized, fascinated by us all.
>
> Miraculously, Joan McCarthy invited me to go with her to hear Billie Holiday; she had two tickets. Never before or after do I remember being invited, or going, anywhere with Joan. Just this one miracle.
>
> Naturally I said yes.

And naturally di Prima loves the concert. "Tonight," she writes, "[Billie Holiday] went still deeper, into a whole other dimension, and took us with her."

The passage, which is an eloquent tribute to Billie Holiday, implicitly asks us to identify ourselves with di Prima and her friends—and to see Joan McCarthy as an outcast: "a woman who was not like any of us." Yet, as she listened, my friend found herself identifying with Joan McCarthy. She began to see di Prima's curt dismissal of the woman ("she held a straight job, had no imagination, nothing in her mind or conversation flew") as cruel, perhaps even unfair. "As Diane has felt the class prejudice of the literary world," my friend writes, "I have felt the sting of elitism within the world of 'artists.'" Joan McCarthy was doing di Prima a favor, after all. Does she deserve this attack—with full name included? McCarthy was, my friend writes, "a woman who perhaps imagined that if Diane di Prima heard Billie Holiday, it might change her life"—which, indeed, it does. Why is di Prima so cruel to her? Because she is not an artist—only someone interested in di Prima and her friends? Why should di Prima repay a kindness with a cruelty?

These questions cannot be answered within the context of the book. We hear nothing more of Joan McCarthy. Yet, for my friend, there were other disturbing moments as well: "I'm content to applaud artists and be supportive," she writes: "I haven't wished for more. In particular, life stories that include extreme selfishness combined with children do not interest me. Deceiving men and then belittling them is not feminist doctrine . . . I like her work very much and what little I know of her as well. That's exactly why I'm so angry to discover that she wasn't all that I wanted her to be."

My friend remains sympathetic to di Prima, and what she wrote me by no means represents her final judgment: "I've written you at least a half dozen unsent letters regarding di Prima's life. Often, I wish I'd never read the memoir. It lands in my thoughts daily. . . ."

How indeed is one to deal with di Prima's anger, fear, willfulness—her paranoid sense of the world as "war" and of herself as one of the very few intelligent people in this life-threatening situation:

> War is everywhere. For me it is everywhere: the War between my parents, the War between myself and the entity they are, the War between all the family and what I have gathered is a hostile world. My father goes out into it and returns discouraged. There is War upon War in my world, and they are all muted, hushed—my parents never argue.
>
> There is also some vast global entity called the War which keeps coming closer . . . In my child's mind they are all one, these Wars . . . And then something else takes over, a fury fills my child's body, almost burns out the circuits: I am in their hands, and they [her parents] are helpless, cowed people. Anger pours through me . . . I will have to *think* to trick them into keeping alive. Into keeping me alive . . . They are bowed: sad, intimidated people, and I suspect even then, somewhat stupid. I'm on my own from here on out.

At one point di Prima describes how she came to believe in "the relative uselessness of men"—an opinion she seems to maintain throughout her life, despite her many connections with men:

> In the turbulent 1930s into which I was born, my grandmother taught me that the things of woman go on: that they are the very basis and ground of human life. Babies are born and raised, the food is cooked. The world is cleaned and mended

and kept in order. Kept sane. That one could live with dignity and joy even in poverty. That even tragedy and shock and loss require this basis of loving attendance.

And that men were peripheral to all this . . . I grew up thinking them a luxury.

Are men relatively useless? Do we have to believe that in order to maintain sympathy for this writer? Di Prima certainly likes some men and dislikes others, just as she likes some women and dislikes others. She is probably unfair to many men in the same way that she is unfair to Joan McCarthy. The male Shunryu Suzuki Roshi, however, "was the first person I ever met for whom I felt immediate and total trust." Di Prima's married lover, LeRoi Jones /Amiri Baraka—with whom she is "in love" for a long period—is presented rather unsympathetically. The book makes it clear why she is angry at him, but less clear why she should love him. For a sense of her deep connection to this brilliant poet we must go to early di Prima poems such as "The Yeomen of the Guard," which ends,

> tomorrow, I said, I shall polish the floor,
> make curtains
> tomorrow I shall come to the door w/ my hair down
> the mistress *par excellence*
> & offer you brandy
>
> you shall brush my hair
> like Charles Boyer in a movie
> & I (like Hedy Lamarr) shall tilt back my head
> & suddenly smile

"To the Spectre of the Lecturer, Long Dead" is particularly moving: it begins, "Why it should all / come clear to me now: betrayal" and ends,

> 8 years after & for the first time it comes as pain
> comes clear
>   what I walked out on
> To turn one's back on love
>   & walk away
> like Casablanca,
>   I hear the roar
> of yr pain/ my pain that I never
> touched, or acknowledged,

> my hands
> pressed over eyelids, hair short too
> not at all
> what you remember

Interestingly, both passages see romance in terms of the movies—which is certainly one way to see romance. (The two films referred to, *Algiers*, 1938, and *Casablanca*, 1942, both take place in exotic locales and deal with doomed, somewhat illicit love.)

But the main point is that the "unfairness" of *Recollections of my Life as a Woman* is preeminently di Prima's, not somebody else's. It arises out of a life which is lived, if possible, to the hilt: "We had no vocabulary for these things," she writes. "No concepts, really for what was happening. Another world was breaking through to ours, and we were awash in it."

Recollections of my Life as a Woman does not offer us a sense of a "complete," "finished" selfhood, not even the "outlaw artist renunciant" selfhood to which di Prima returns often. The book is passionate moments, extraordinary events, and powerfully-held ("usually strong and vociferous") opinions. Whether the opinions are "correct" is another matter. They are unquestionably di Prima's. I believe my friend's discomfort with this book is precisely the right reaction to it. It is the price both di Prima and the reader pay for the book's "willingness to peer into darkness. Struggle for Truth." Di Prima is utterly determined not to be like the people of her parents' world—and that determination leaves its mark on her. "I proceeded to break the rules of that Italianate familial world, one by one," she writes. (Note, however, that her opinion that men are "relatively useless" arises directly out of "that Italianate familial world" which she claims to be rejecting.)

> Disappointment or loss marked the men of that world. And silence; one simply didn't talk about it.
>
> Disappointment and silence marked the women too. But there the silence lay deeper. No tales were told about them. They did not turn from one career to another, "take up the law," but buried the work of their hearts in the basement, burned their poems and stories, lost the thread of their dreams.

Such honesty and eloquence are characteristic of the entire book and make it an enormously important document of the late Twentieth Century. Di Prima's story is by no means everyone's—she is in many ways a very odd person and contradictions abound—but there are living insights here which you will find nowhere else.

I want to close this essay with a long, searing, marvelous passage from the book. This statement is at once beautifully written, enormously insightful, and obviously true. It's a kind of underside to di Prima's famous poem, "Rant"—and ought to be required reading for anyone even considering being a poet. Di Prima is told by a "prospective editor at Knopf" that an influential neighbor of hers is "vociferously against publishing [her] work, which—he declared—wasn't poetry at all." She comments,

[It] may be that I had run into one of my first real encounters with class prejudice in the literary world. This is something that nobody talks about much, but it is very very real. There are to this day accepted and prestigious modes of entry into that world that are based simply on race, gender, class and/or money, and everybody knows about them and nobody acknowledges them.

Take, for example, the simple expedient of going to one of the right literary colleges, and while there using family dollars to start a slick but arty literary magazine. Many prestigious writers will happily send you work, if your "product" looks tasteful and expensive. And one name leads to another, of course. Presto, before you know it you are not only an editor and publisher, but a *writer*, for god's sake, a literary personage to be reckoned with (whether you can really write a word or not). You instantaneously wield a certain amount of power, and—unless you do something unspeakably gauche—no one is going to venture a word against you.

And this is only one of the more innocent and harmless methods of becoming part of the literary landscape.

Look at what it takes in the way of financial backup to be available to travel and read your work at the ridiculously low rates they offer at first. How much money you need to show up in the right places at the right times: poetry conferences, arts festivals, or to publish endlessly in non-paying "little magazines," spend a small fortune on postage, spend the equivalent of a part-time job in work hours on gratuitous (often inane and pompous) literary correspondence, etc. There is simply no way to persist in all these activities, and not only persist but convey a sense of ease and pleasure in them, in the "literary life," per se, no way, I tell you, to have the time, space, and finances to continue these games indefinitely, without some kind of private income. So that you are free to make your decisions not based on what will help you survive for the next month, what will get the rent paid and food on the table, but on what will aid and abet your literary career, keep you visible, by god, put you at the right conference, in the right city, the right anthology or magazine, the right agent's or publisher's office at the right moment.

And all the other denizens of that world, your fellow-literary-playmates-whatever want and need your unspoken assurance that the living is easy, that no unsightly issue such as the bills, or medicine for the kids, or the bouncing check you wrote the airline to get there to do that reading in the first place, is on your mind when you show up to play with them. They crave this assurance of ease.

It is a gentleman's life for sure, and my upstairs neighbor—who had no doubt won his own place in that life with just the right mixture of money and academia, subservience and arrogance—was quite right in sensing that I was an upstart who had no place in it at all.

In years to come I would encounter the same barriers time and again; they would rise up in response to my politics, my mode of dress, my deliberately cultivated Italian/American manner, New York accent, the concerns of the characters in my short stories, the street slang in my poems.

Or I would stand stubbornly in the wings at some powerful and prestigious university, refusing to go on, demanding payment in front for some lecture or reading, while the powers-that-be assured me that the check would arrive in the mail in about two months. It was painfully clear at those moments that I was *not* one of the boys, and it worked against me. It still does, in spite of the alleged gains of the women's movement. In spite of the vague prestige and respect that simply surviving to the frontier of old age brings an artist, and especially a woman artist, in this all-devouring century.

I showed that passage to still another friend, a poet; he commented, "God bless Diane di Prima for telling out."

Recollections of my Life as a Woman is an instance of a kind of book one sees less and less these days. It is an interesting phenomenon of current publishing that mass-market books often appear with "Questions for Discussion" at the back. I would have found such questions appalling when, in my adolescence, I read—one would rather say *absorbed*—Thomas Wolfe's autobiographical novel, *Look Homeward, Angel.* Wolfe's book seemed to speak to me directly—to see into my soul. That, it seemed to me, was the purpose of a novel: to enlarge selfhood, to give us a vision of ourselves which we recognized as simultaneously true and missing from our lives. The only "question" which arose was how to deal with this invasion and expansion of consciousness. I felt that the experience of Wolfe's book made me stronger, more certain of myself: it inspired me to attempt to create such an experience in others. I did *not* see the book as something to be "discussed"—though I would of course have listened to a discussion were one available. It seemed to me that the central purpose of the book was to change my life—and that is exactly what it did.

Publishers are extremely canny: they realize that, these days, the way most people initially experience novels is in the classroom—that the audience for novels is "educated" people, people who are used to "questions for discussion." From this point of view, a book is not something which speaks to what Wolfe called "the buried life"—Wolfe subtitled *Look Homeward, Angel* "A Story of the Buried Life"—but the central focus of a discussion group: an object which will prod us to "express ourselves," to offer our individual "opinions." *Look Homeward, Angel* left me feeling that an enormous number of possibilities had awakened in me—but I was also stunned, something like speechless, hardly in a state to offer my "individual opinion." To do that, I would have had to diminish the force the book had on me—and continues to have—and I had no wish to diminish the book's force: rather, to explore it, to see where it might lead.

Recollections of my Life as a Woman is a memoir of Diane di Prima's individual life, and we can discuss it in those terms—compare her version of "Beat" experience to that of Jack Kerouac or Michael McClure or see the book as a Feminist document in which the primary focus is the author's struggles as a woman artist. But the book is more than that. It is a book like *Look Homeward, Angel.* It means to take hold of us and turn us around ("convert" us). It is revolutionary in the only way that a book can really be revolutionary: it forces us to *alter our consciousness.* Its anger is ultimately liberating and energizing, its passion and commitment to art boundless. It has the courage to present a di Prima who "wasn't all that I wanted her to be." Yet, like Rilke's statue, it is saying, "Du mußt dein Leben ändern"— "You must change your life."

Poems Are Not Tattoos

Francisco X. Alarcón, *From the Other Side of Night*
/ Del Otro Lado De La Noche: New and Selected Poems

> the poor
> signature of
> my illiterate
> and peasant self
>
> giving away
> all rights
> in a deceptive
> contract for life
> —FRANCISCO X. ALARCÓN, "The X in My Name"

In the Afterword to this important collection (University of Arizona Press, 2002), Manuel de Jesús Hernádez-G insists on the "unity" of Francisco X. Alarcón's life and work. Hernádez-G asserts that this poet presents us with "a unified erotic and activist vision," that Alarcón has "a unified Chicano poetic voice, one that is both communal and activist."

Whenever I come across such assertions of "unity," I immediately begin to look for the contradictions, the "sub-texts," which such statements seek to evade or deny. In Alarcón one does not have to look far. Francisco X. Alarcón identifies himself with the working class, yet he is the product of "elitist" institutions such as Stanford University; he identifies himself with the outlaw, even with the criminal, yet he is having mainstream honors heaped upon him: he was recently presented with the Fred Cody Award for Lifetime Achievement from BABRA, the Bay Area Book Reviewers Association; he was a strong candidate for California Poet Laureate. This is not to say that Alarcón's view of himself is in any way hypocritical or even inaccurate: only to say that it is complex, multiple. We owe Alarcón a debt not because he achieves some sort of dubious "unity" in his life and work but because he is able to live with the manifold contradictions of his nature and situation and can give them free and varied expression—can even allow them to comment on each other. "Being a Chicano gay poet who has crossed several social, cultural, linguistic, and sexual barriers, borders, and taboos," he writes in "The Poet as The Other," "I have experienced a life full of contradictions and differences. . . ." In "Reclaiming Ourselves, Reclaiming America" he adds, "My face, my body, my soul are in constant turmoil."

From the Other Side of Night stretches from Francisco X. Alarcón's first book, *Tattoos* (published in Oakland in 1985) to new, not-yet-collected poems. It opens with the title poem from *Tattoos*:

>   poems
>   fill up
>   pages
>
>   tattoos
>   puncture
>   flesh

That is the entire poem. There is scarcely any "imagery" (though one feels something in that word "puncture") and no "narrative" whatsoever: only two statements. Yet the juxtaposition of the statements opens up a number of questions. What in the world do tattoos have to do with poems? They seem to exist in utterly different worlds. Yet: do they? How can we find a *connection* between these notions? Are pages a kind of skin? (One thinks of parchment.) Are tattoos a kind of writing? Is a person who writes poems likely to sport tattoos? Are poems "elitist" while tattoos are "working class"? Is there a sexual element at work here? (Alarcón is an openly gay man.) Aren't both tattoos and poems attempts at self-expression and the creation of beauty?

These various questions are posed, not answered. When he first began to write the work in *Tattoos*, Alarcón was told that what he was writing was not poems. He answered, "Yes, that's right: they're tattoos!" Alarcón did not wish his work to "fill up" pages. (Indeed, much of his work has been called "minimalist" precisely because it *doesn't* "fill up" a page.) But he did wish his work to "puncture flesh": to touch us, even to pierce us. (Born in Los Angeles, Alarcón grew up in Guadalajara, Mexico—a country of intense Roman Catholic imagery: one wonders if there is a slight hint here of the spear that "punctures" the flesh of the Savior. In the opening poem of *Sonnets to Madness and Other Misfortunes* Alarcón numbers himself among those who were born "marcado," branded—the mark of Cain but also perhaps "tattooed." And might that punctured flesh imply just a touch of the sadistic?)

The various "worlds" alluded to in these questions suggest the complexity of Alarcón's situation—and the necessary doubleness of his art, which exists in both English and Spanish versions. (His art is, like his identity, "mestizo"— mixed.) At times, as Alarcón suggests in "Un Beso Is Not a Kiss," the English version does not serve the Spanish well. Sonnet XXIII of *Sonnets to Madness and Other Misfortunes* has

> bailando combatamos la tortura
> de la tristeza que sólo la locura
> cura con manos llenas de fortuna

This is translated by Alarcón's longtime translator, Francisco Aragón, as

> dancing let us resist the torture
> of sadness that only madness
> with its plentiful luck can cure

The English makes a valiant effort to catch some of Alarcón's intricate rhyming ("torture / cure," "sadness / madness") but it is unable to do justice to the central phrase "la locura / cura," which finds healing ("cura") in madness ("locura"). (It has been suggested that Alarcón is not a "curandero" but a "*lo*curandero.") Similarly, one of the primary themes of Alarcón's work is the problematical relationship between the *I* and the *we*—and, even more importantly, the shift from the *I* to the *we*. There are certain words which haunt this poet: one is dark or darkness ("oscura"—another word involving "cura") and another is "otro" ("other"). Sonnet X has "*uno* no es nada" ("*one* is nothing") and goes on to assert that "un día uno so tropieza con el otro" ("one day, one runs into the other"). At the end of the poem the poet is finally able to say "us," which in Spanish is *nosotros*, a word affirming community by literally "including" the "other": *nos-otros*. Conversely, a passage in "Plegaria de amor" ("Love Plea"),

> que soy
> el duelo
> de tu melodía

is translated as

> I am
> the mourning
> of your noon

There the English suggests a pun on "mourning/morning" which is not in the Spanish.

Interestingly, though Alarcón is an excellent reader of his work, he sometimes rushes through the English version of a poem and immediately moves on after reciting it. This may indicate nothing more than a poet's lack of interest in a poem written some time ago—a constant problem for people who are called upon to read their work frequently. Yet it's also possible that this poet, whose first language was Spanish, is a little anxious to prevent the listener from scrutinizing his phrases too closely. People whose command of a language is problematical will often speak quickly in order to prevent the listener from noticing their possible lapses.

Don't mistake my argument. Alarcón is a fully functional speaker of English, and his poems are a great pleasure to read in both Spanish and English—a fact which is no small achievement of his work. Yet tensions necessarily exist, even in his recitations, and they are part of the fabric—the challenge—of his work.

From the Other Side of Night begins with a presentation of the poet as a "shadow" (another of Alarcón's frequently-appearing words); he is a creature of "darkness"—a person whose very light ("luz") must be described as dark ("oscura"). Alarcón does not in any way glamorize or justify criminal behavior, but, as he says, his "ethnicity, class origin, and sexual orientation" bring him to represent himself as a "fugitive," a criminal "acusado de todo":

> I've had
> to bear
> the days
> anonymously
> like a shadow
> slip
> through the city
> without raising
> suspicions . . .
> My crime
> must have
> been

as huge as
the darkness
found in
my punishment

above all
I've sought
the mute
company
of night

I've learned
to fake
nearly everything
but
still
when next to you
I'm given away
by the empty
pounding
of my heart
("Prófugo / Fugitive")

"Shadow," "night," "darkness" are all defining words of this period. "For a long time," he writes in "Reclaiming Ourselves, Reclaiming America," "I was a person without an image . . . How could I possible identify or associate myself with this body of mine when almost everything around negated me?" As the concluding lines of "Prófugo / Fugitive" make clear, the subject of this particular poem is specifically the speaker's guilt-ridden homosexuality. Yet Alarcón also speaks of Chicanos as a whole as "shadows," and they too are experiencing "a dark / and cruel / night." "Whole peoples were forced to perceive themselves as the defective copies of idealized realities," Alarcón goes on. "Vast territories of this continent were to be projections of imposed models from the 'Old World,' first 'New Spain,' and later, other European cultural models like the French and the British as well as the newer Anglo-American ones." In "Patria" he describes his "gente" as

foreigners
in our own

native land
giving away
everything
they haven't
yet stolen
from us

reduced
to shadows
carrying
inside
our eyes
a dark
and cruel
night

Yet to be Chicano and to be gay are not the same thing—any more than a poem is the same thing as a tattoo. Some of the work in *From the Other Side of Night* suggests that Alarcón's own immediate family was none too happy with his sexual orientation:

my father
and I greet
each other

guarded
as if
sealing

a truce
on a
battlefield

we sit down
to eat like
two strangers
("My Father")

His poetry is hardly encouraged by his mother. In "Advice of a Mother" she says,

it hurts to see
you this way

wasting
your eyes
and your time

with those things
you call
poems

The poet's problem in this early work is to find a way of speaking which can assert *all* aspects of his identity more or less simultaneously—despite the fact that these aspects may be in considerable conflict with one another. The poems are "minimal" in the sense that they depend on few words and on silence—they are elliptical and suggestive rather than assertive—but they are constantly alive with the tensions and sorrows of Alarcón's life. He is not a writer who coldly calculates his merely formal possibilities. "I am a writer," he told an interviewer, "who creates poetry in a fit of passion." In his essay, "The Poet as The Other," he adds,

> What would we call that moment in life in which the precarious nature of our existence without warning is exposed and suddenly everything we accept, believe, take for granted, seems to succumb to the unrelenting questioning of our mind? For some, these are symptoms of what is known as mid-life crisis. For me, these are just some of the very conditions in which poetry frequently comes to me. As a Chicano poet who also celebrates being gay, I have come to realize that I write desde afuera del margen mismo de la sociedad (from the outside of even the margin of society), and that for some, even my own gente, I represent the ultimate Other.

Both the poet and others "weep" in Alarcón's work.

The young Alarcón's relationship with his grandmother, from whom he learned Spanish, offers him solace—*"mijito* / don't cry / she'd tell me"—yet eventually his *abuela* "went far away." He sees himself as an "Imprisoned Poet," a "Natural Criminal":

I am
a nomad
in a country
of settlers . . .

My crime
has been being
what I've been
all my life

Even the darkness of his skin seems to be in doubt: "I used to be / much much darker / dark as la tierra / recién llovida." He sees the world as "tan real" ("so real") yet himself, "deep inside," "tan incierta / tan irreal" ("so uncertain / so unreal"). He longs to "set / [his] body on fire":

I want
no memory

rather to embrace
every instant
to a frenzy

Various poems suggest a call to political activism ("Las flores son nuestras armas") and to an increased exploration of his sexuality—which itself has its "dark" aspects:

with your gray hair
I've made now
a long rope
you tell me
wrapping it
around my neck
("My Hair")

Yet with *Quake Poems* and *Loma Prieta* (1989/1990: the word "prieta" means "black, dark"; the entire phrase means "dark hillock") and even more with *Snake Poems: An Aztec Invocation* (1992) the poet enters into an entirely new phase of his identity. The devastating Santa Cruz earthquake of 1989 is seen—rather amazingly—as an opportunity ("oportunidad") for a transformation and a "healing" not only of the Santa Cruz community but of Alarcón himself. In a poem printed only in Spanish the lover is described as "víctima del / terremoto / del amor / y la pasión" ("victim of the / earthquake / of love / and of passion"). Instead of representing himself as the lonely, dark ego—the "ultimate Other"—Alarcón, in a moment of Whitmanic transformation, suddenly sees himself as absolutely everybody around him:

> I lost my home
> my china my store
> I broke my arm
> the back of my neck
>
> I didn't know
> what to do
> I ran I froze
> I cried I laughed
>
> I thought about
> the children
> I panicked I prayed
> I was helpless. . . .
> ("First-Person Eulogy")

"For once," the poet comments, "this pronoun / *I* . . . included / each and every one."

Personal transformation, an inclusive rather than an excluded *I*, an entry into a space which is at once historical and mythic, and an understanding of the poet as shaman are central facts of *Snake Poems: An Aztec Invocation*, a remarkable book written in English while Alarcón was living in Mexico and published in the year of Christopher Columbus's Quincentennial. In Mexico, Alarcón came upon a book written by *another* Alarcón—Hernando Ruiz de Alarcón (1587-1646). This Alarcón, who may have been Francisco's ancestor, did terrible things to the Indians—who were also Francisco's ancestors. But Hernando Ruiz also produced a book, *Treatise on the Superstitions and Heathen Customs That Today Live Among the Indians Native to This New Spain* (1629)— a book which preserved much of the very culture which the author and his conquistador companions were actively destroying. In a pantheistic moment—a moment in which he perceived the entire earth as alive— Francisco had earlier written, "Todo es un cuerpo inmenso" ("Everything Is an Immense Body"). For Hernando Ruiz, the Indians believe

that the clouds are angels and gods worthy of worship. They think the same of the winds because they believe these forces live everywhere, in the hills, mountains, valleys, and ravines. They believe the same of the rivers, lakes, and springs because they offer wax and incense to all the above.

Snake Poems represents Francisco X. Alarcón's active entry into a mythic space which also offers the possibility of "healing." At the center of the book is the magical Nahuatl phrase, "Nomatca Nehuatl"—roughly translated as "'I myself,' magical formula for personal empowerment found in most Nahuatl spells. . . ." In a way, "Nomatca Nehuatl" is simply the Aztec equivalent to *Shazam*: a magical phrase which utterly transforms the speaker and brings him suddenly into a larger life—what Alarcón calls "this boundless / desire / of being":

> I myself
> I, Quetzalcoatl
> I, the Hand
> indeed I, the Warrior
> I, the Mocker
> I respect nothing . . .
>
> Come forth
> spirits
> from the sunset
> from the sunrise
>
> anywhere you dwell
> as animals
> as birds
>
> from the four directions
> I call you
> to my grip . . .
>
> come forth
> knife
> to be stained
> with blood
>
> come forth
> cross my path

At this point Alarcón is no longer "víctima" of anything, whether earthquakes or love. He has arrived at a selfhood which has transcended the personal ego and which identifies itself with the active universe of Aztec belief:

I myself
the mountain
the ocean
the breeze
the flame

the thorn
the serpent
the feather
the Moon
the Sun
("Nomatca Nehuatl")

If, in "Mestizo," he had written, "my feet / recognize / no border," he can now assert not only the "borderless" but the "boundless." "In order to understand history and be able to exorcize the past," he writes in "Reclaiming Ourselves, Reclaiming America,"

> We need to reenact all the misunderstandings, confrontations and contradictions, all the suffering and havoc brought about by the so-called "discovery" of this continent by Europeans . . . We need to bring back the deceased in order to continue living. We have to reclaim our suppressed tongues and spirits, our burned homes and fields, our slaughtered mothers and fathers, our enslaved sisters and brothers. By reclaiming ourselves, we will be reclaiming America.

It is precisely this "reclaiming" that *Snake Poems: An Aztec Invocation* enacts. It is an attempt to redefine the Western tradition not by going to other traditions—to Buddhism, for example—but by finding positive but neglected elements within the tradition itself. (Alarcón points out that his "tonal"— his sign—in the Nahuatl tradition is the coatl, the serpent, a word which forms half of the name of the ancient god, Quetzalcoatl, "the feathered serpent.") In "Reclaiming Ourselves, Reclaiming America" Alarcón asserts that 1492 marked the beginning of "the Conquest by Sword, Cross, and Grammar." *Snake Poems* is one indication of the emergence of another sort of consciousness, "the liberating praxis of a new Mestizo / Mestiza . . .

consciousness": "a fluid ontology in which any notion of 'self' must include the 'others'" and which avoids "neat demarcations like subject/object, human/ nature, us/them, and other similar dichotomies common [to] Western thought and mythologies."

In "Maternal Home," Alarcón writes of his "canceled" childhood. *Snake Poems* opens him not only to the deep past of history but to his deep personal past, which, like the historical past, can be "reinterpreted." Like the "buried" Aztec culture, the poet's childhood suddenly comes alive: "let us arrive," he writes,

> as children
> to this huge
> playground—
>
> the universe

This discovery of "the inner child" and of the possibility of canceling his "canceled" childhood opens Alarcón into new areas of exploration. "We'll only be free," he writes in *Sonnets to Madness*,

> when we become
> little boys and girls once again
> who squirm with joy as we explore
> the marvels, the wonders of the world

Alarcón's wonderful children's books arise out of this impulse—which has Christian as well as Indian resonances—to explore childhood. At about the same time, he also begins to write sonnets—a form which is quite different from the poetry he had earlier produced. These poems were collected in *De amor oscuro / Of Dark Love* (1991) and *Sonnets to Madness and Other Misfortunes / Sonetos a la locura y otras penas* (2001). Alarcón's models here are Federico García Lorca (who wrote a book called *Sonetos del amor oscuro*) and Pablo Neruda. Neruda, says Alarcón, "liberated the sonnet in his book, *Veinte Poemas de Amor y Una Canción Desesperada (Twenty Poems of Love and One Song of Despair)*." Alarcón's sonnets are fourteen lines, unrhymed, and roughly hendecasyllabic; he refers to them as "versos libres." The sonnets explore earlier issues in various ways; they are frequently—as sonnets often are—love poems, and at times they deliberately echo the language of earlier work. In the early "Raíces / Roots" the poet asserts,

> I carry
> my roots
> with me
> all the time
> rolled up
> I use them [*me sirven*]
> as my pillow

The "Chicano Dedication" to *Sonnets to Madness* has

> there are so many prisons, so many silences,
> so many deaths forbidding my life—
> my roots serve me [*me sirven*] also as pillow

Sonnet XVII of *Sonnets to Madness* brings together many of Alarcón's themes:

> we've stopped being monologues
> black, moonless, starless nights,
> books no one dared to write,
> torn pockets, forgotten tombs
>
> our waves overwhelm the jetties now,
> raging rivers roar beneath our bridges
> we're summoned by the wind's rebellion,
> hurricanes surge from our chests
>
> we've turned the road into a garden,
> our scars grow inward
> —like plants—and blossom words
>
> tearing down prison walls we delve
> into the forest like humming birds—
> we drink the nectar from our mouths
> (*Sonnets to Madness*, #XVII)

Earlier selves remain, and at times assert themselves, but the mastery of this recent work allows none of these selves to dominate the others. The concluding words of *From the Other Side of Night* are a kind of litany of earlier themes: *cura, nos, uno, otro, la noche,* even "wounds" (*las heridas*), a rich word which suggests personal and historical pain as well as those early tattoos which "puncture / flesh." Each of these words/themes takes its place as part of an ongoing and constantly problematical music:

> para curanos
> uno a otro
> —como la noche
> las heridas

> to soothe
> —like the night—
> each other's
> wounds

Even "childhood" gets redefined here. It is no longer a specific time of one's life but an active principle asserting a deep connection to the universe. Alarcón's tender and imaginative *abuela* told him, "*mijito* / don't cry," but finally "went far away." "Tlazolteotl" is the everlasting "Goddess of Love / Goddess of Death / Eater of Filth / Mother of All Seasons." The poet prays to her,

> Mother of the Rivers
> cleanse your son
> with waters flowing
> from the Fountain of Youth

> Mother of the Hummingbirds
> dry off his last tears
> kiss each aching bone
> dress him in morning flowers

"We have to empower ourselves by bringing together what has been disjointed, by recognizing ourselves in others, by accepting and celebrating who we are," Alarcón writes in "The Poet as The Other": "Everyday we are witnesses of the annihilation everywhere of ancient and communal ways of life." It is this process of self-empowerment and the achievement of communal modes that *From the Other Side of Night* documents in a rich and satisfying way. Indeed, the poet goes even further in his call for "a new eco-poetics grounded in a heritage thousands of years old that upholds that everything in the universe is sacred":

> For me, this new liberating Mestizo/Mestiza consciousness not only embraces "others" as equal and unique human beings but also calls for a new global awareness of the "oneness" of all living creatures and of nature as a whole. This vision of the "oneness" of all life is shared by many of the ancient Earth worshipping religions, the shamanistic spiritual traditions of Native peoples in the Americas, Siberia, and other parts of Asia. In the Western cultural tradition, "mystics" (saints, visionaries, poets, and other outcasts) have left moving testimonies of their own epiphanies and encounters with this "oneness" of all creation . . . Ultimately [the] poetic "self" dwells in the "collective" consciousness and/or sense of "oneness" with the surrounding ecosystems. When doing public readings of *Snake Poems*, I usually start by reciting a short invocation that comes from "Prayer to Fire" and burning of some sage and copal (tree resin). Since this ecopoetics is eclectic, I believe it should also appeal to all the senses . . . Then I ask everybody in the audience to join me in calling the four directions according to the Nahuatl tradition . . . [One] of the main purposes of this ecopoetics is to reconcile the internal split of many Mestizos (also felt by most people currently living on the planet) which is a direct result of the relentless world expansion of the West which involves conquering, colonizing, and exploiting indigenous peoples, their cultures and their lands.
>
> ("Reclaiming Ourselves, Reclaiming America")

If there is some sentimentality and even self-pity in Alarcón's work, that is the case with most writers who attempt to reach an audience larger than that of the poetry coteries. (What is more sentimental and self-pitying than "popular song"?) "I knew I was different," Alarcón writes in "The Poet as The Other": "I had some intuitions about the personal and social consequences of this fact. Acting on this difference essentially meant transgression." *La locura / cura.*

Glenn Spearman

The Musa-physics: Myth-Science-Poetics

> Most people don't have any idea of what improvisation is . . . It means the magical lifting of one's spirits to a state of trance . . . It means experiencing oneself as another kind of living organism, much in the way of a plant, a tree—the growth, you see, that's what it is . . . It has to do with religious forces.
> —CECIL TAYLOR, quoted in Michael Ventura, *Shadow Dancing in the U.S.A.*

> "I asked him, 'Are you dying?' He said, 'No.'"
> —Glenn Spearman's wife, Shantée Baker Spearman, on the night before his death

The death in 1998 of tenor saxophonist Glenn Spearman brought to an end his brilliant career as free jazz composer, player, teacher, and all-round energy source. Spearman was only fifty-one when he died, and in the notes to his last CD, *Blues for Falasha*, his associate Larry Ochs writes, "This recording, which seemed like the beginning of something new in his music, now must instead serve as a memorial . . . We're left to imagine where his music might have headed next."

Spearman's longtime friend and associate, bassist/painter Benjamin Lindgren, says, "He would tell us, 'When we hit the stage it's balls-out music,' and he was always feeding music to the band to take it to the next level. Life for Glenn was always deep and spiritual, and he was cliché-free, going for the heart of whatever he was doing." Spearman himself insisted that he was part of a long tradition: "It's one music from Louis Armstrong and Fats Waller," he said, "it's one continuous push to bring beauty in[to] a world of madness and frustration."

I knew Spearman and participated with him and Lindgren in some memorable poetry and jazz sessions, one of which was recorded and broadcast on KPFA in Berkeley. Discussing his methods of improvisation, Spearman said to me, "Any individual note refers simultaneously to a number of keys." I immediately thought of James Joyce's *Finnegans Wake*, in which any individual word refers simultaneously, by puns, to a number of contexts. Spearman's remark seemed to me Joycean thinking applied to music, so it came as no surprise when he told me that he was an enthusiastic reader of Joyce, and particularly of *Finnegans Wake*.

It was also no surprise to discover that Spearman, who loved crossing over categories, wrote poetry and produced visual art. Shortly before he died, he told me how pleased he was that he had managed to publish *The Musa-Physics* (Ascension Publication, 1996), his book of poems and drawings. Like his music, his poetry is at once baffling, powerful, fragmentary, learned—"spiritual":

> AFTER many
> multiplications ALL IN GOD
> REJOYCE, paint dancing the scene, as
> blood flows to be in rain, reflective
> absorbed continuance, MYTHOLOGY,
> YOU YOURSELF, REALISM
> PROCLAIMS the corners of the earth,
> the exotic spirit BIRTHS things beyond
> HER, yet the breath in BIRTH must be
> confirmed as flow to with from beyond
> to beyond, full liberty full freedom. . . .

The capitalized words are like emphasized notes he might play. The passage, which ends with a statement about "everlasting song," maintains a number of contexts in constant juxtaposed activity. "GOD" is there, as is the pun on James Joyce's name, but so is "dancing," "blood," "rain," "reflective / absorbed continuance," mythology, realism, etc. Spearman "hears" the word "breath" in the word "birth," and both words are essential to his concept of "full liberty full freedom." But most important of all is the fact of movement: "to with from beyond." The title of the piece from which I have excerpted these lines is "Gawwal; musician, rags; motion," but the lines are a recapitulation (as one recapitulates musical themes) of an identical passage in another poem, "EAGLE FLYERS, MAMBO SAMBA." Their repetition indicates not only their musicality but how important they are to this book.

The concept of "music" in poetry is usually a rather loose, metaphorical, inexact one. Spearman, however, uses words exactly as he uses notes:

> BREATH TEXTURES ITSELF; A
> HOLLOW RING, surface resistance
> non-dimensional, inside leading, a
> SPACE place, hollow, but not empty,
> denoting sound . . .

Reading such passages, one thinks *gesture*: Spearman is "throwing" words on paper in the same way that an action painter might throw pigment on canvas. At any individual moment, *everything* is relevant. One fails to understand these poems if one fails to understand the muscularity which animates them.

Discussing "American Action Painters," art critic Harold Rosenberg asserted that "At a certain moment the canvas began to appear to one American painter after another as an arena in which to act—rather than as a space in which to reproduce, redesign, analyse or 'express' an object, actual or imagined. What was to go on the canvas was not a picture but an event . . . The revolution against the given, in the self and in the world, which since Hegel has provided European vanguard art with theories of a New Reality, has re-entered America in the form of personal revolts. Art as action rests on the enormous assumption that the artist accepts as real only that which he is in the process of creating . . . The artist works in a condition of open possibility. . . ."

Rosenberg's remarks were published in 1952 and applied only to painting. But surely Spearman understood poetry—as he understood music—to be "an arena in which to act," not "a space in which to reproduce, redesign, analyse or 'express' an object"—e.g., a given tune or a given set of chords. From the point of view of "action," all art tends towards performance, and the theme of performance, particularly musical performance, haunts *The Musa-Physics*:

> Black waves,
> > partial to currents
> and modal attitudes,
> for moving
> stiff, western systems
> 10th power
> > diminished.
> > flatted structures
> move between cracks,
> as spirit is pervasive.

> ✑

> > inherent—oratorio,
> > > for voices in solo
> orbit
> the thunder of
> > music stars

Even errors (misspellings, for example) become part of the structure. The point is not to create something "finished"—a work of "art"—but to enter into a state of consciousness which is profoundly "other" than the everyday. As we waited impatiently and, it seemed, endlessly for our microphones to be adjusted by the technicians in the recording studio, Spearman suddenly said, "As far as I'm concerned, this is a spiritual event." It was exactly what we needed to hear. Bassist Benjamin Lindgren had previously told me, "The idea is to get 'high,' not with dope, with the music."

Their point was similar to what Cecil Taylor meant when he described improvisation as "the magical lifting of one's spirits to a state of trance . . . experiencing oneself as another kind of living organism."

The "religious forces" to which Taylor refers are not the kind which insist on one sort of morality or another; they do not involve "action" in that sense. Rather, they are essentially *transformative*. They thrust us into an area in which everything is in flux. The music or the poetry or for that matter the drawing becomes the means by which the artist holds himself in an openness to spirit. Whatever comes into the art space comes into it and is dealt with accordingly. For many people, this state of radical openness is nothing more than an assertion of chaos and should be rejected. For Spearman, however, the art space implies a constant listening for patterns; it is alive with possibilities of order:

> THE SAME SOUND IN
> DIFFERENT PLACES, THE TENSION OF
> RHYTHMIC OPPOSITION, CHANGING
> PARTS, DISORDERING THE MUSICAL
> SYNTAX, A MOVING SURFACE OF
> MUSICAL MEANING MUSICAL
> FREEDOM THE MANIPULATION OF
> CREATIVE DISRUPTION ENHANCING
> TRANSFORMATIONS OF MUSICAL
> INVESTIGATION.

Glenn Spearman's life ended on October 8, 1998. But his influence continues, both in the United States and in Europe. "My thing is thematic improvisation," Spearman said in an interview quoted by jazz critic Larry Kelp. "I write traditional thematic ideas that are not relegated to key, and are not relegated to time . . . I write what I hear."

The Musa-Physics is a powerful meditation on a life lived as improvisation. The author's keen intelligence constantly thrusts us back into an awareness of what we're doing while, at the same time, his intuitions and passions drive us forward. It is an amazing effect. The book suggests certain passages in Jake Berry's *Brambu Drezi* or Ivan Argüelles's *Pantograph*. It is akin to moments like this in Clark Coolidge's early work:

> massed disguise, pleats of calcomine train
> of elevator, finely key boreal watch hits
> wrist with slick thongs, red yellow
> "watch that!" hate a long rim of dial rub

But Spearman is an original. His music was probably capable of reaching further than his poetry—he was after all primarily a musician—but his poetry, about which he was quite serious, reaches far enough:

INTOXICATION IS A NUMBER, CALLING YOU FROM HERE TO THERE. STEPS NUMBERED ALONG THE WAY. THE NUMBER IS NOW. HIDDEN ESSENCE IN A SOUND MATTER, AS ONE TONE ONE BEAT ONE BREATH, BECOME *TO* EUCLIDIAN FUNCTIONS, SYMBOLS OF THE HOW.

A Very Brechty X-mas!

A Theater Review

When a televangelist announced that Christmas was the season of rejoicing, a doubtful spectator remarked, "Oh, so that's what we're doing—rejoicing." Brian Katz, Artistic Director of the Custom Made Theatre Company in San Francisco, clearly doesn't believe that's what we're doing. The program to his new production, *A Very Brechty X-mas!*, announces, "There is not enough written about the link between poverty and war. Look at who serves, who is shedding their blood in the deserts and mountains overseas. Read the obits (in the papers brave enough to print them) and see who is doing the dying."

Real Christmas is an orgy of buying—Greed Rampant. It is all about spending money (read "giving") in the midst of a mythology of utter bliss and fulfillment. Literary Christmas, on the other hand—*A Christmas Carol*, "The Gift of the Magi"—is all about Happy Poverty, poverty that manages to give its gifts no matter what the financial setbacks may be. Neither of Custom Made Theatre's two plays—*Candaules, Commissioner* by Daniel Gerould and *The Exception and the Rule* by Bertolt Brecht—is directly about Christmas, but they are both about poverty, not what Lawrence Lipton once named "voluntary poverty" but real, brutal poverty, the kind that rarely inspires people to orgies of consumerism.

Gerould's Vietnam-era *Candaules, Commissioner* is the first and very much the weaker of the two plays. A radio version was presented on station KPFA by the Actors Workshop during the Vietnam War. The play probably seemed topical and intense at the time—dealing with a war whose real *raison d'être* was denied by the people who were causing it. There are some amusing moments in *Candaules, Commissioner*—and it is directed by the very capable Brian Katz—but the plot is far too predictable. Worse, it is far too *bourgeois*.

The bourgeois family frequently images itself in art is as a triangle: two men and a woman. One of the men is older (a "father" in some sense), the other is a "son." What are the men doing? They are—what else?—fighting over the woman, who is the "prize." In 2006, the political implications of *Candaules, Commissioner* tend to be submerged in its Oedipal subtext—

which unfortunately now rises blatantly to the surface. The play attempts to explore the tensions between a husband and wife as well as the tensions between a master and servant, but in fact all it does is rehash the favorite subject of bourgeois drama: the "triangle." Gerould attempts to add a "twist" to this hoary situation—the son wins the mother and then *rejects* her—but, unlike Brecht, he is not able to re-imagine the terms of his story. The play is worth seeing not because it is a neglected masterpiece but because of some terrific performances by the Custom Made Theatre cast. All three actors— Jay Martin as Candaules, Perry Aliado as Gyges, his driver, and Katja Rivera as Candaules' wife Nyssia—are wonderful and beautifully cast. Aliado and Rivera especially bring a reality to this material which the author didn't quite manage to achieve.

Oh yes, there is some "nudity" in the play—as we of course know beforehand—and Gerould plays with our awareness of the nudity: Candaules is stripped of his clothing, so we think, "Oh, the man will be the nude one." He is left in his fig-leaf underwear, however, and lo, it is the woman who must be naked. The woman nude, the man in underwear: where have we seen that before?

It was precisely *against* the bourgeois theater with its "eternal triangles" that Bertolt Brecht directed his considerable energies. *The Exception and the Rule*—in an excellent new translation by the director of the play, Lewis Campbell—is a delight and a reminder of the deep pleasure of thinking. Here, thinking is not opposed to emotion; in the hands of masters like Brecht and Shaw, thinking *is* emotion. We are moved not because an attractive woman displays her body but because thinking moves us, changes us. Poet Bob Perelman once wrote, "My mind changed me." That is precisely the area of *The Exception and the Rule*, which attempts, in terms of bourgeois theater, to be an "exception," not "the rule." Brecht understood that a debate was emotional, that it was theater, and, even more importantly, it was theater that managed to avoid the sentimentality which saturates even excellent bourgeois plays. Is it possible to write about something other than "love"? Don't we feel strongly about many things? Brecht was an avid reader of Kipling—to the extent that he stole some of Kipling's lines for his lyrics: "Gunga Din" is probably more relevant to *The Exception and the Rule* than is *Romeo and Juliet*. What happens in that master-slave relationship? What kinds of feelings arise?

The play divides into two parts: the first is an action—a merchant beats and, under the inaccurate assumption that he is being attacked, finally murders his porter; the second is a discussion of that action: was the man in any way right to do what he did? Why did he do it? A whole panoply of sometimes hilarious contradictions and false assumptions emerges as the matter is "considered" in court—and of course, since it is a Brecht play, the court arrives at exactly the *wrong* decision. The play ends with a poem:

> Thus ends
> The story of a journey.
> You have heard and you have seen it.
> You have seen the commonplace.
> It happens all the time.
> But we ask you just this:
> Though it isn't strange,
> Find it estranging.
> Though it is usual,
> Find it unexplainable.
> Though it is common,
> Let it astound you.
> Though it's the rule,
> See it as an abuse.
> And when you find abuse of power,
> Work to make it right!
> Work to make it right!
> Work to make it right!

Translator/director Lewis Campbell understands the ensemble nature of Brecht's consciousness—its continual focus on various characters, on issues that transcend individual psychology—and has even added to the ensemble effect by keeping the entire cast onstage throughout. Brecht's use of song is a reminder of the roots of drama in the figure of the Homeric singer: his plays are frequently *told* by someone, he thinks of them as *epic*, not in Cecil B. DeMille's sense of epic but in the sense of the tale of the tribe sung to eager, judgmental listeners by the local Bard. Happily, Campbell commissioned Robert E. Lesoine to write music for the play's many songs. Lesoine, who is experienced with cabaret, manages the amazing trick of writing music that sounds like Kurt Weill without in the least sounding derivative. And Campbell's cast is just about perfect. AJ Davenport plays the judge and gifts us with still another wonderful performance. (I've never seen her be anything less than excellent.) Carson Creecy IV is suitably wild-eyed and furious as the merchant; Richard Wenzel is very fine as the Guide, and sings beautifully;

Benjamin Pither's Porter is always human and sympathetic, never descending to the Christ figure, and his singing is also excellent; Leah Dashe is beautiful as the Porter's wife, though her singing occasionally has some pitch problems. Stefin Collins, John Jamieson, and Linda McPharlin are all fine in the play's smaller roles.

But the real "star" of this play is the spirit of Bertolt Brecht, puffing on his cigar, amused, ironic, compassionate but also alive with righteous anger. And always *theatrical*. He was able to see far beyond the bourgeois "triangle drama" into the heart of another reality altogether. His plays keep asking, *Is this sufficient? What else is there?* What better question to ask in the holiday season? "To not always find it natural . . . just because it is."

Seven Passages From A Notebook

Plus A Poem

1.

"She's a Language writer," said WBAI's Janet Coleman to me. Coleman was speaking of a writer she liked. In a way, that statement was odd. What we call "Language writing" arose out of a discussion—often a fierce and heated discussion—conducted by a group of writers located primarily in California and New York. Lyn Hejinian told me that Bob Perelman's "Talks" series was instituted as a forum for the presentation, discussion and criticism of the work these writers were producing. I am not speaking here of criticism of Language poetry from poets *outside* the group. I am speaking of criticism of Language poetry from poets *within* the group. Language poetry arose out of an argument people were having about the nature of poetry. Now, it seems, Language poetry has become a *style* of writing which anyone can adopt—without debate or discussion. You can say, "She's a Language writer" and expect to be understood. Doesn't that mean that the movement *as* a movement—something *in motion*—is over? Isn't that the shift from something deeply in question—argued about by the participants—into something fixed: a style, a way of writing? You might as well be writing sonnets.

2.

I think the concept of "honesty" arises out of various Puritanical impulses. Puritans want people to *choose* one thing or another—indeed, at the expense of another. The great Puritan epic, *Paradise Lost*, is all about a *wrong choice*. I think this is tied to "honesty": "What I really feel is this . . . "—and you leave out all the things that glimmer around a subject and perhaps contradict it. It is of course good form in our society to be on the side of "honesty"—emotional and intellectual. No one would tell you that honesty isn't a wonderful thing. And yet: is it? Does it hide something which might call it into question? Is there a sense in which it is a denial and not an affirmation? Nietzsche is one of the very few who would attack honesty in the name of healthy lying. I'm afraid—to be as honest as I can possibly be—I agree with him. "Honesty" demolishes fictions: fictions, I think, are life. Puritans like nothing more than to demolish fictions, to destroy myths. But I think that myth is the only adequate way to understand the world—and that the Puritan position is itself in fact (what else?) a fiction, though it is a fiction claiming a moral superiority which it does not actually possess. It is the supreme arrogance of Puritanism that it believes its one fiction takes utter precedence over all other fictions: Puritan "honesty" is thus a kind of monotheism. The question is not whether one supports lies ("evasiveness") or truth ("honesty"): the question is what kinds of fictions give life, what kinds give death? . . .

To a friend who asked questions: People tend to believe in "honesty" as an absolute: it's *always* a good thing. And people get praised for their "honesty"—not necessarily for any particular kind of honesty, simply for being "honest." But, if there are no absolutes, it's possible that the virtue of honesty has its limitations, even its negations—especially when it becomes anti-mythology. I'm afraid I have a deep distrust of things Puritan—not to mention things everybody praises. In at least some senses, "honesty" is *anti* imagination: *Tell the truth, be honest, don't lie.* To praise "honesty" is to praise not making fictions. Is that what we wish to tell our poets? Is that any way to arrive at new myths? Isn't "honesty" an aspect of the Puritan distrust of the imagination—the impulse that made them close down the theaters in Shakespeare's time?

3.

Do tough guys in Brooklyn still say *dese* and *dose* for *these* and *those*? The Greek words for god and goddess are, respectively, *theos* and *thea*. The Roman words are *deus* and *dea*. . . The Romans were tough guys, too.

4.

When I was in New York over forty years ago—1960? 1961?—I wished to make a journal like this but had great difficulty doing it. Now, the words flow forth. Adelle says, "That's because, then, you *wanted* to be a writer. Now, you *are* a writer." Undoubtedly, I lacked confidence then. But, even more, I lacked *subject matter*. Now, I have subjects aplenty. If you are lucky, time will give you subjects—a great gift—and these will form the base of your perceptions. Never—or only rarely—fully conscious, subject matter will nudge you into language. It constantly colors your words, making your words mean more than they seem to initially. The word "dark" in Dana Gioia's work is subject matter. And subject matter is history.

5.

Collage has been called, by Jerome Rothenberg and others, *the* art form of the twentieth century, and collage by its very nature moves *against* the idea of private property. Did T.S. Eliot ask permission of all the people he quoted in *The Waste Land*? The possible hazards of the collagist's sometimes cavalier appropriation of materials were demonstrated when San Francisco artist Jess sent his "Tricky Cad"—an homage to/surrealist parody of "Dick Tracy"—to Dick Tracy's creator, Chester Gould. Gould was furious and threatened legal action. Jess hastily removed the "Tricky Cad" section from his book, *O!* (1960).

6.

"Poet, / Be like God" (Jack Spicer, "Imaginary Elegies"). The problem with this formulation—hardly original with Spicer—lies in the notions of "world" and "creativity." God creates *ex nihilo*, out of nothing: there is no "world" until God "creates" it. The poet's "creativity" is not like that. The poet *inhabits* a world which is always impinging upon him/her. The poet "creates" *from that world*, not from nothing. Consequently, the poet's "creativity" is significantly different from God's; it is closer to that of the jazz musician who is always reacting to something given: a set of chords, a tune. Spicer's line expresses the desire to forget that fact, to imagine oneself as without precedent, without history.

7.

Is what we call "love" a fiction which masks something else? Can the same word reasonably refer both to what a child feels towards his parents and to what a man feels when he desires a woman? The word is covered over with so much history, much of it metaphysical and in many ways outmoded. Even people who don't believe in the metaphysics use the word—it haunts our psyches and our language. How would we describe what we call "love" if we were to step outside all that? Do two people "endure life's joys and sorrows together" or does such language, so often used, actually obscure the real "relationship" between a man and a woman? The classic definition of "faith" is from St. Paul, Hebrews 11:1: "Faith is the substance of things hoped for, the evidence of things not seen." Doesn't that sound like a definition of fiction, filled as fiction is with desire ("things hoped for") and, certainly, with "the evidence of things not seen"? Further: Mightn't it be a definition of madness? Isn't madness shot through with desire? Don't mad people sometimes see things which aren't there? What happens if we step outside all that—all that language about love? What doors open? What doors close? What is the bond between a child and a parent if we no longer use the word? What is the "relationship" between a couple? What, indeed, is a "couple"—is it related (and *how* is it related?) to "coupling," sexual activity? What causes the bonds between people? Should we say "love" causes the bonds? Have we said anything when we say that word? Or is the word an empty word, essentially meaningless—perhaps merely a way of affirming indirectly the presence of a god who in fact isn't there but whom we nevertheless identify with "love" ("God is Love") and who would exist even *less* than he does if his existence were not constantly being upheld by the fact of people's constant talk about "love"? I once told a little girl who asked about the existence of Santa Claus that many things were "real" even if they didn't exist. What is "love" in our culture?

A Poem Of Departure

for Edouard Muller

I heard a woman sobbing
Outside my window
Late last night
But when I went to look
She'd gone
I heard a woman
Weeping
But could
Not find her
I heard a woman wailing
As if she felt
The weight
Of everything
As she passed by
My window
Open to the dark
She was it seemed
Beyond

Any

Possibility of consolation
In desolate
Constringency—

As she gave herself to
Sorrow
Weeping
For no reason
I could know or see

Appearing Ink

Garrison Keillor and *The Hudson Review*

1. *The Debate*

The April, 2004 issue of *Poetry* contains a debate between Dana Gioia and August Kleinzahler over Garrison Keillor's book, *Good Poems*; the book is a selection from poems read by Keillor on his daily *Writers Almanac* program.

A number of my friends have written poems which have been read aloud by Garrison Keillor. The most recent of these was Robert Sward's "God is In the Cracks" from *Rosicrucian in the Basement*:

> "Just a tiny crack separates this world
> from the next, and you step over it
>   every day,
> God is in the cracks."
> Foot propped up, nurse hovering, phone ringing.
> "Relax and breathe from your heels.
> Now, that's breathing.
> So, tell me, have you enrolled yet?"
>
> "Enrolled?"
>
> "In the Illinois College of Podiatry."
>
> "Dad, I have a job. I teach."
>
> "Ha! Well, I'm a man of the lower extremities."
>
> "Dad, I'm fifty-three."
>
> "So what? I'm eighty. I knew you
> before you began wearing shoes.
> Too good for feet?" he asks.

"*I. Me. Mind:*
>   That's all I get from your poetry.
>   Your words lack feet. Forget the mind.
>   Mind is all over the place. There's no support.
>   You want me to be proud of you? Be a foot man.
>   Here, son," he says, handing me back my shoes,
>   "try walking in these.
>   Arch supports. Now there's a subject.
>   Some day you'll write about arch supports."

Keillor's smooth baritone was equal to the task of Sward's poem, and he read it quite well. And, indeed, Sward's odd, funny poem *is* a "good poem"; Sward was later told by Keillor's staff that the poem received many favorable comments.

I came upon Garrison Keillor's *A Prairie Home Companion* a good many years ago. I liked it at first but found myself growing increasingly bored. People often compare Keillor to old radio comedian Fred Allen, but Keillor has none of Allen's bite—none of Allen's surprises. And, unlike Allen's, Keillor's show is suffused with nostalgia—not just nostalgia for the "good old days when life seemed simpler," though that is certainly there, but nostalgia for old radio itself. *Why, do you remember the days when people used to listen to the radio? . . . It was a "theater of the mind!"* Keillor's celebrated Lake Wobegon monologues began to seem more and more predictable, more and more soporific. In addition, the relentlessly even tone of his voice seemed to suggest a kind of smugness, a sense of self-satisfaction. (Kleinzahler insists that "Keillor embalms whatever . . . he reads within the burnished caul of his delivery. . . . ") Finally, I just gave up on Keillor.

Now, in addition to the weekly variety show, Garrison Keillor has been reading poems on the radio. Since, under the auspices of Berkeley, California station, KPFA, I do that too, I was curious to hear what he was doing. I listened to a few of his programs; he didn't read badly, but he didn't do anything stunning either. Anyone who has heard the unforgettable *sounds* Antonin Artaud made in his "radiodiffusion," *Pour en finir avec le jugement de dieu,* knows that there is another world of "poetry" out there which Garrison Keillor never approaches.

Gioia quotes, approvingly, this passage from Keillor's remarks:

I expected to include plenty of Whitman here and discovered, reading him, a sort of seasickness at all those undulating lines of Uncle Walt's perpetual swoon over grass and leaves and camerados. There are good poems there, and it's a mistake to omit them, but Walt is the Typhoid Mary of American Lit: so much bad poetry can be traced back to him (and not brief bad poems, either), he gave so many dreadful writers permission to lavish themselves upon us.

It is not surprising that Keillor reads nothing but short poems on his show ("and not brief bad poems, either"—ha ha). Keillor's remarks here are not only inaccurate, they are actively stupid. If we are going to talk about someone being "the Typhoid Mary of American Lit," Garrison Keillor might be a better candidate than Walt Whitman. (Oprah Winfrey, perhaps Keillor's model in literary endeavors, might be another.) I read aloud Whitman's magnificent, "not brief" poem, "Out of the Cradle Endlessly Rocking" on one of my KPFA programs. I know what an extraordinary experience it is to perform that poem. After hearing the program, some listeners phoned in to tell me they hadn't realized what an amazing poet Whitman was until they heard me read him aloud. Keillor is not offering amazement; nor is he offering the listener a way of entering Whitman's sometimes difficult poetry. His remarks suggest that he himself is unaware of the deep music of Whitman's longer work. (On another show I played a recording of Orson Welles reading selections from *Leaves of Grass*; it too was an extraordinary experience.) What Keillor is saying here is not good criticism and it is not intelligent writing: it is simply an unexamined prejudice which the author is happy to hand along to his readers. He'll be glad to read you some Whitman so long as Whitman conforms to Keillor's understanding of what constitutes a "good poem." Thank you, Mr. Keillor, for one more stupid thing said about Whitman; I guess they won't be reading much of him—or of the "bad poems" Keillor says he has fostered (by Ferlinghetti? Ginsberg?)—around Lake Wobegon. Oh, "the perpetual swoon over grass and leaves and camerados." Is there a touch of homophobia in those words "swoon" and "camerados"? Are there any gays at Lake Wobegon? Are there any Italians?

As for Marianne Moore, Keillor says she is "a dotty old aunt whose poems are quite replicable for [by?] anyone with a thesaurus." Will any of Keillor's fans be likely to read a Marianne Moore poem after reading that? Are these lines from Moore's "What Are Years?" the ravings of "a dotty old aunt"?

> What is our innocence,
> what is our guilt? All are
>   naked, none is safe. And whence
> is courage: the unanswered question,
> the resolute doubt,—
> dumbly calling, deafly listening—that

> in misfortune, even death,
> encourages others
> and in its defeat, stirs. . . .

One can ask: Is what Keillor's doing genuinely "expanding the audience for poetry"? Or is he merely expanding (or cementing) an audience for Garrison Keillor and for the kind of writing Keillor chooses to call "poetry"?

For Keillor clearly espouses a *kind* of writing. "I find it wise," he says, "to stay away from stuff that is too airy or that refers off-handedly to the poet Li-Po or relies on your familiarity with butterflies or Spanish or Monet." Adds Kleinzahler, "'So I'll be feeding you mostly shit,' is what Garrison could well go on to say." "*Good Poems*," writes Gioia in a considerable understatement, "is not a volume aimed at academic pursuits":

> The book *Good Poems* most closely resembles is Hazel Felleman's once ubiquitous and now unspeakably unfashionable *Best Loved Poems of the American People* (1936), which sold 1.5 million copies to our parents and grandparents.
>
> Memorability is the core of Keillor's aesthetic, but significantly, he does not invoke the traditional mnemonic powers of rhyme and meter. On the contrary, he has a decided preference for the plainspoken free verse of writers like Raymond Carver, William Stafford, and Robert Bly. If not verbal music, then what makes language stick in the mind? . . . Keillor locates memorability in storytelling. "What makes a poem memorable is its narrative line," he asserts. "A story is easier to remember than a puzzle."

If Keillor is insensitive to "verbal music," preferring "plainspoken free verse," and if he believes that the essential thing about a poem is its "narrative line," then how are we to tell a poem from a brief short story? Are the poems he reads nothing more than Lake Wobegon monologues in another guise? For his audience, I suspect that they are. Certainly Keillor does not adjust his persona to the poems; rather, he adjusts the poems to his persona.

Gioia and Kleinzahler are writing about exactly the same thing—except that their points of view differ on the value of that thing. "Everything Keillor does," writes Kleinzahler, "is about reassurance, containment, continuity": "Gentleness and good manners are the twin pillars of the church of Keillor." Gioia points out that his "working-class mother had a well-worn copy [of *Best Loved Poems of the American People*] on the bookshelf next to the almanac, and she literally did love a great many of the poems that Hazel Felleman provided." Kleinzahler points out Keillor's resemblance to Edgar Guest (1881-

1959), who, like Keillor, had a radio show and whom Gioia's mother might have listened to or read. (Unlike Guest, Keillor does not write his own poems.) Edgar Guest's most famous poem begins, "It takes a heap o' livin' in a house t' make it home"—more home-fed nostalgia. Guest's poetry sold extremely well during his lifetime, but no one reads him now. Gioia makes a reference to Ezra Pound: "Despite having been born in Hailey, Idaho, Ezra Pound is absent from Keillor's pages for reasons, I suppose, having to do with the poet's subsequent travels"—and goes on rightly to describe Pound's "Homage to Sextus Propertius" as "magnificent and mostly forgotten." I suspect that Keillor wouldn't touch Ezra Pound or Sextus Propertius with a ten-foot pole!

There is a kind of "domino theory" sometimes expressed about poetry. *At least they're reading poetry; maybe they'll go on to read BETTER poetry.* Billy Collins today; tomorrow, Gertrude Stein. But the domino theory is no more accurate here than it is in the realm of politics. Rilke was surely right when he said that, in order to read poetry, you must "change your life." American mass culture seems to foster the illusion that if something is good, it must be good for *everybody*. But not everybody is willing or even able to change their lives—and that's perfectly all right. Kleinzahler is most amusing when he announces that *poetry is not good for you*. And his vision of "poetry workshops presided over by a dispirited, compromised mediocrity," with students "critiquing and being critiqued by younger versions of the same" certainly rings true. But I don't think he's right that "the better animals in the jungle aren't drawn to poetry anymore." Poetry's unique relationship to consciousness will always bring people to it—including "the better animals in the jungle," god help them. But Gioia is right, too: given Keillor's considerable limitations, and given the limitations of his sense of "poetry," he is doing a pretty good job. He is reading some poems on the radio, and some of them are undoubtedly "good poems." If he reads them well, more power to him. If Keillor's were the only understanding of poetry available—and for some people it is—woe for the art of poetry. But, happily, it is still possible to stumble upon something else, something better, something that will tell you that poetry allows you to enter a "new life," a *vita nuova*, and that, because of it, you will never be the same; something that will cause you to understand that poetry, like all really powerful things, is not only reassuring but *dangerous*:

> Just a tiny crack separates this world
> from the next, and you step over it
> every day.

∽

Like August Kleinzahler, *Poetry*'s editor Christian Wiman also takes up the theme of poetry's possible (even probable) death when he writes, "Poetry as we know it in twentieth-first century America *can die*, will die without a committed audience that is larger than its practitioners, and those of us for whom the art is important must ask ourselves hard practical questions about its survival." This sounds to me oddly *political*—rather like the exhortations people make when they are trying to convince you to vote for someone. Unless you vote for X, look at all these horrible things that are likely to happen. (The phrase "Poetry as we know it" sounds suspiciously like the cliché "Civilization as we know it.") "A culture might evolve or devolve," writes Wiman, "to the point where its poetic impulses and appetite are completely satisfied by pop songs and advertisements." There are people who say things like that, but they are not usually people who have experienced poetry very deeply. (I don't mean this as a comment about Wiman, whose work I have reviewed favorably.)

Speaking personally, I began with "pop songs and advertisements"—until someone suggested that I read a real poem, Gray's *Elegy Written in a Country Churchyard*. At that point I realized the limitations of pop songs and advertisements. Deconstructed, Kleinzahler's "the better animals in the jungle aren't drawn to poetry anymore" is really nothing more than the familiar complaint that "poets aren't being read enough—*I'm* not being read enough." Certainly Garrison Keillor's *Writers Almanac* is not the place in which "hard practical questions" about the survival of poetry will take place. Keillor doesn't even begin to suggest the imaginative possibilities of poetry on the radio—not least because the only voice Keillor presents is his own. (And it is not even "his own" voice; it is, as Kleinzahler says, his "poetry voice.") Garrison Keillor does have an audience, however, and it may be that poets are so desperate for an audience that they are willing to take Keillor far more seriously than he deserves to be taken. Why can't poets be American Idols too?

2. *The Hudson Review*, 55th Anniversary Issue
(Vol. lvi, No. 1, Spring 2003)

Sacrificing
to the four quarters
I find the winds responsive
—FREDERICK MORGAN, "The Priest"

I was with [Allen] Ginsberg in Paterson, N.J., in the late '70s, at a reading of William Carlos Williams' work. I walked into the room, and Ginsberg said, "What are you doing here? You love Wallace Stevens!"
—DANIEL HALPERN

The current issue of *The Hudson Review* is a celebration of the magazine's 55th anniversary. In an instance of interesting synchronicity, Lawrence Ferlinghetti's City Lights Book Store—in many ways at the opposite end of the esthetic spectrum from *The Hudson Review*—is celebrating the 50th anniversary of its founding. The new *Hudson Review* features *Along These Lines,* "an historic CD: 55 Years of *Hudson Review* Poetry with readings by W.S. Merwin, Anthony Hecht, Daniel Hoffman, Maxine Kumin, Galway Kinnell, X.J. Kennedy, Philip Levine, Marilyn Nelson and many others"—a compilation narrated by Dan Stone and produced by Stone's Speakeasy Literary Audio (www.speakeasyaudio.org). But it was Lawrence Ferlinghetti who, over forty years ago, said—and recorded—

> The trouble with the printed word is, it is so silent. Let poetry return to its first purpose—the oral message. Let there be a law against *writing* poetry. It should be spoken, then recorded.

Even the often "writerly" William Carlos Williams announced at a poetry reading given about 1950, "The modern poem . . . should be *heard.* It's very difficult sometimes to get it off the page. But once you hear it, then you should be able to appraise it."

∽

Michael Pakenham, writing for the *Baltimore Sun,* called *The Hudson Review* "a monument of civility": "It comes out of a small office in Manhattan four times a year, with a circulation of about 5,000 copies. Even with an estimated ten or so readers for every copy, the readership, in terms of a mass market, is minuscule."

Founded in 1948 by Frederick Morgan—who was to be its editor for fifty years—along with Joseph Bennett and William Arrowsmith (Princetonians all), the *Review* describes itself as dealing "with the area where literature bears on the intellectual life of the time and on diverse aspects of American culture":

It has no university affiliation and is not committed to any narrow academic aim or to any particular political perspective. The magazine serves as a major forum for the work of new writers and for the exploration of new developments in literature and the arts. By consistently maintaining its critical standards and a commitment to excellent writing, *The Hudson Review* has made a significant impact on the international literary climate. It has a distinguished record of publishing little-known or undiscovered writers, many of whom have become major literary figures.

Among the many already-famous writers published in the magazine were Thomas Mann, Wallace Stevens, Ezra Pound, T.S. Eliot, Dylan Thomas, William Carlos Williams, Eudora Welty, and Robert Graves. Anthony Hecht, James Merrill, Saul Bellow, Louis Simpson, Anne Sexton, Sylvia Plath, A.R. Ammons and Theodore Roethke were published there at the beginning of their careers.

Given the amount of political furor stirred up over Pound's receiving the $1000 Bollingen Award for *The Pisan Cantos* in 1949—despite Karl Shapiro's objection that "the poet's political and moral philosophy ultimately vitiates his poetry and lowers its standards"—Morgan's publication of Pound's work was a small act of courage. Pound's version of the Confucian *Analects* appeared in the *Hudson Review's* Spring and Summer issues in 1950; his version of Sophocles' *The Women of Trachis* appeared in the Winter issue, 1953-4. Seven of the later Cantos appeared between 1954 and the end of 1956. It should be noted, however, that Pound's version of the Confucian *Odes* was regarded by Charles Olson—a follower of Pound's—as a complete betrayal of the master's liberating earlier work. "The dross of verse. Rhyme!" Olson fulminated in "I, Mencius, Pupil of the Master":

> that Confucius himself
> should try to alter it, he
> who taught us all
> that no line must sleep,
> that as the line goes so goes
> the Nation! that the Master
> should now be embraced by the demon
> he drove off! . . .
>
> We'll to these woods
> no more, where we were used
> to get so much.

It was Pound who persuaded Morgan to publish Jaime de Angulo's "Indians in Overalls." Because one of *The Hudson's Review*'s editors had attacked him in another magazine, William Carlos Williams was initially reluctant to submit work. Eventually, however, he was persuaded and maintained a high opinion of the magazine throughout the rest of his life.

Though Morgan insists that "we never adopted the New Criticism as the only method to use" and asserts that "we resisted deconstruction when all the major universities fell for it hook, line, and sinker," the magazine was known for many years as a principal outlet for the New Criticism, a movement which took its name from John Crowe Ransom's book, *The New Criticism* (1941) and included such figures as Cleanth Brooks, Allen Tate, Robert Penn Warren, R.P. Blackmur and Ransom himself. Though Morgan visited Ezra Pound at St. Elizabeth's, it was not Pound but Allen Tate—Southerner and New Critic—who had the strongest influence on the magazine. In "*The Hudson Review*'s Early Years," an interview with Morgan conducted by Michael Peich in 1997, Morgan says, "Unlike Allen Tate, Ezra Pound was a hectoring kind of would-be mentor" who "wanted to tell me exactly what to do issue by issue": "I disregarded almost all the specific advice he favored me with over the next several years." Tate, on the other hand, whom Morgan met and studied with at Princeton, "was always friendly and encouraging." Morgan remarks on the CD that it was Tate who "gave us the most inspiration or instigation to publish." In the Peich interview he adds, "We wanted from the very beginning to have a strong critical component [in the magazine], in the sense that we'd be reviewing important new books and covering developments not only in literature, but in music, theatre, dance and the visual arts."

Though *The Hudson Review* is proud of its "distinguished record of publishing little-known or undiscovered writers," its focus was never on the Modernist "new"—as in Pound's "Make It New" or Baudelaire's "Au fond de l'Inconnu pour trouver du *nouveau*" ("In the depths of the Unknown to find something *new*"). Nor did it focus on the Surrealist "marvelous"—a version of the "new." The focus of *The Hudson Review* was rather on "excellent writing" and on "critical standards." "I think," Morgan observes on the CD, "the idea was to publish the *best* poetry." Such an emphasis necessarily places the magazine in a more-or-less conservative position. "Excellence" according to whom? *Which* "critical standards"? (Karl Shapiro thought that Pound's "political and moral philosophy" lowered that poet's "standards." By publishing Pound, Frederick Morgan indicated that his "standards" were different from Shapiro's.)

In 1998, Morgan gave the editorship of the magazine to his wife, Paula Deitz, who had been with *The Hudson Review* for thirty years; Morgan currently maintains an advisory role. It is Paula Deitz who is primarily responsible for this anniversary issue, though I suspect that the issue still reflects her husband's sensibilities. If *The Hudson Review* was once something of a bastion of the New Criticism, since the late 1970s it has been something of a bastion of a very different movement: the New Formalism. This issue features Dana Gioia, David Mason, R.S. Gwynn, Mark Jarman, and others whom we associate with that movement. "It was like, sort of in the air, this kind of new group of poets," Morgan remarks on the CD about the New Formalists. "They converged on *The Hudson Review,* partly because they knew the magazine already and liked it . . . They're remarkably cohesive, and they were a very pleasant change from the generation who were all neurotic as could be and alcoholic and crazy. You know, they [that generation] were just impossible people: Lowell, Berryman, Schwartz, Jarrell, that crowd."

∽

[T]he so-called "work" of oral art . . . is always live performance. It is really not a "work," but an action.
—WALTER J. ONG, S.J., *Interfaces of the Word* (1977)

People will not read my poems, but when I read to them I can spellbind. Everything engages, all my faculties converge here, and I become for
this brief time transcendently myself.
—WILLIAM EVERSON (1956)

The CD accompanying *The Hudson Review* is in part a reflection of its opening article, Dana Gioia's "Disappearing Ink: Poetry at the End of Print Culture." The essay begins with an announcement of revolution—a rather startling thing to find in the pages of *The Hudson Review*:

We are currently living in the midst of a massive cultural revolution. For the first time since the development of moveable type in the late fifteenth century, print has lost its primacy in communication.

"A spectre is haunting Europe"! And not only Europe.

There is no doubt that Gioia's essay is brilliant and considerably extends our understanding of a situation in which "writing exists but is no longer the primary means of public discourse." "Books, magazines, and newspapers are not disappearing," he goes on—and "disappearing" is an important word in this essay—"but their position in the culture has changed significantly over the past few decades, even among the educated. We are now seeing the first generation of young intellectuals who are not willing to immerse themselves in the world of books. They are not against reading, but they see it as only one of the many options for information . . . The decline of print as our culture's primary means of codifying, presenting, and preserving information isn't merely a methodological change; it is an epistemological transformation."

In the midst of "the end of print culture," however, the art of poetry—or at least some aspects of the art of poetry—is experiencing a resurgence. Verse, Gioia argues, "has changed into a growth industry, though its rehabilitation has happened mostly off the printed page":

> Without doubt the most surprising and significant development in recent American poetry has been the wide-scale and unexpected reemergence of popular poetry— namely rap, cowboy poetry, poetry slams, and certain overtly accessible types of what was once a defiantly avant-garde genre, performance poetry.

Gioia cautions, however, that the term "poetry" "now encompasses so many diverse and often irreconcilable artistic enterprises that it often proves insufficient to distinguish the critical issues at stake"; instead, he proposes the terms "literary poetry" and "popular poetry." "Literary poetry" designates "all written, high-art poetry of whatever school"; "popular poetry" indicates "the new forms of verse that have emerged outside the official literary culture." There are four significant aspects to popular poetry: it is oral; it emerges from outside established literary life, involving "innovation from the margins"; it is "overwhelmingly, indeed characteristically, formal"; and—amazingly enough for poetry—it has considerable popular appeal: it is "commercial." (One of the glories of "Disappearing Ink" is Gioia's serious and informed discussion of rap.)

These four trends "that appear so obvious" in popular poetry "also exist less overtly in the established literary world":

> The most conspicuous difference between literary poetry and the new popular poetry is that one is written and the other predominantly oral. Those features seem irreconcilable, do they not? And yet, who would dispute that the contemporary American poet's primary means of publication is now oral—namely the poetry reading? Poets of every school now reach more people through oral performance—

in person, by broadcast, through video or audio recording—than they generally do through print. Books remain the basic medium for literary poetry, but paradoxically an author's print readership now heavily depends on attracting an audience initially through oral performance.

"Literary high-art poetry," Gioia argues, "is now in the process of breaking up into at least four distinct literary forms, each based on a fundamentally different relationship between spoken and typographic language." Performance poetry, emerging "out of the medium of the poetry reading," "is not rooted only in language":

> Instead, it recognizes and exploits the physical presence of the performer, the audience, and the performance space. The text is only one element in its artistic totality . . . Though its historical origins are in literary poetry, performance poetry is now a different art, and its fundamental irreconcilability with literary poetry becomes more apparent each year.

The second form into which literary high-art poetry is breaking up is "oral poetry": "The new oral poetry differs from performance poetry in that it uses words—rather than the artist's total physical presence and performance space—as its raw material. In the context of popular entertainment, oral poetry takes the form of rap and cowboy poetry, but "among literary poets, the new oral verse is called 'Spoken Word' poetry, and it has developed a substantial and serious following. In the San Francisco Bay Area, for example, there is already a sophisticated community of Spoken Word poets. . . ." Gioia here mentions my work as one instance of Spoken Word poetry.

The third form high-art literary poetry is becoming is "audio-visual": "There is no trendy new name . . . because this aesthetic most closely resembles our traditional conception of poetry. It focuses on the creation of verse that can work equally well as a typographic entity and a spoken performance." Such verse must, however, face "the conflicting demands of the visual aesthetic of Modernist poetry and the new orality of mass culture."

The final form high-art literary poetry is becoming is "visual poetry": "At one end of this aesthetic, the work can be read aloud . . . At the other end of this visual aesthetic, as in concrete poetry, the text cannot be realized in any meaningful sense as spoken language."

"The decline of print culture," Gioia goes on, "has been especially hard on literary poets since it has broken down the elaborate cultural machinery by which they once reached their audience":

Traditionally a poet's readership and reputation was influenced mainly by four interrelated factors—journalistic review, serious (usually academic) literary criticism, anthologies, and general press coverage. All four means of reaching the literary reading public have diminished notably in the last few decades.

Gioia then adds some eloquent passages about "the rise of the new bohemia"—which is for him an extremely significant and hopeful development. "The near monopoly that the university so recently enjoyed in the stewardship of poetry now seems to be dissolving in the face of economic, demographic, and technological changes":

> The academy's role in supporting new poetry is not disappearing [again the word "disappearing"—ed.]. Writing programs and English departments continue to play a decisive role in contemporary letters. But the larger literary world that surrounds the university has changed so significantly that the academy's position in literary culture is being transformed . . . American poetry is presently returning to a more historically typical, an intellectually healthier situation where the university's role is balanced by a strong non-academic literary culture . . . Today, for the first time in fifty years, the vast majority of young American writers now live and work outside the university.

Anyone deeply involved in the whirl-a-gig poetry world will appreciate the truth of Gioia's arguments. A poet who opens himself up to this world soon discovers that it is in constant motion: it's not that there is no there there; it's that the number of there's is often surprising and baffling. "Poetry" is not one thing but a complex web of activities, some of which are very much at odds with one another. In a situation in which our poets laureate often speak for the art as a whole—poetry "is" this, poetry "is" that—Gioia's important essay demonstrates how genuinely dense the actualities of the situation are. In addition, he gives us a terminology by which we can make some sense of the chaos that faces us. Most essays dealing with poetry as such are really nothing more than the manifestation of one partial view—often one sentimental, partial view. "Disappearing Ink" is a genuine beginning, something which we can use as we try to assess what is happening to poetry as a whole—if in fact one can even speak of "poetry as a whole."

Having said so much, however, I want to make a few criticisms—and to approach the subject from a point of view which is quite different from Gioia's. Two small points: I wish he had mentioned the considerable number of books on tape—a significant phenomenon in the current literary scene.

(Margaret Atwood's fascinating new novel, *Oryx and Crake*, appeared simultaneously as text and as tape.) In addition, despite the "end of print culture," certain aspects of publishing are doing quite well. My wife reads mystery novels and so do many of her friends: they are constantly exchanging the books, giving each other information, locating new ones—quite excited by the activity of reading. These mystery novels, by authors such as Sue Grafton and Elizabeth George, are, I believe, books for educated people who don't have the "time" to read "seriously" but for whom reading is an important part of their self-understanding: they *see* themselves as "readers" even though they realize that there are certain kinds of books they no longer have the energy to undertake. "Romance novels" may serve something of the same function.

There is also a small error of fact in "Disappearing Ink." Gioia writes that "bookstores like Chapters in Washington, D.C. or Cody's in Berkeley have presented literary programming equal to that of major universities, and it has been free and open to anyone who walked in the door." I don't know about Chapters, but Cody's Poetry Series does charge a nominal fee.

Gioia does a fine job in differentiating the various kinds of "poetries" at large in our world. What Gioia does not suggest is the possibility that these various "poetries" can interact, interrelate—to their mutual illumination. We see more and more books which are a combination of text and CD, but we do not see much use of these modes in interrelationship. Every medium has both strengths and limitations. Modern technology has caused a number of media—print, CD, cassette, video—to be more or less equally available to the poet. These various modes can be used to *comment* on one another, though, admittedly, for the most part they have not been used in that way. Towards the end of my poem, "Gershwin," there appears the following passage: "[Chord: E major]." On the CD accompanying the book, you hear the chord being played. On the other hand, the poem also contains a drawing I made of Gershwin—an instance of the visual possibilities of the page. You can't get the sound of the chord from the page, but you can get it from the CD; you can't get the picture of Gershwin from the CD, but you can get it from the page.

Finally, there is the issue of "Modernism." In "Notes on the New Formalism," one of the essays collected in *Can Poetry Matter?*, Dana Gioia writes that "the modern movement, which began this century in bohemia, is now ending it in the university . . . Ultimately the mission of the university has little to do with the mission of the arts." "Free verse," he asserts, "the creation of an older literary revolution, is now the long-established, ruling orthodoxy, formal poetry the unexpected challenge." "It's time," he suggests in "Can Poetry Matter?," "to experiment." In "Disappearing Ink" he refers to "the now-antiquarian assumptions of Modernism and the avant-garde" and to Modernism's "typographic poetry."

Gioia's attack on "Modernism"—which is indeed, despite Yeats' status as a "Modernist," associated with free verse—is a way of clearing the field for a new movement, a movement in which "traditional forms" (and the "New Formalism") play a significant role. What Gioia is doing here is not very different from what spokespeople for any new movement are likely to do. Yet in approaching the problem in this way Gioia is not being "traditional" but modernist. "Modernity," writes Paul de Man in *Blindness and Insight*, "exists in the form of a desire to wipe out whatever came earlier, in the hope of reaching at last a point that could be called a true present, a point of origin that marks a new departure." Such a definition of Modernity sounds exactly like what Gioia is doing in *attacking* Modernity. "Modern," suggests Frederick R. Karl in *Modern and Modernism*, "is the onslaught of new knowledge that [forces] rethinking in every field." "Inevitably," Karl goes on, "Modern . . . devours itself."

Indeed, Gioia is Modernist is other respects as well. The problems he is dealing with—problems having to do with the relationship between the visuality of text and the aurality of speech—were first enunciated by Modernism. It is not odd that Gioia should be raising such questions—they are burning issues and he is one of the few critics courageous enough to be confronting them head on—but it is odd that he should be raising them in the context of an attack on Modernism. Gioia associates literary Modernism with the *visual* and "the new popular poetry" with the *aural*: "an early Modernist poem in free verse distinguishes itself from prose by certain typographical conventions such as empty space and line breaks that visually disrupt the standard page rule of the right-hand margin" whereas "oral poetry uses apprehensible auditory patterns, such as rhyme and meter, to command the special attention an audience gives to the heightened form of speech known as poetry."

Gioia's references to "the visual aesthetic of Modernist poetry" are in some respects, I believe, a misrepresentation of literary history. Surely, the great ancestor of Modernism's "visual aesthetic" is Stéphane Mallarmé's *Un coup de dés, A Throw of the Dice Will Never Abolish Chance*, a poem published in 1897. I have argued elsewhere that *Un coup de dés* gave birth to an extraordinary series of experiments with typefaces, with white space, with patterns, with letters (in Apollinaire as well as E. E. Cummings), with "field" techniques, with all sorts of essentially visual phenomena. But Mallarmé insists that his visual innovations are an attempt to represent *sound*—that the poem is a *score* for speech:

> Everything happens by a shortcut, hypothetically; story-telling is avoided. Add to that: that from this naked use of thought, retreating, prolonging, fleeing, or from its very design, there results for the person reading it aloud, a musical score. The difference in the printed characters between the preponderant, secondary, and adjacent motifs, dictates their importance for oral expression; the disposition of the characters: in the middle, on the top, or the bottom of the page, indicates the rise and fall in intonation.

The idea of the printed poem as a "musical score" shows up in other poets as well. Charles Olson's famous, wonderfully energetic, sometimes confused essay, "Projective Verse" (1950), reads like an announcement of "the Spoken Word revolution":

> What we have suffered from, is manuscript, press, the removal of verse from its producer and its reproducer, the voice, a removal by one, by two removes from its place of origin *and* its destination. For the breath has a double meaning which latin [*sic*] had not yet lost.

Olson's denunciation of the "verse that print bred" is part of an attempt to espouse another mode which he calls "projective" and which is centered on "the breath, . . . the breathing of the man who writes, at the moment that he writes."[1] For Olson too the page is a "score." The typewriter, "due to its rigidity and its space precision . . . can, for a poet, indicate exactly the breath, the pauses, the suspensions even of syllables, the juxtapositions even of parts of phrases":

> For the first time the poet has the stave and the bar a musician has had. For the first time he can, without the convention of rime and meter, record the listening he has done to his own speech and by that one act indicate how he would want any reader, silently or otherwise, to voice his work.
>
> It is time we picked the fruits of the experiments of Cummings, Pound, Williams, each of whom has, after his way, already used the machine as a scoring to his composing, as a script to its vocalization.

In insisting that New Directions publish a facsimile of his typescript in *Ground Work: Before the War* (1984), Robert Duncan was firmly in the tradition of

Mallarmé and Olson. "All 'typographical' features,'" Duncan writes, "are notations for the performance of the reading"; "The cadence of the verse, and, in turn, the interpenetration of cadences in sequence is, for me, related to the dance of my physical body. My hands keep time and know more than my brain does of measure." *Ground Work: Before the War* is probably the oddest-looking book New Directions ever published, and subsequent books by Duncan—all published posthumously—have not resembled it.

But these various efforts raise a question. If the typewriter is only the vehicle by which the poet makes known his "vocalization," why not abandon this last link with what "print bred"? Why not move entirely into the realm of the spoken? Thomas Parkinson once remarked to me that he thought Charles Olson's natural medium was the tape recorder—or, as we would now say, the CD. David Antin is one instance of a poet who has attempted to incorporate speech into his writing: books such as *Talking at the Boundaries* (1976) and *Tuning* (1984) deliberately blur the distinction between the "talk" and the "poetry reading"; their "texts" have been generated by Antin's spontaneous rap as he addresses an audience. Language poet Steve Benson also works in this manner.

Do the spatial innovations of such writers (Olson insisted that he was *post*modernist) affect the way we hear or recite their poems? Yes, of course they do—but that is not all they do. In many ways Gioia is quite right about the association of Modernism with the visual: the way these poems *look* on the page is necessarily part of how we react to them—however much their spacing may affect the way we "hear" them. The point of what these poets are doing is neither the page as such nor the oral/aural as such, but *the problematical way in which the page and the oral relate to one another*—which is precisely the problem Gioia is considering. Surely these poets (particularly Olson) deserve at least a mention in Gioia's essay, but they do not receive one. Here, perhaps, the author's commitment to a kind of poetry outweighs even his own keen historical sense. In addition to enunciating the problem of print vs. speech, these writers are all mighty proponents of free verse, a poetic practice Gioia argues is currently somewhat outmoded, even "antiquarian." It is of course true that interest in "formal modes" has grown by leaps and bounds—and Gioia is in many ways responsible for that growth. For many, the rhyme and meter of popular song has found its way into the serious consideration of poetry, has in fact functioned as a bridge to that consideration. When asked about Charles Bukowski as a "model" for the young, New Formalist poet Timothy Steele answered, "I think you're much better off taking a pop star, because heaven knows, Lennon-McCartney and Dylan write in meter, so you at least get something of the art from them."[2]

∽

The fact is that Gioia, perhaps single-handedly, has brought a kind of writing which at one time was entirely associated with the "literary"—with the *read*—into the realm of the "spoken"—a realm usually associated with a very different kind of writing. That is part of what is "new" about "The New Formalism." *The Hudson Review* rightly boasts of having included the Pulitzer-Prize-winning Wallace Stevens in its early issues. But Gioia himself points out that Stevens was practically a stranger to the "oral message" and quotes the poet grousing that the "public reading of poetry is something particularly ghastly." It is precisely the ancestors of "the Spoken Word revolution" that *The Hudson Review* did *not* publish. To the casual observer, Gioia may seem to be attempting merely to revive the neglected traditions of "rhyme and meter"— and in part, of course, that is what he is doing. But "Disappearing Ink" is one indication of the fact that what Gioia is doing is not only "new"—that Modernist term—but more or less without precedent. And, amazingly, he has brought the entire *Hudson Review* along with him.

Some of the *Hudson Review* poets read quite well on the CD. X.J. Kennedy is always a joy to hear, and one could wish for more from Daniel Hoffman. (Hoffman has published many fine books over the years, but his early *A Little Geste and Other Poems*—1960—has always been a favorite of mine.) Dana Gioia, Philip Levine, and David Mason read well and read excellent work. R.S. Gwynn's "Before Prostate Surgery" and "Leda" are both delightful—and an interesting pairing. ("Leda" is printed in the issue.) Other poets do not fare as well at the microphone. Whatever possessed W.S. Merwin to write—and then read in his "poet's voice"—the unfortunate lines, "It is wine that I will not drink / I will not drink it / Not I / this wine," published in *The Hudson Review* in Spring, 1973. Galway Kinnell recites a passage from his famous but rather over-rated "The Avenue Bearing the Initial of Christ into the New World"—a poem I always felt was inspired by the work of Allen Ginsberg. The younger poets—Ginger Andrews, Michael Donaghy, and Catherine Tufariello—do not seem as compelling as the older ones. Noted U.K. poet Donaghy's longish "Black Ice and Rain" sounded to me like an attempt to "modernize" Browning by references to people like Curtis Mayfield—but gave us nothing Browning hasn't already given. I transcribed these lines from the CD:

Just so: the past falls open anywhere
Even sitting here with you. Sorry!
You remind me of a girl I knew.
I met her at a party much like this
But younger, louder, the bay
So fat, the night so sticky you could drown
And we shouted Art at each other
Over sole and cold beer in the crowded kitchen . . .

Some of the finest moments on the CD are supplied by Frederick Morgan as he reminisces about the magazine's history and reads—beautifully—some of the poems published in it. Wallace Stevens' wonderful "The Course of a Particular" is perhaps the finest poem read on the CD, and Morgan reads it quite well. It was published in the magazine's Spring1951 issue and can be found in Stevens' *Opus Posthumous*. Edwin Muir's fine poem, "The Animals" (Winter 1952), also read by Morgan, is perhaps better seen than heard. Since this poet is no longer well known, I thought to include the text in this essay. The poem plays upon Nietzsche's observation, made in *The Uses and Abuses of History*, that "the animal lives unhistorically":

They do not live in the world,
Are not in time and space,
From birth to death hurled
No word do they have, not one
To plant a foot upon,
Were never in any place.

For by words the world was called
Out of the empty air,
With words was shaped and walled—
Line and circle and square,
Mud and emerald,—
Snatched from deceiving death
By the articulate breath.

But these have never trod
Twice the familiar track,
Never never turned back
Into the memoried day;

All is new and near
In the unchanging Here
Of the fifth great day of God,
That shall remain the same,
Never shall pass away.

On the sixth day we came.

Though Morgan is an excellent poet (his book, *The One Abiding*, with an introduction by Dana Gioia, recently appeared from Story Line Press), he does not read any of his own work on the CD.

The readings collected on *Along These Lines* suggest that none of these writers is placing "writing" as such in question. There is not a single moment in which the CD presents something which *cannot* be represented on a page. These are poets—often very fine poets—who are not in this sense questioning the limitations of their art. Yet, as "Disappearing Ink" makes clear, Gioia *is* doing that—and so the CD does indeed have "an historic" significance. Under Gioia's influence, the current *Hudson Review* is a testimony to the fact that "history" is never anything but in motion.

When William Carlos Williams insisted that "the modern poem . . . should be *heard*," he was echoing a statement we come upon often over the course of the twentieth century. Readers have frequently remarked about poetry that they "understand" it better when they hear it than when they read it silently, or that the poem "on the page" seems different—better— after they have heard the poet read it aloud. Such readings are *transformative*. Dylan Thomas was a master of such readings: his beautiful renditions of his poems placed in question our capacity to read them silently. There is nothing on the *Hudson Review* CD which does that. It is interesting to hear the poets, but the work they read can be understood perfectly well through silent reading: it is not *transformed* by their reading. When the Beat poets read poetry to jazz accompaniment or when my wife Adelle and I perform multi-voiced poems—whatever the value of such performances—*an attempt is being made to transform the poem as it exists on the page*: we are doing something which silent reading cannot represent. If we recall the fact that poetry begins with oral recitation—and that Homer is represented as being blind and therefore without any relationship to the visual art of "writing"—we realize that the printing of poetry too represented a "transformation": it was no longer necessary to *hear* someone (a specific person in a specific place) read the poem aloud; we could "see" it instead.

For various reasons, written poetry has always maintained an uneasy relationship to poetry's oral past—a past which, paradoxically, was to some extent preserved through works of writing. I suggested in my book *O Powerful Western Star* that at the heart of Western poetry is a split, a confusion, a multimedia situation which is never resolved but which remains in a continual, and at times enormously creative, state of tension. What Walter J. Ong calls "the new orality" of the electronic era has caused critics—Gioia among them—to recognize this hidden history of poetry, a history which was not made clear by earlier critics: certainly not by the New Critics, for whom the poem was entirely a written object. The fact is that Modernism is steeped in the performance of poetry—Dylan Thomas was firmly in the tradition of Yeats, Pound and Marinetti when he took to the radio—but the critics who made Modernism famous completely ignored this aspect of its history. Ironically, it was only by *analogy* with presentations in the electronic media that poetry found its way into the current "national consciousness." To put it bluntly: *poetry is the one branch of "literature" which has a performative aspect; it is the one branch of "literature" which can be made to resemble rock-and-roll.* (The narrative elements of drama—the other performative literary activity—make it a very different experience from the rock-and-roll show.)[3]

If we are to maintain ourselves as a "literate" people, a people interested in "literature"—and *at the same time* maintain our interest in the electronic media—the "Spoken Word revolution" is one way to do it. Though the Spoken Word movement has not yet produced its Shakespeare, it nevertheless *combines* the electronic with the written. It is important to note, however, that the Spoken Word movement does not arise entirely from within poetry itself—though the Black Mountain poets and the Beats were definitely precursors. The current issue of *The Hudson Review* demonstrates that poetry remains as divided and confused as it ever was. The Spoken Word movement arises out of the need to find some sort of balance between the literary and the electronic, which is to say it arises out of that very crisis of writing which it simultaneously expresses and to some degree resolves.

⌀

The Hudson Review is rightly proud of its past—its version of "excellence"—and it should be proud as well of this fascinating 55th-anniversary issue. But the reader should be aware that there are kinds of writing—even of "excellent writing"—which have never appeared in *The Hudson Review*. This, quoted in its entirety, is from Larry Eigner's book, *Readiness Enough Depends On*. It would never have appeared in *either The Hudson Review* or Lawrence Ferlinghetti's *City Lights Review*:

phonepole

a tree

big sky

great cloud

The kind of inspiration that many people drew from Donald Allen's famous 1960 anthology, *The New American Poetry*—in which Eigner *did* appear and which featured Olson's "Projective Verse" essay—was never to be found in *The Hudson Review*. Did *any* of Allen's contributors appear in Morgan's magazine? Poems such as these—the first by Charles Bukowski, the second by Charles Olson—had to interest someone other than Frederick Morgan in order to reach their audiences:

the mockingbird

the mockingbird had been following the cat
all summer
mocking mocking mocking
teasing and cocksure;
the cat crawled under rockers on porches
tail flashing
and said something angry to the mockingbird
which I didn't understand.

yesterday the cat walked calmly up the driveway
with the mockingbird alive in its mouth,
wings fanned, beautiful wings fanned and flopping,
feathers parted like a woman's legs,
and the bird was no longer mocking,
it was asking, it was praying
        but the cat
        striding down through centuries

would not listen.

I saw it crawl under a yellow car
with the bird
to bargain it to another place.

summer was over.

∽

I have made dialogues,
have discussed ancient texts,
have thrown what light I could, offered
what pleasures
doceat allows

But the known?
This, I have had to be given,
a life, love, and from one man
the world.

Tokens.
But sitting here
I look out as a wind
and water man, testing
And missing
some proof

I know the quarters
of the weather, where it comes from,
where it goes. But the stem of me,
this I took from their welcome,
or their rejection, of me

And my arrogance
was neither diminished
nor increased
by the communication

2
It is undone business
I speak of, this morning,
with the sea
stretching out
from my feet.

Yet *The Hudson Review* remains: a monument to "civility," intelligence, and a vision of literature which, though necessarily partial, is deep, courageous, and beautifully mannered. And this is true despite the powerful sense of "loss" which this 55th-anniversary issue so frequently manifests. The first word of Gioia's essay is "disappearing"; the last word is "listening," not "reading": "Even if there are *fewer readers*"—my italics—"people will be listening."

American Literature

A paper delivered at the University of Damascus,
Damascus, Syria, October, 2003, revised for this book

I am a sort of "accidental tourist" in Syria. My wife Adelle and I are here because our son Sean, who is doing research on the nineteenth-century figure Sheikh Khalid Naqshbandi, invited us to visit. It was Sean who arranged this lecture, working through the good offices of the American Cultural Center, and it is he and his wife Kerry who are hosting us and guiding us throughout the visit. I have presented several programs dealing with Arabic poetry on my radio show, "Cover to Cover," which originates in Berkeley, California—but I am far from being an expert on that subject.

Writing of early Arabic poetry, one critic remarked, "Arabic poetry at the time of the *Jahiliyya* (the pre-Islamic era in Arabia) was rooted in the oral and developed within an audio-vocal culture; . . . this poetry did not come down to us in written form but was 'anthologized' in the memory and preserved through oral transmission . . . Two basic principles of pre-Islamic poetry were that it should be recited aloud and that the poet himself should recite his own poem."[1]

In addition to this talk on American literature, you will hear a choral poem, "Overture," recited aloud by "the poet himself"—along with his wife. The tradition of oral recitation by "the poet himself" has begun to spring up again in the United States, though for a long time a more "writerly" tradition had replaced it. As I came into poetry in the 1950s, I felt very strongly that the writerly tradition needed an infusion of oral energy.

∽

It's no easy task to talk about American literature and American culture in a short space. There is much, I'm sure, which you already know—and perhaps much as well about which you may be mistaken, just as Americans are often mistaken about Arab culture. More, not less, interchange between our countries is necessary: getting to know another person has many twists, turns, and surprises; getting to know another culture has even more.

Should I talk about rock and roll, about rap, about American Classical music, about American literature (novels and poetry but also history books, self-help books, sociological books, cook books, even comic books), about sports, about relationships between ethnic groups, about gender relationships, about American media (films, radio, television, newspapers, drama), about communications in America, about ways of travel, about the use of the Internet—about what someone called, many years ago, "the lonely crowd" of consumers or about the mass of happy consumers regularly postulated by American television programs? Should I talk about the look of American cities and the shapes of their buildings? All these things are relevant but can hardly be covered in a short period. In addition, two people may be looking at the same thing but registering it in entirely different ways. A nineteenth-century British reviewer, faced for the first time with the astonishing verse of the American poet, Walt Whitman, remarked: "Mr. Whitman seems to believe that because the Mississippi River is long and the Missouri River is wide, every American is God." That is of course not at all what Mr. Whitman believed, but one can understand how the reviewer arrived at his opinion.

A friend told me that a literate, intelligent European—a friend of his—made a surprising remark about American literature. The European said that, while he often read American novels and poetry, he felt that they were never *about* anything. They were enjoyable, even very enjoyable, but at some deep level they had absolutely no subject matter. It is interesting that—in a widely-quoted remark—the creators of a popular American television program, *Seinfeld*, made a similar observation: they announced that *Seinfeld* was "about nothing."

Is it possible for *anything* to be about nothing? Shakespeare remarks in a resonant moment in *King Lear*, "Nothing will come of nothing." Yet Western Culture insists that *everything* came from "nothing," that the entire universe was created *ex nihilo*.

I think what the European meant was that American literature often had no easily defined, obvious *subject matter*. This poem, "The Vampire" (1897) by the British poet Rudyard Kipling, is about the bad end people come to if they fall in love with an adventurous female:

> A fool there was and he made his prayer
> (Even as you and I!)
> To a rag and a bone and a hank of hair
> (We called her the woman who did not care)
> But the fool he called her his lady fair—

(Even as you and I!)

But what exactly is the subject matter of this untitled poem (c. 1861) by the American Emily Dickinson?

> Wild Nights—Wild Nights!
> Were I with thee
> Wild Nights should be
> Our luxury!
>
> Futile—the Winds—
> To a Heart in port—
> Done with the Compass—
> Done with the Chart!
>
> Rowing in Eden—
> Ah, the Sea!
> Might I but moor—Tonight—
> In Thee!

Is the "Thee" of the poem God or a human lover? There is no easy way to tell. The poem seems to name some sort of longed-for ecstasy: "Ah, the Sea!" But it is not quite clear what sort it is. What exactly does the word "Wild" mean here? An abandonment to sexuality? And what is "luxury"? The poem's true subject seems to be the fact that the poet has *felt* something. For Kipling, feeling something is merely the *condition* of the poem. Of course he feels something about the kind of woman he is naming, and this is what he has to say about it; Kipling insists upon asserting a social context in which such a woman can be described. Dickinson's poem is a powerful assertion of feeling—but there is no definite social or even religious context in which the feeling takes place. The poem, like feeling itself, is mysterious, not quite to be pinned down. Feeling is like the ocean: "Ah, the Sea!" In addition, there is perhaps the suggestion that there is a force (or a condition) which ordinarily moves *against* feeling—"Futile—the Winds—/ To a Heart in port"—and so it is exceptional for the poet to be feeling something. Feeling is not present at all times but is a thing to be longed-for, conjured up, an *if only*.

Dickinson's contemporary, Ralph Waldo Emerson goes even further in his essay on "Nature" (1836):

> Standing on the bare ground . . . all mean egotism vanishes. I become a transparent
> eyeball; I am nothing; I see all; the currents of the Universal Being circulate through
> me; I am part and parcel of God.

Like Emily Dickinson, Emerson describes a sudden dissolution of the ego, a state which is utterly different from the state in which he usually exists—and he announces further that in the midst of that state he is, precisely, "nothing." American literature at such moments is definitely "about nothing"—a "nothing" which deliberately removes itself from the web of social situations and interactions which exists all around any individual person or object; a "nothing" which achieves, precisely, the obliteration of "everything." Emerson's passage names a desire to exist out of the world, to be elsewhere— to be "nothing." God's creation—Nature itself—is necessarily *something*. To become "a transparent eyeball" is to achieve an ecstatic condition in which whatever is flows through you. At such moments you are not likely to be making judgments about one kind of woman rather than another—or about one kind of employment rather than another or about whether people doing a certain job are receiving fair wages or about whether one political system is better than another.[2] "I am nothing," writes Emerson, "I see all." "Wild Nights! Wild Nights!" writes Emily Dickinson.

Why should this be the case? Why should this longing for what Emerson called "the Transcendental" be so important in American literature and American culture? Why is American literature so deeply about *escape*—and, often, about the failure of escape? "Which of us has not remained forever prison-pent?" asked the novelist Thomas Wolfe in his great book, *Look Homeward, Angel* (1929), "Which of us is not forever a stranger and alone?":

> Remembering speechlessly, we seek the great forgotten language, the lost lane-end
> into heaven. A stone, a leaf, an unfound door. Where? When? O lost, and by the
> wind grieved, ghost, come back again.

You must understand that American culture is a relatively recent thing. America as a nation dates back only about two hundred and twenty-five years. The Englishmen who "settled" the country initially thought of themselves as Englishmen, not as "Americans." And it was precisely as Englishmen that they undertook a rebellion against King George. The question of what constitutes an "American" haunts American culture. How can we have a culture if we don't know who we are? Or perhaps it is the culture which *determines* who we are. What kind of identity do we have if we have done this, that, or the other thing? What do our actions say about us? And, even more pertinently, who exactly is "us"?

The United States has a long, confusing tradition of utter diversity. What "constitutes" culture in this country is a crazy quilt of contributions from all sorts of specific cultures. Poet Ishmael Reed has coined a name for this situation: "MultiAmerica"—not a single, unified entity but a soup of various elements which are in a constant state of movement.

In the anthology, *Unsettling America* (1994), editors Maria Mazziotti Gillan and Jennifer Gillan take this sense of movement as the primary fact about America: "We chose poems," Jennifer Gillan writes, "that directly address the instability of American identity and confront the prevalence of cultural conflict and exchange within the United States . . . We hope to highlight the constant erecting, blurring, breaking, clarifying, and crossing of boundaries that are a consequence of the complex intersections among peoples, cultures, and languages within national borders, which themselves are revised constantly."

Gillan's eloquent words recall those of Alexis de Tocqueville, whose *Democracy in America* appeared in the original French (and in an English translation) between 1835 and 1840. In America, writes de Tocqueville, "continual changes are . . . every instant occurring under the observation of every man"; there is "universal tumult," an "incessant conflict of jarring interests"; "everyone is in motion."

As these quotations suggest, "the instability of American identity"—its "unsettling"—is an old story, but it is one which is continually hidden under the rhetoric of stability and constancy, a rhetoric which has furnished many a politician with comforting platitudes about "family values" and "Americanism." The tensions that arise out of genuine difference, out of what may be in fact utter incompatibility, are what Americans must simultaneously deny and deal with on an everyday basis. *It is in fact precisely this perception of incompatibility—of diversity, history—that American writers are trying to escape.* The thrust towards some kind of perceived "unity" is very strong in the American character—"I am nothing; I see all"—but so is the drive towards chaos. If Walt Whitman is writing a poetry which celebrates "the Union of these States," he is also writing a poetry which is in many ways supremely chaotic. His "Song of Myself" is one of the great structureless poems in the English language.

At a high point in his trilogy of novels, *USA* (1938), John Dos Passos cries out, "all right we are two nations." At the present moment in the United States, we are not two but hundreds of nations, each in a state of simultaneous alienation and connectedness. It was the great task of the now defunct twentieth century to make clear the fact that, however much we failed to acknowledge it, chaos—or "multiplicity"—was the actual condition of living in the United States, indeed in the entire world. Two American writers immediately come to mind: T.S. Eliot and Ezra Pound—both of whom in a sense sacrificed themselves to their burgeoning sense of diversity. This is the beginning of Eliot's famous poem, *The Waste Land*—a poem which, I'm told, is well-known in the Arab world:

> April is the cruellest month, breeding
> Lilacs out of the dead land, mixing
> Memory and desire, stirring
> Dull roots with spring rain.
> Winter kept us warm, covering
> Earth in forgetful snow, feeding
> A little life with dried tubers.
> Summer surprised us, coming over the Starnbergersee
> With a shower of rain; we stopped in the colonnade,
> And went on in sunlight, into the Hofgarten,
> And drank coffee, and talked for an hour.
> Bin gar keine Russin, stamm' aus Litauen, echt deutsch.
> And when we were children, staying at the archduke's,
> My cousin's, he took me out on a sled,
> And I was frightened. He said, Marie,
> Marie, hold on tight. And down we went.
> In the mountains, there you feel free.
> I read, much of the night, and go south in the winter.

It is as if the poem is spoken, not by an individual, but by a crowd of people whose various voices are being registered on the poet's sensibility.

Puritanism is one of the great traditions of the United States, and I believe that one of the defining characteristics of Puritanism is its insistence that we make *choices*. The great Puritan poem, John Milton's *Paradise Lost* (1667), is about a *wrong choice*. In this, as has often been observed, Puritanism goes very well with consumer Capitalism, which also insists that we make choices: this product rather than that one. The richness of the passage from *The Waste Land* does not lie in its insistence on an either/or mentality. It lies in allowing a number of isolated contexts to "speak" to one another, to touch, to "illuminate" one another. T.S. Eliot was a deeply divided man; *The Waste*

Land was his attempt to find a "form" which would have room for all aspects of his complex personality. He himself doubted whether the poem succeeded. Ezra Pound edited *The Waste Land*—cut it somewhat severely— and received credit in the printed version as "il miglior fabbro," the better craftsman. Asked by an interviewer whether Pound's editing "changed the intellectual structure of the poem," Eliot answered, "No. I think it was just as structureless, only in a more futile way, in the longer version." Eliot remarked that, as he wrote the poem, "I wasn't even bothering whether I understood what I was saying."[3]

What exactly was Eliot saying? At the time he wrote *The Waste Land*, which was published in 1922, both he and Ezra Pound had been studying the English poet Robert Browning, whose "dramatic monologues" are among the jewels of English literature. In a "dramatic monologue," the poem is "spoken" by a single person—someone who is not the poet—and we deduce the speaker's situation from what he says: the effect is as if someone took one of the soliloquies from a Shakespeare play and presented it, entirely apart from the play, as an individual poem. Both Pound and Eliot wrote "dramatic monologues"; the most famous of these is Eliot's brilliant "The Love Song of J. Alfred Prufrock" (1917), but Pound wrote several as well. Browning's dramatic monologues can be extraordinarily complex in their implications, but they always maintain themselves as the utterance of a *single* speaker. Both Eliot and Pound began to formulate the idea of an individual poem spoken by *various* speakers with little or no attempt to clarify the distinction of the speakers from one another: voices simply *appear*. One might call such poems dramatic multilogues or polylogues. Eliot is aware, however, that such a poem implies not only an esthetic method but a *self* which may be "structureless." In what may have been a moment of panic, he added a footnote to *The Waste Land* in which he insisted that the poem—which utterly explodes the idea of a single speaker—was in fact a dramatic monologue, the utterance of the single speaker, Tiresias:

> Tiresias, although a mere spectator and not indeed a "character," is yet the most important personage in the poem, uniting all the rest. Just as the one-eyed merchant, seller of currants, melts into the Phoenician Sailor, and the latter is not wholly distinct from Ferdinand Prince of Naples, so all the women are one woman, and the two sexes meet in Tiresias. What Tiresias *sees*, in fact, is the substance of the poem.

Tiresias is indeed understood in Classical mythology to be androgynous, an "old man with wrinkled dugs," as Eliot puts it. But he is not understood to be simultaneously young and old—and there are young and old speakers in *The Waste Land*. It is difficult to see how this figure who is "not indeed a 'character'" can be said to "unify" the poem—to "become" all the other characters. Rather, Tiresias appears merely as one more voice in a poem which is full of voices.

Eliot remarked that in writing *The Waste Land* he had "more to say than one knew how to say" and had "something one wanted to put into words and rhythm which one didn't have the command of words and rhythm to put in a way immediately apprehensible."[4] What was not "immediately apprehensible" to Eliot was the depth of his own perception of multiplicity: *The Waste Land* is a poem which cannot be regarded as the utterance of a single individual, yet in a desperate attempt at "unifying" his "structureless" poem, Eliot asserts that it is—that this "dramatic multilogue" is in fact a dramatic monologue. Pound had similar problems in asserting the "coherence" of the *Cantos*, crying out at one point "I cannot make it cohere" and ending in an embrace of silence:

> Do not move
> Let the wind speak
> that is paradise

In 1916 the American industrialist Henry Ford made the famous remark that "history is more or less bunk." In 1934, thinking of the *Cantos*, Ezra Pound wrote in *ABC of Reading* that the "epic" was a poem "*including* history" (my italics).[5]

American literature is in many ways an attempt *both* to evade and to "include" history. In her brilliant, peculiar poetry, Emily Dickinson deliberately *ignores* (fails to notice) the immense fact of the Civil War, whereas Walt Whitman seeks to incorporate the War into his work as primary subject matter. The need to evade history—to become "nothing"—may arise because what Eliot called "the historical sense" is immensely powerful and threatening. In that ongoing crisis which constitutes American literature, the writer is necessarily thrown back not on the particular issues which create a subject matter—what that European would have called a book's being "about something"—but on the very conditions of writing itself, conditions which American literature is constantly attempting to define and justify. *What kind of history can arise out of a multicultural situation? How can history be simplified, turned into myth? The Waste Land* and *The Cantos* can be seen as poems whose formal strategies—embodiments of "the new"—come into conflict with the authors' deep and enduring sense of the complexity of the past.

Though 2003 is very far from 1776, the nameless country called The United States was born of revolution and became the complex focal point of a number of utterly divergent traditions. The vitality of these traditions gives the lie to the idea of "the melting pot," a concept formulated by Israel Zangwill in 1908: "America is God's crucible, the great melting pot where all the races of Europe are melting and re-forming."

"MultiAmerica" is not a melting pot but a conversation among people who both agree and disagree—and who live *with* one another in an extremely problematical way, a way which is constantly "unstable," constantly attempting to define itself. That is the problem facing American literature as a whole. It draws upon so many traditions and even, as in Eliot's and Pound's work, on so many languages that the possibility of its utter lack of unity is very great. Perhaps it will be the burden of the twenty-first century not to despair at this fact but to recognize a new definition of "unity": not something all-embracing, not something which insists on touching absolutely everything, but a looser coalition in which various patterns and peoples emerge. In a famous passage from his book, *Philosophical Investigations,* the philosopher Ludwig Wittgenstein attempts to find an "essence" for the subject of "games"—a single quality without which a game cannot be considered a game. Wittgenstein is unsuccessful in this attempt. What he finds instead of a single quality—an "essence"—is

> a complicated network of similarities overlapping and criss-crossing: sometimes overall similarities, sometimes similarities of detail.
>
> I can think of no better expression to characterize these similarities than "family resemblances"; for the various resemblances between members of a family: build, features, colour of eyes, gait, temperament, etc. etc. overlap and criss-cross in the same way.—And I shall say: 'games' form a family . . . And we extend our concept . . . as in spinning a thread we twist fibre on fibre. And the strength of the thread does not reside in the fact that some one fibre runs through its whole length, but in the overlapping of many fibres.

Similarly, commenting in *This is Not a Pipe* on the work of the French philosopher Michel Foucault, James Harkness writes, "Things are cast adrift, more or less like one another without any of them being able to claim the privileged status of 'model' for the rest. Hierarchy gives way to a series of exclusively lateral relations . . . Painting becomes an endless series of . . . variations set free from a theme."

Such a vision of "variations set free from a theme" does not insist on reducing everything to *one*—to an "essence"—but on remaining *tentative*, open to whatever possibilities may occur. It is this openness to history—"the overlapping of many fibres"—matched with its opposite number, the frequent attempt to avoid history altogether, that is one of the great "traditions" of American culture. The American critic Harold Rosenberg paradoxically referred to Modernism, a movement of which Eliot and Pound are central figures, as "a tradition of the new"—and that word "new" is highly resonant in America. (The United States is often referred to as "The New World"—as opposed to Europe, "The Old World"—and one of the central mottos of Pound's *Cantos* is "Make It New.")

One can make a case for the tradition of the new arising out of Puritanism, with its desire for remaking the world—its desire for immediate apocalypse. But in its rejection of various elements of the past (the "old"), in its desire for inclusiveness, for incorporating into itself a wide range of both "high" and "low" culture, the "tradition of the new" is also *anti* Puritan—even to the point of embracing the irrational. That deeply American invention, "free jazz"—in which each instrumentalist is free to choose whatever key signature he wishes—is one way in which the tradition of the new is currently manifesting itself. Some people hear this music as deeply liberating; others hear it as pure chaos.

Yet Puritan traditionalism maintains a strong presence as well; along with the tradition of the new, there is an equally strong interest in the exclusive, the limited, the *old*—an interest in what Herman Melville memorably called in his novel *Billy Budd* "forms, measured forms." From this point of view, history, the Old World, Europe, even Asia all arrive with a vengeance. Indeed, ethnically-oriented literature—of considerable importance in the United States with its mélange of identities—affirms *both* European and non-European traditions; and both traditions frequently *change* when they come into contact with the "New World." (Of course, for Native Americans, the term "New World" is hopelessly Eurocentric: they were here *before* the transplanted Europeans. And for Africans brought to the United States in slavery, this country was hardly "the New World" but a world of pain and loss.)

American literature thrives on such ambiguity, on the plunging into history as well as the attempt to transcend (evade) history entirely—not to mention the attempt to transform history. In its effort to respond to *everything,* its all-inclusiveness, this literature frequently encounters the need to create forms which justify its own existence. Why should we have a literature at all? Aren't we simply a branch of *English* literature? Often— in Ernest Hemingway as well as in Emily Dickinson—*feeling something* becomes the only real criterion of value.

American literature is in its depths a *root* literature, one that is always seeking foundations which, in turn, remain forever just out of reach. It is in a way a literature of pure quest, of being—in the words of one of its most famous practitioners, Jack Kerouac—*on the road.* And the examples of Kerouac and Charles Bukowski (among others) suggest that it is also frequently a *transgressive* literature, one which is constantly repeating the revolutionary gesture of its "founding fathers" and which, as a consequence, requires someone or something to play the role of "England." For many writers, the "status quo" plays this role, and so American writers deliberately and vociferously turn away from the status quo. Melville admired Hawthorne for his ability to say "NO! in thunder": "the devil himself cannot make him say *yes*." And Clotaire Rapaille suggests in *The Culture Code* that "our rebellious period never really ended": "we never killed our king because we never actually had one. . . ." For Rapaille, this notion "explains why we are so successful around the world selling the trappings of adolescence: Coca-Cola, Nike shoes, fast food, blue jeans, and loud, violent movies":

> The American culture exhibits many of the traits consistent with adolescence: intense focus on the "now," dramatic mood swings, a constant need for exploration and challenge to authority, a fascination with extremes, openness to change and reinvention, and a strong belief that mistakes warrant second chances. As Americans, we feel we know more than our elders do. . . .

Indeed, America's most "popular" celebrities are frequently celebrated for embodying an "anti-establishment" stance, a stance which often turns out to be their primary means of being *in* "the establishment." (Think of Elvis.) If, as is commonly believed, we are a country of self-determining "individuals," then we are necessarily a country of outsiders, people deeply distrustful of "belonging" to anything. America may be in this sense a country of permanent, self-willed *exiles*—how many of its writers are precisely that?—and the existential condition of exile is often what its literature is "about." "Might I but moor—Tonight / in Thee!"

Added for this book:

Forgive me, but it seems to me that the notion of the death of God allows us to see more clearly some of the ramifications of what it means to live amid complexity. It allows us to abandon the need for an overall unity, a divine "plan" that accounts for everything. It allows us to see ourselves not as monologues but as multilogues—and to accept that fact as something which does not need "correction." *The notion of the death of God is of course nothing but a myth, a story, just as the notion of God is noting but a story. But it is a story which has different baggage from the story of God and which may therefore be of considerable use. For some time now, we have been watching American Culture collapse around us—watching its tremendous failures; yet American Culture—like Western culture as a whole—has within itself the means of its own renewal: it is large enough and diverse ("chaotic") enough to be able to re-create itself into an image in which we can truly live. But we need to genuinely redefine things if that is to happen. As Eliot and Pound among many others have shown, "multipicity" is not merely a social and political fact: it is a fact of consciousness—and to affirm "God" and "individuality" is to affirm precisely the things that once liberated us but which have become the deepest of our oppressors. It will be the task of the twenty-first century—and particularly the task of poetry, and art in which language comes to the fullest comprehension of itself—to tell new stories, to create new pathways in which insight may occur.*

And all this is to say nothing about still another problem: the problem of choosing which aspects of a complex history to believe. Booksellers will tell you that books of history sell extremely well in this often-forgetful country—and those books frequently become films, a medium which is in a way a *branch* of "American literature." Gore Vidal points out in *Screening History* that American movies are often entirely fictional assertions of a past that exists only in the imaginations of Hollywood screenwriters and directors. That is subject matter for still another paper. American literature, like America itself, remains deeply "unsettled," divided, problematical, in question. "Do I contradict myself?" asked Walt Whitman in a famous passage from "Song of Myself,"

> Very well I contradict myself.
> (I am large, I contain multitudes.)

Thank you for the opportunity to present these points of view. *Salaam aleikum. Ma'a s-salaama.*

Overture: Chorus

for two or more voices
recited by my wife Adelle and me at the University of Damascus
in conjunction with the "American Literature" speech

that the hummingbird's wings are of a remarkable rapidity he had noted often
        nothing could be done   the shift of his breathing   had to begin
12 o'clock and he still hadn't had a   dermal sensation
        the block of the governor   is therefore revealing
the muck of the plains   living blues   a means of reversing
            whereof is so manifest
such crooked crooked paths, such ways this palace hides
            wit and power, to study the travail
new adventures list he undertake
            the way and its power   leading to the outside
in the eyes of the law   a long time, & ideas rise up
        toward toward gratification   inhaling   exhaling   rise & fall
I name that audacitywith   him a hundredfold   intellect does, & the soul
            I name that audacity whose courage unmanned
                in the form that is
with the heavenly heart   excitations unbounded
                INDOLENCE   indolence and distraction
directly the roots of   towards punishment, towards

THE ORIGINS
AND HISTORIES   *simultaneous with:*   who can tell in such matters?
OF CONSCIOUSNESS   he blackened his face, his bowels

DISPATCHED FROM THE EARTH BY HIS BROTHERS
HE BEGAN TO   star of the magi: regeneration
BREATHE AGAIN   temperance: self-control

FOR A LONG TIME NOW I HAVE FELT THE VOID   a peculiar token
LIKE THE PLAGUE

                                                                a power

creating in the soul a craving of the greatest force wild animals
size of the altar   indispensable for those who are to apprehend his meaning aright
our most logical form the syllogism   like consternation spread
has the greatest force   and the big hat with the turquoise-inlaid eye
at the bottom of her soul   "Look! Niña! It is the general!"   on the vermin of
the house   *holding back*   the lymphatic milk of fishes   made in silence
through the way   more literary than music though so-called "music"
the swarming "population"   lo for this little while   sugar curse Eve fish-hook!
from the freshness of my eyes   little boat and a smell of
the revolver
ready
          come oh bird settle a moment
                                        EXPERIENCE ANYTHING a bullock wagon
the tramp of feathers the thunder drop the white snake
for a long time now I have felt the void like the
plague it is the
revelation   a formidable call to the forces that impel the mind
we do not see it as it is but as it has been fashioned

                    moving heads on rollers
                    animated hieroglyphs
                    a disinclination or resistance

rolling eyes, pouting lips, muscular spasms
mirrors, shoots, sources,   (limbs!)
in a pier is burning (east, east is burning!)
the old man drew, in a black spirit, hugely, *against,*
in the flickering light, again, against,
in the earliest march, courageous,
far more astounding   astounding—

        the days in which

sweetbriar, nebraska

at the spring at sunset   *simultaneous with:*

the knight in disguise

who knows

the would-be merman

the foolish queen

adventures while singing

when Peter Jackson preached in old church

factory windows are always broken

"this is the price I pay

for the light I shall someday see"

began to rivet, it
shared persuasion
no sight of the highway
for a long long time
your sweet dividing
informs the statement
endlessly there
its effect to force
since pleasure's divided
remove our ideas
offspring of a union
amphibians reptiles
forced to rise
at a height above
hot winter's weathers
the book of breath
opes his eyes
a break of Yoga
that old old man
he draws, in a black spirit, hugely

——————————

and what if my body die

of this small inland town

BUT
draunk in tears no bird great beds of poppy only asleep dissolved
in thunder jars no guardian nine times battered to wear & weaving
oh keep him safe reveal him whose he was and who he was with the peak
of the mountain & his bones were boulders the Egyptian asp ship onward she
bore a child (clop-clop of horses) stored assembled and disassembled

the

startling impact of their loud bursts of noise as they arrive
    at unpredictable intervals of the stream—

the lines which spread   the theater's alchemy
at night, anyway
                  in a tight

net

                  the huge

when I saw that the light appeared I was astonished
    & again fell down, fell dead away

this is indeed the spirit of wisdom, the Eastern source
        preserving their antiquity

for none of the pleasures I have is equal to what is given me

    the lines which spread   the theater's alchemy

some of these seem much older than was thought
        God's "immanence" or "indwelling" in the world

a particularly searching theory of the Shekinah

        the King on his throne

followers developed in great detail

      most shameful sinners, burned

the process of creation burns, there are two versions of it, in *Genesis,*

      in short, before all else, entirely practical
        works of the Chariot

my hopes for the theater are, strictly speaking, "idealized"
logos in vacuum

innermost joy   bound by love

these are the   manifestations

the next morning I communicated to my teacher

lines that spread

Post Script

The Death of Philomene Long

Two people have told me the same story about Philomene's sad last days. She complained to both Marsha Getzler and Mary Kerr of a terrible "cold" which made her cough and sent her to the bathroom all the time. Marsha was puzzled—"sounds more like a flu"—and Mary actually raised the possibility of pneumonia. I doubt that Philomene was the sort of person who easily went to her doctor because of a "cold." Mary had asked her for a donation for a fund-raising auction but Philomene told her she was too weak to get to the post office.

Philomene was supposed to come up here and was planning to stay with us some months ago, but she ended up canceling the trip. Her death is a real blow to the Venice scene. "None so keen as Philomene." All those old "Venice Beachniks" are dying off. Black Ace recently did a tribute issue to Tony Scibella.

This is Philomene's "Eulogy for Tony Scibella" from that issue:

Last year when my husband poet John Thomas died, Tony wrote to me—"Philomene: aye, lass & what can i say? I'll see u in September & maybe we can say 'JOHN' w/ o crumbling."

These last days I have tried, unsuccessfully, to say "TONY" without crumbling.

There is a saying in Zen: "All know the Way. Few actually walk it."

Tony knew—that enlightenment does not care how you get there. The Great Path has no gates. Thousands of roads enter it. Reach for it and you will miss. Let it loose and it will follow you.

Tony understood—that those who speak do not know. The quieter you become the more you will hear. The highest purpose is to have no purpose at all. And then nothing is left but to have a good laugh.

On October 28th and 29th, 2003, as much of Southern California was burning and the sun hurled solar storms at earth, Tony received his death as he, in life, received his Muse—Her fiery winds of silence descending like a gull into his open palms.

Frankie once had a vision of Stuart "waiting at the gate." That gate has been swinging so much lately that it is just about jammed open.

Perhaps because of their great reach into silence for the word—poets seem to speak louder after death. They are here.

Philomene Long, d. August 2007

Is it possible to imagine a smiling tidal wave bearing flowers and a guitar?
And rushing into a room to give them to you?
Is it possible to imagine Philomene
Who imagined herself so beautifully?
Is it possible to imagine
The love she bore to her husband John
So that his death was only the slightest interruption of their conversations?
Death, pooh!
"I do tend to fill up a room," she said.
What happens really is that the room suddenly feels cold.
Whatever happened to the sun? it asks. *Will it ever return?* it asks.
And then it sees Philomene
So it wraps itself around her, curls up at her feet like a kitten, covers her like a cloak
It becomes a MUCH livelier room,
Offers witticisms, flirts with everyone, quotes Rumi (its favorite poet).
Philomene could make a room talk
But she also listened
Is this not the first lesson in compassion?
What waves of intellect come from Philomene when she speaks
What flowers of poetry
What echoes of music as from instruments.
There are no smiling tidal waves bearing flowers and guitars.
Everyone knows that.
But there was Philomene

There was Philomene

Notes

Introduction

1. See http://www.nytimes.com/2003/07/27/arts/music/27TARU.html. Cited July, 2004.
2. Willard Bohn, *The Dada Market: An Anthology of Poetry* (Carbondale and Edwardsville: Southern Illinois University Press, 1993), pp. xii-xiii.
3. Philip Pullman, "The Republic of Heaven," *The Horn Book* (November/December 2001), p. 655.

William Butler Yeats

1. In *W.B. Yeats and Tradition* F.A.C. Wilson writes, "the bird is the traditional symbol for the purified soul . . . and Yeats employs it consistently in this sense. One thinks of his manuscript reference to the 'birds that I shall be like when I get out of the body'. . . ." In "Meditations in Time of Civil War," the image of the "stare" is *opposed* to the image of the "honey bee." (The word "stare," which Yeats explains is the West of Ireland expression for "starling," is echoed in "Two Songs From a Play": "I saw a *staring* virgin stand. . . .") Cf. "As at the loophole there, / The daws chatter and scream. . . ." Footnote 2 below suggests the meaning of honey bees in "Meditations."
2. Yeats' early poem, "The Lake Isle of Innisfree," isn't usually taken to be one of the poet's more esoteric pieces, but a number of its details—the water, the honey, the bee and its hive, the color purple, the number nine, the beans—come straight out of Porphyry. Indeed, in the context of Porphyry, the repeated lines in "Meditations in Time of Civil War"— "honey bees / Come build in the empty house of the stare"—may well be ironic, even mocking. "The sweetness of honey signifies, with theologians," writes Porphyry, "the same thing as the pleasure arising from copulation, by which Saturn, being ensnared, was castrated."
3. In *W.B. Yeats and Tradition*, F.A.C. Wilson points out that, according to Thomas Taylor, Dionysus—who shows up explicitly in *The Tower* in "Two Songs From a Play"—"is a symbol for spirit in its descent into matter." Wilson quotes Taylor:

This fall . . . is very properly represented as a cruel dismemberment and a disaster, for life in the physical world is a curse. Dionysus could stand only to lose by abandoning his true nature. . . .

In falling, the soul "'becomes bound in body as in a prison.'" "The ceremony of cutting out the heart as a symbol of eventual resurrection," Wilson goes on, "dates back to Egyptian funeral rites":

When Jupiter takes the body of the slain god from the Titans and commits it into Apollo's keeping, the myth represents the rescue of the spirit of man from a merely material existence. . . .

Two Modernists & A Beat

1. Remembering that language sometimes reverses letters, as in the cases of morphe/form or ciel/ceiling: An early form of "sparrow" is sparwa.

sparwa / passer

Take the s sound of passer and put it at the beginning of the word, so that it's spaer or spa-er—isn't that close to sparwa and sparrow? Instead of pas-, we have spa-: a reversal. Language too has its dyslexia. (And this is to say nothing of the -wa / -ow reversal of sparwa and sparrow.)

2. In "The Black Boy Looks at the White Boy," James Baldwin rightly characterized such passages as "absolute nonsense . . . and offensive nonsense at that." Like Elvis Presley, Kerouac seemed to express something like a "black" sensibility, but, like Elvis, he wasn't black. At the same time, like Elvis, Kerouac was *criticized* (at times viciously) for being "improper," "wild," "anti-intellectual"—i.e., (in the racist sense) "black." "There were people," Norman Mailer told Bruce Cook in *The Beat Generation*, "who made a career out of attacking the Beats." The ability of the Beats to survive such criticism depended on their considerable talent surely but also on the fact that they were, after all, white males living in a world which tended to empower and mythologize white males. The whole point of Mailer's essay is to *provide a way of empowering Mailer, and, by extension, other white people, particularly white males.* It has nothing to do with African Americans. "I had tried," Baldwin added, "to convey something of what it felt like to be a Negro and no one had been able to listen: they wanted their romance."

3. There is a typo in *Howl on Trial*'s presentation of the text of "Howl": line 9 of the opening section, "who got busted in their public beards" should be "who got busted in their pubic beards." The mistake is understandable: "Howl" is definitely a poem that makes the pubic public.

Remains To Be Seen

1. Interview, *Towards a New American Poetics*, ed. Ekbert Faas (Santa Barbara: Black Sparrow Press, 1978), p. 71.
2. Interview, *Sagetrieb*, vol. 4, nos. 2 & 3 (1985), p. 111.
3. *Towards a New American Poetics*, p. 65.
4. Robert Duncan, *The Truth & Life of Myth* (Fremont, MI: The Sumac Press, 1968), p. 7.
5. Interview, *Soup* magazine (1980), p. 35.
6. Robert Duncan, "The Homosexual in Society (1944, 1959)," *Jimmy & Lucy's House of "K,"* no. 3 (January, 1985), p. 51.
7. *Jimmy & Lucy's House of "K,"* pp. 51-52.
8. *Towards a New American Poetics*, p. 78.
9. *Towards a New American Poetics*, p. 72.
10. *Soup*, p. 51.
11. *Soup*, p. 33.
12. Interview, *Line* (Spring Fall, 1986), no page number given.

Unassimilable

1. Cf. these passages from *The Dragon and the Unicorn* (1944-1950):

> [A]s the dual,
> The beloved, is known and
> Loved more and more fully, all
> The universe of persons
> Grows steadily more and more real.
> Eventually loss or pain
> To the least of these, the most
> Remote known person of the
> Other, is felt personally
> Through the intense reality
> Of the dual.

        * * *

> What we realize
> In the beloved is the
> Growing reality of
> All the others.

Cf. also Rexroth's notorious remark, "I write poetry to seduce women and to overthrow the Capitalist system. In that order."

2. In *American Poetry in the Twentieth Century* (1971) Rexroth asserts that "KPFA has been the single most powerful cultural influence in the [San Francisco] Bay Area."

3. In the late sequence, "The Silver Swan" (1974-1978), Rexroth represents the process of "unselving." A female apparition comes to him and asks,

> "Lover, do you know what Heart
> You have possessed?'
> Before I can answer, her
> Body flows into mine, each
> Corpuscle of light merges
> With a corpuscle of blood or flesh.
> As we become one the world
> Vanishes. My self vanishes.
> I am dispossessed, only
> An abyss without limits.
> Only dark oblivion
> Of sense and mind in an
> Illimitable void.
> Infinitely away burns
> A minute red point to which
> I move or which moves to me.
> Time fades away. Motion is
> Not motion. Space becomes Void.
> A ruby fire fills all being.
> It opens, not like a gate,
> Like hands in prayer that unclasp
> And close around me.
> Then nothing. All senses ceased.
> No awareness, nothing.
> Only another kind of knowing

Of an all encompassing
Love that has consumed all being.

Despite the theme of "unselving"—and the assertion that "My self vanishes"—nothing in Rexroth's language actually places the ego sense in question. Rather, the effect of the passage is something like "Look what happened to *me*!" It still depends on ego assertion. The interplay of various voices one finds in Pound, Eliot, Duncan and Olson is rarely to be found in Rexroth—though Rexroth does insist in his introduction to *The Collected Longer Poems* that his work embodies "the interior and exterior adventures of two poles of a personality."

4. David Kipen, *The San Francisco Chronicle*, 1/25/03. In "Rexroth Rediscovered," an article written for the *LA Times*, Dana Gioia suggests that Rexroth has suffered the fate of the regional writer—neglect from the East:

> Rexroth's place in the American literary canon, like that of many Californian poets such as Robinson Jeffers, William Everson, Josephine Miles, Yvor Winters, Robert Duncan, and Jack Spicer—remains open to critical debate. Consistently ignored or underrated by the Eastern literary establishment, these poets continue to exercise an active influence on West Coast writers, and they continue to be read, though largely outside the academy.

Interestingly, *The Dragon and the Unicorn*—which is probably Rexroth's central utterance—takes place for the most part in Europe. Rexroth's primary publisher was New Directions, which in 1958 published Lawrence Ferlinghetti's *A Coney Island of the Mind*. Had Rexroth written anything that sold like Ferlinghetti's book, his status as a "Western writer" would have been utterly transformed.

5. Rexroth puts it in a more positive way in *The Dragon and the Unicorn*:

> Keep uncompromised;
> Stay poor; try to keep out from
> Under the boot; love one another;
> Reject all illusions; wait.

> * * *

> There is no need to assume
> The existence of a god
> Behind the community
> Of persons, the community

Is the absolute. There is no
Future life because there is
No future . . .
　　At
The heart of being is the act of
Contemplation, it is timeless.

Adrienne Rich

1. I confess to being somewhat puzzled by Rich's assertion in *The School Among the Ruins* that "After Apollinaire & Brassens" is partly derived from Georges Brassens' song "Le Pont des Arts." I'm familiar with Brassens' work but have no recollection of that title. There is "Le Vent," which has

> Si par hasard,
> Sur l' Pont des Arts
> Tu crois's le vent, le vent fripon
> Prudenc' prends garde à ton jupon.

and "Les Ricochets," which has

> . . . On s'étonn'ra pas
> Si mes premiers pas
> Tous droit me menèrent
> Au pont Mirabeau
> Pour un coup d'chapeau
> À l'Apollinaire
> À l'Apollinaire

   but I've been unable to find anything called "Le Pont des Arts." I think Rich means to refer to "Le Vent."

2. In "Blood, Bread, and Poetry" Rich writes, "I should add that I was easily entranced by pure sound and still am, no matter what it is saying; and any poet who mixes the poetry of the actual world with the poetry of sound interests and excites me more than I am able to say."

Shadow of the Vampire

1. In a way, Buffy is Nina's great-granddaughter. A phrase from the script, "shadow of the vampire," was used as the title of an excellent recent film dealing with the making of *Nosferatu*. The visual motif of the vampire's menacing shadow appears throughout Murnau's film and furnishes Gioia with the cover image of his book.
2. Gioia states that he took most of the characters' names and the locale from the original version of *Nosferatu*—the director's cut. Evidently the names were later changed into something closer to Stoker's novel. Gioia's thinking about the film was influenced by "The Deadly Space Between," the chapter on *Nosferatu* in Gilberto Perez, *The Material Ghost: Films and Their Medium.*
3. The suggestions of Christ in "piercing your side" are by no means accidental. Gioia seems to have modeled his poem on these lines, spoken by Christ, in Charles Causley's devotional sonnet, "I am the Great Sun":

> I am the great sun, but you do not see me,
> I am your husband, but you turn me away.
> I am the captive, but you do not free me,
> I am the captain you will not obey.

> I am the truth, but you will not believe me,
> I am the city where you will not stay,
> I am your wife, your child, but you will leave me,
> I am that God to whom you will not pray.

   Gioia quotes the passage in his essay, "The Most Unpopular Poet Alive, Part II" (*The Dark Horse*, Spring 1998).
4. The word "lonely," like the word "dark," tends to haunt this poet. Gioia calls his wonderful essay on Weldon Kees, "The Loneliness of Weldon Kees"; he titled his essay on his childhood reading from a line by Yeats, "A Lonely Impulse of Delight."
5. Baudelaire, quoted in Jeffrey Coven, *Baudelaire's Voyages.*

Annie Finch

1. In "Coherent Decentering: Towards a New Model of the Poetic Self," Finch writes that "if we look closely we are not likely to perceive our selves as discrete entities. I am aware that my own selfhood, let alone the self voicing my poems, is not a clear and simple unit separate from everything else in the world. Our 'Selves,' insofar as they seem to exist at

all, are more likely to come to our awareness as a shifting progression of moods and thoughts, contingent on circumstance, culture, and context, open to many interpretations." Further on, she writes of being "bewildered by the apparent need to act as a coherent central lyric Self to write poems" and comments that "the 'I' is not unified." "[T]he decentered, multiple point of view . . . can thrive in the 'mechanisms' of syntactic coherence," however:

> The coherent methods of decentering the lyric Self that I have explored include syntactic density and innuendo; lexical and metaphorical subtext; and the questioning of "objects" and use of multiple speakers. Most of all I have found my tools in the defamiliarizing repetition of conspicuous word and sound patters, or "form." When I began to write in patterns, I found a nonverbal vocabulary of coherent decentering and vatic containment that could channel the balance of energy and form, chaos and pattern I felt in nature and in language . . . As a poet, I find syntactic coherence a key element of the beauty and strength of the language. And as a postmodern woman, I want to honor the core of my experience as a self that I know is not a self. . . .Much more precious to me than aleatory dynamics or primary process, now, is the counterpoise of energies that incorporates, as all balance does, opposing forces: center and circumference (to use Dickinson's terms), coherence and incoherence, boundary and core.

2. "Metrical Diversity: A Defense of the Non-Iambic Meters" is the title of an essay Finch published in a book she edited, *After New Formalism: Poets on Form, Narrative, and Tradition.* In the essay she writes, "The long hegemony of free verse has finally cleared our ears of the stifling and artificial associations that haunted metrical verse, particularly non-iambic verse, at the beginning of our century. The field is, in a sense, clearer for metrical verse, especially non-iambic verse, than it has been for many generations." For all her interest in form—indeed, because of it—Finch takes to heart Pound's famous advice (quoted in *The Ghost of Meter*) "to compose in the sequence of the musical phrase, not in sequence of a metronome." She asserts that "The tension between conflicting meters, a source of beauty and excitement, would disappear without metrical diversity."

3. Cf. "You reach through your mouth to find me" in "Over Dark Arches," "Here is his open mouth" in "Elegy For My Father," and "Now the worshipping savage cathedral our mouths make will lace / death and its food" in "Wild Yeast." The words "seed" and "dark" haunt the book, as does the idea of water; there are also many suggestions of the womb—caverns ("Meeting Mammoth Cave"), for example. The ocean—often present—is also a womb . "Over Dark Arches" is a dialogue between a mother and her breast-feeding child. Such clusters suggest an attempt to invoke the archetypal mother—particularly the mother as goddess. Persephone appears explicitly in the title poem, but "seed," "dark," and womb all suggest her presence.

4. Finch's "Elegy For My Father" is one of the most beautiful poems in *Calendars*—a rich, gorgeous meditation on death:

> Here is his open mouth. Silence is here
> like one more new question that he will not answer.

The presence of Hart Crane (the best French poet in the English language) in the superscription suggests the influence of 19th-century Symbolist poetry on Finch's work. In *The Ghost of Meter* she comments that "a significant part of Whitman's influence on American free verse came by way of French poets." Finch's phrases "silent orisons" and "offerings of silence" are perhaps half-conscious echoes of Mallarmé's "Musicienne du silence" ("Sainte").

5. It can be argued that Pound's *Cantos* are an attempt to move away from iambic pentameter and towards triple meters:

> And then went down to the ship,
> Set keel to breakers, forth on the godly sea, and

is epic language which deliberately avoids iambic pentameter and tends towards triple meters. Pound arrives at this attempt through his study of Classical meters. Finch is no Classicist, but her work resembles his in this regard. Pound was also experimenting with the possibilities of long and short vowels in English verse; Finch makes no such attempt.

Appearing Ink

1. Unlike Gioia, Olson does not regard rhyme and meter as *necessarily* oral devices: the ear "once had the burden of memory to quicken it" but "rime & regular cadence . . . merely lived on in print after the oral necessities were ended." Gioia insists that "auditory poetry virtually always employs apprehensible formal patterns to shape its language . . . [T]he practice of arranging some auditorily apprehensible feature such as stress, tone, quantity, alliteration, syllable count, or syntax into a regular pattern is so universal that it suggests that there is something primal and ineradicable at work. Metrical speech not only produces some heightened form of attention that increases mnemonic retention; it also seems to provide innate physical pleasure in both the auditor and orator." Of course all verse depends upon pattern and repetition. The question is how "regular" that pattern and repetition has to be. Olson quotes Pound's famous advice, formulated in 1912, to "compose in the sequence of the musical phrase, not in sequence of a metronome," but it should be noted that, though he does not say so explicitly, Olson is offering an alternative to conventional

free verse as well as to rhyme-and-meter. Gioia's poem, "Being Happy," included in this issue of *The Hudson Review*, is written in "free"—but not "projective"—verse. One should perhaps also mention the fact that actors regularly memorize prose, which does not have the "mnemonic device" of a "regular pattern."

2. The remark is quoted in Brendan Bernhard's article, "Perhaps These Are Not Poetic Times At All: Poetry and Los Angeles at the Millennium," collected in *The Misread City: New Literary Los Angeles*, an anthology edited by Scott Timberg and Dana Gioia. I was surprised to discover that the anthology was dedicated to Ray Bradbury and—me.

3. Gioia's interest in opera is another instance of his interest in performance. In "Sotto Voce," an essay included in his book, *Nosferatu,* Gioia argues eloquently for the opera libretto as a significant literary form.

American Literature

1. Adonis, *An Introduction to Arab Poetics*, translated by Catherine Cobham (Austin: University of Texas Press, 1990), pp. 13-14.

2. In saying this, I don't mean to suggest that America lacks a powerful tradition of literature of social protest. One could easily produce a paper longer than this one on that subject alone. But the themes I am trying to enunciate here are certainly central ones and are, I think, distinctively American. Still, one can hardly imagine a more American figure than Woody Guthrie, and he is certainly associated with social protest. American optimism—and its dark brother, American despair—is another theme I have failed to mention in this paper.

3. Donald Hall, "Interview with T.S. Eliot," *Writers at Work: The* Paris Review *Interviews* (New York: Viking, 1963), p. 96.

4. Ibid.

5. In *Jefferson and/or Mussolini* (1935) Pound wrote, "Genius . . . is the capacity to see ten things where the ordinary man sees one, and where the man of talent sees two or three, *plus* the ability to register that multiple perception in the material of his art."

Jack Foley's poetry books, all of which feature accompanying CDs or cassette tapes on which he performs with his wife Adelle, include *Letters/Lights — Words for Adelle, Gershwin, Adrift* (nominated for a BABRA award), *Exiles,* and (with Ivan Argüelles) *New Poetry from California: Dead / Requiem.* His *Greatest Hits 1974-2003* appeared from Pudding House Press. Two companion volumes of Foley's essays and interviews, *O Powerful Western Star* and *Foley's Books:California Rebels, Beats, and Radicals,* appeared from Pantograph Press. *O Powerful Western Star* received the Artists Embassy Literary/Cultural Award 1998-2000. Since 1988, Foley has hosted a show of interviews and poetry presentations on Berkeley radio station KPFA; "Foley's Books," a column of reviews, appears in the online magazine, *The Alsop Review.* Foley's play, *The Boy, the Girl, and the Piece of Chocolate* was recently made into a film by Alabama filmmaker Wayne Sides.